T0339763

A MEDICAL DOCTOR EXAMINES
LIFE ON THREE CONTINENTS

# A MEDICAL DOCTOR EXAMINES
# LIFE ON THREE CONTINENTS

## A PAKISTANI VIEW

S. Akhtar Ehtisham

Algora Publishing
New York

Library of Congress Cataloging-in-Publication Data —

Ehtisham, S. Akhtar, 1939-
   Through a Pakistani's eyes: life on three continents / S. Akhtar Ehtisham.
      p. cm.
   ISBN 978-0-87586-633-8 (trade paper) — ISBN 978-0-87586-634-5 (case laminate) —
ISBN 978-0-87586-635-2 (ebook) 1. Ehtisham, S. Akhtar, 1939- 2. Pakistani Americans—
Biography. 3. Physicians—Biography. 4. Political activists—Biography. 5. Pakistan—
Social conditions. 6. Medical care—Pakistan. 7. Great Britain—Social conditions—1945-
8. Medical care—Great Britain. 9. United States—Social conditions—1945- 10. Medical
care—United States. I. Title.

   E184.P28E35 2008
   909.82092—dc22
   [B]
                              2008037936

Front Cover: (from top left clockwise):
A Pakistani warms his hands over a bonfire in Karachi. Image: © AKHTAR SOOMRO/
epa/Corbis.
The Makkah Masjid mosque is seen on the Hyde Park landscape. Image:© DARREN
STAPLES/Reuters/Corbis.
Pakistani religious students take computer lessons in the main madrassah or Islamic
seminary in Wana. Image: © MIAN KHURSHEED/Reuters/Corbis.
Indiana University students. Image: © Steve Raymer/CORBIS.
Pakistan - Islamabad - Islamic Fundamentalist Protest. Image: © Warrick Page/
Corbis.
Pakistan - Islam - Muslims Prepare for Eid. Image: © Warrick Page/Corbis.

I dedicate this narrative to my mother Zakia Ehtisham, who was the most formative influence in my life.

# TABLE OF CONTENTS

# PREFACE

This narrative is based on the experiences of my life over the last six decades in India, Pakistan, the UK, Canada and the United States. I have included a brief survey of historical forces which have had an impact on the events and have molded my generation.

I was a witness to a large part of the unprecedented changes our world went through in the twentieth century. Discoveries in science and innovations in technology transformed industry, warfare and health care beyond recognition. Colonialism gave way to economic dominion. International capitalism defeated fascism and overcame communism. National capitalism was overtaken by corporate imperialism, which ushered in an era of seemingly invincible globalization.

I witnessed the establishment of a religion-based state of Pakistan firsthand. Because of my leftist leanings I had a special interest in Israel, another state based on religion. I lived through a resurgence of religious fanaticism and bigotry. At the time of the fall of the Soviet Union, I was in transition between Pakistan and the US. I had observed the precipitous descent of the former socialist bloc, China and Cuba excepted, into the status of the client states of the West.

I had studied the methods of neo-imperialists. When subtle manipulation did not work, agents in place overthrew legitimate governments in Indonesia and Iran and many countries in the Caribbean and South America. When *agents provocateurs* were not successful, client states were exhorted to invade their neighbors. If all else failed, aggression for regime change became a viable option after the collapse of the Soviet Union. The insidious takeover of national wealth by global corporations, given legal cover by the World Trade Organization (WTO), aided and abetted by the World Bank (WB) and International monetary fund (IMF), working through financial hit men and local stooges, had led to pauperization of untold millions. Genetic engineering technology has made hundreds of thousands of farmers in the Third World redundant. Tens of thousands of land workers in India alone have committed suicide.

Today, native fascist, military and hereditary regimes are propped up by force of arms, their own and those of the neo-imperialists. They plunder the resources of the land and spend little on social services. Improved health care, heightened consciousness of health hazards and diet, lower infant mortality, and higher life expectancy have enhanced the quality of life in the West. The same factors have added to the misery of the people in the East, as lack of education, family planning and proscription of birth control by the clergy, have led to a population explosion.

I share an unsettling and unsettled lifestyle with persons born during the middle decades of the twentieth century into genteel but poor families of the United Provinces (UP) in Northern India. This class of people, in spite of their modest means, was respected by high and low. We boasted of lineage from Arab ancestors who had migrated to India long ago via Iran.

We got infected with the Pakistan virus. Hindu–Muslim relations deteriorated. Sporadic communal riots broke out in pre-independence days. Unemployment, which had been high in the middle decades of the twentieth century, was somewhat relieved by World War II. Another steep rise in the ranks of the jobless came in 1945. Young Muslim men migrated to Pakistan and filled the vacuum caused by the exodus of non-Muslims.

The early period in Pakistan, in spite of lack of basic amenities, was exhilarating. We were living a dream. The assassination of the first Prime Minister, Liaquat Ali Khan, in October 1951, marked the beginning of the end of ethnic fair play in the country. Discrimination against non-Punjabi Mohajirs (immigrants) remained covert till the advent of Ayub's martial law. Bhutto's rule saw nearly total alienation of these people. Zia further accentuated the process. We became unwanted in the land of the pure.

I have, in my time, attended a public reception for Jinnah, heard Gandhi, Nehru, Azad, Patel, and Liaquat live, and shaken hands with prime ministers, presidents and military dictators of Pakistan and two British Prime Ministers, Wilson and Heath. I have a more than passing acquaintance with US congressmen.

As a callow youth I had joined independence processions, seen *lathi* (baton) and tear-gas charges. I observed firsthand a Police-student riot in my hometown in independent India. I saw with my own eyes, the plight of refugees coming from Pakistan to India, and was in turn a refugee myself. I disrupted classes and harangued students and teachers in 1956 to join Anti-West procession protesting seizure of the Suez Canal. I, with other students, agitated against the martial law regime in 1961, and was briefly a state guest. In 1964 I treated casualties in an ethnic riot led by Gohar, son of Ayub Khan, the president of the country. I watched the civil war (East Pakistan-Bangladesh) on TV in the U.K. In the 1980s, I was curfew bound for weeks in Karachi. In a nightmarish replay of 1964, I looked after victims of ethnic civil war in Karachi in 1984–1991.

I was working in a clinic in Scotland and was nearly driven out of my mind when I saw 9/11 on TV. My eldest daughter Eram worked in the building next door. I did not get any news of her for six hours. Fortunately she had not gone to work that day.

I am not a social scientist and have presented events from a layperson's perspective. I have, of necessity, focused on Pakistan and the US, but other south Asian and European countries mirror more or less the conditions prevailing in the two countries.

## INTRODUCTION: A SOUTH-ASIAN LIFE OF OUR TIMES

### "UDAAS NASLAIN"

An acclaimed Urdu writer has dubbed our generation "Udaas Naslain" (the sad generation). He could have called it lost or transitional as well, because the people born in post 1857 colonial India and more specifically the ones born in independent India and Pakistan since 1947 are still groping for their identity and have been in transition for decades. Those born in the first three decades of the twentieth century opened their eyes in a society revitalizing and rejuvenating itself through an epic struggle to throw off the yoke of foreign rule. The ones born later saw a society disintegrating and imploding on itself. It was the culmination of several millennia of history going back into murky prehistoric times. They share a unique, though tragic heritage.

Immigrants to India from Pakistan have been successfully assimilated in the country to which they were forced to relocate. Muslims in India, though well on the road to full acceptance, are still vulnerable to religious-fascist hate mongers. Descendents of Urdu, Gujerati, and other non-local linguistic groups who migrated to Pakistan, are still called Mohajir (immigrants) sixty-one years after Independence (2008).

India, after pursuing an egalitarian policy during the rule of the Nehru dynasty, finally succumbed to the blandishments of Global Capital. Pakistan had fallen into the trap of "mutual defense" pacts in its early years and has finally, and I must say logically, descended into near anarchy and fundamentalism.

Since the collapse of the Soviet Union, Western imperialism has had its way with the Third World. A few countries remain as outposts of social progress, and lately the winds of change have been blowing across Latin America and parts of Asia, but forces of socialism remain under siege.

The US emerged onto the global playing field in the late nineteenth century starting with President McKinley attack on the Philippines.[1] But the real US ascendency occurred after World War II. Fending off any tendency toward Socialism in favor of corporate-led capitalism, working through covert CIA operatives and through the Christian Church as well, Washington trained and supported regimes that terrorized the intellectual class with tens of thousands of murders, live burials, mutilations and rapes. Millions fled into exile. Capital went along in the name of freedom. In the end, George W. Bush added a messianic touch to the acquisition and control of the oil buried under the sands of the Middle East.

After long centuries of internal ebbs and flows, India had achieved a syncretic culture, which accorded respect to all faiths and gave a lesson of tolerance of the other point of view. The British colonists of the nineteenth century resurrected old enmities to enable them to set one group against another again so that they could rule the country.

In the Indian independence movement, the capitalist class supported the leading party, the secularist Indian National Congress, but the first two presidents were devout Hindus and objected to the "welfare socialism" of Nehru. The religious-right wing coalition soon took over and consigned economic reforms to the dust-heap of history. The other party, the Muslim league, used the pull of religion to secure the interest of the feudal class created by the colonists as a prop for their rule and as a reward for betraying their own people. Sixty years on, the state is still doing it successfully as religion does not allow expropriation of property, however acquired.

India was a fabled land of fertile soil, glorious rivers, magnificent forests, majestic mountains and gorgeous valleys. The legendary riches lured people from all over. Later they "discovered" the sea routes used for millennia by Africans and Polynesians. Europeans, seeking spices to make poorly preserved food edible or driven by famine and religious persecution, started arriving in the late fifteenth century.

Some married local women and never went back. They would later and gradually, intermingle with earlier arrivals and indigenous groups. New languages, and religious practices would be shared, and mores, customs, and traditions synthesized into whole new concepts. William Dalrymple in his book *White Moghals* states, "India always had a strange way with conquerors. In defeat it beckons them, it then slowly seduces, assimilates and transforms them."

Those were the early days of religion. People worshiped natural phenomena. They were afraid of what they would face after death and invented gods who would help them at the end of life and rites to propitiate the different deities

---

1 *Empire's Workshop* by Greg Grandin.

who, they came to believe, if unhappy, caused disasters. Religious conflicts were rather subdued. People would occasionally fight for the pre-eminence of their own favorite god, but would soon come to a compromise, venerating both deities. People fought over pragmatic issues — land, food and women. Allegiance was owed to the family, clan, tribe, community and local ruler, in that order. The concept of nationalism was to come much later.

Over time a social hierarchy developed, with the ruler at the top, and a supporting cast of greater and lesser feudal lords living it up, on the produce of the land and the toil of peasants. Brahmans, like people of religion elsewhere, were very much a part of the feudal system. Their temples were endowed with large land holdings. Traders formed the third class and artisans and farmers the fourth. Untouchables were probably remnants of the indigenous population, reduced to the status after defeat at the hands of invaders. An arrangement initially based on division of labor, over time degenerated into a rigid, unalterable and fossilized caste system.

This went on millennium after millennium, till the advent of Muslims about a thousand years ago. They brought the first "divinely" inspired religion to India. Religion hither to had been sacerdotal, polytheistic and pragmatic. Muslims insisted that there was only one God, with no lesser gods. They brought, moreover, a rigid structure of religious practices. But what made it rather less palatable was that the adherents were not allowed to drink alcohol or use other intoxicants. They could not listen to music, except devotional, or indulge in dancing or other revelry. About the only concession they made was that a man could have as many wives as he could afford and have conjugal relations with slave girls, a practice which had Koranic sanction.[1]

In practice, however, the dogma was not and could not be strictly enforced. Sufis, adherents of a particularly tolerant, some would even aver permissive, branch of Islam, had given sanction to music and dancing. Muslim rulers, nobles and others drank wine, smoked pot, enjoyed music and dancing as their Hindu contemporaries did.

Victorious Muslim men married Hindu women. Some shrewd Muslim princes and nobles married Hindu princesses and highborn women as a matter of policy. Emperor Akbar married a Rajput princess and appointed her brother commander of his army. This princess Jodha Bai[2] was the only one of his many wives to give him a son. Moghal rulers were, henceforth, genetically as much Indian as central Asian.

The luck of the Moghals finally ran out. Akbar's grandson, Shah Jehan, had four sons. The eldest, Dara Shikoh, crown prince, was a poet, philosopher and a

---

1 *The Koran* — Surah Nisa — on women.
2 It is a reflection of the change of times that a late forties movie "Moghal e Azam" depicting the story was a popular hit. A 2007-8 Akbar and Jodha movie on the same theme was proscribed by several states in India.

Sufi. He would have been a second Akbar but with all the Emperor's forces and resources at his command, the second son Aurangzeb bested him. Aurangzeb skillfully exploited the latent resentment of Muslim fundamentalists in the court, who passionately hated the nativization of the court and covertly helped the in-surgent army. Muslim zealots hail him as a religious hero, but he imprisoned his father, killed two brothers and chased the fourth one out of the country — all patently against the teachings of his religion. He spent nearly all the years of his reign at war and in fact spent more of his time and energy fighting Muslim Sultanates in the south of India than he did fighting Hindu Rajahs. The perpetual state of war, together with internecine conflict over succession after his death, sapped the strength of the Moghals.

Hindu zealots and fanatics have similarly mythologized the Maratha chief-tain Shiva Ji and insist that he was fighting for the Hindu religion and nation. However, there was no concept of a Hindu–Muslim political divide, much less that of nationality, at the time. Second, leading commanders in Shiva Ji's army were Muslims. Further, he had forged alliances with neighboring Muslim rulers against Aurangzeb.

Europeans had obtained trade concessions and permission to build trade set-tlements in coastal towns, acting as tax collectors and later as regents, ostensibly of the Indian crown. In the process, they suborned the local princes and nobility and acquired land and property. Indian kings did not have tight physical control over their whole territory and of necessity ruled through royal appointees. They and the court in Delhi would simply ignore minor incursions into their territory. Worse, the rulers had traditionally ignored the seas and had neglected the navy. Indians would pay a high price for that complacency. Things went from bad to worse, till the writ of the last Moghal Emperor was restricted to the few acres of the Red Fort of Delhi.

Foreigners built forts, fought with each other and, made and broke alliances with local warlords. The English triumphed at the end of the day, defeating and subjugating regional rulers, usually by trickery, pitting one against the other. They were helped by the defeat of Napoleon in Europe, which made the French withdraw from the contest. But they were not able to establish their supremacy in India till the 1757 battle of Plassey in Bengal. The only credible resistance the British met after Plassey was in the south of India, at the hands of Hyder Ali and his son. The British finally controlled most of India.

Indians could not tolerate the overbearing attitude of the foreign rulers and rose in revolt in 1857. That turned out to be a futile and hopeless gesture, doomed to failure due to internal divisions inherent in a decadent people.

The elite took several decades to mount opposition to the occupation. For two decades nationalism overrode all considerations but sectarian, religious and other divides lurked in the shadows and a divided and debilitated India emerged in 1947. The two new dominions lost no time in getting at each other's throats.

Post World War II, the world also saw an existential struggle between capitalism and socialism. Capitalist countries unabashedly used religion in the conflict. They were helped in the war by satrapies and collaborators created by the colonists in their dying days. Neo-imperialists took over from decadent colonists and the new methodology was to control all the assets of the world, not by physical occupation but through financial burden imposed in the name of aid, given directly or through the agency of the World Bank and the International Monetary Fund.

With the collapse of the Soviet Union, multinational corporations and the Western governments beholden to them came into their own. Prior to that, the leaders of neo-imperialist powers had crushed only Central, Latin and South America and a few countries in Asia. Now the whole world became their playground. Muslims, who had been the most vociferous in opposing the infidel communists, ironically or as some would say justifiably, became the foremost victim of the rapaciousness of the neo-colonists.

Optimists find signs of senescence in the new overlords and point to their dependence on China, the resurgence of Russia and to the winds of change blowing across South America. They insist that the pace of history has quickened so that empires decline and fall in several decades rather than several centuries. Others disagree. They argue that once neo-imperialism disengages from Iraq, it will again resort to manipulation through agents. The non-capitalist world would then again be subject to total control and be reduced to ever-worsening abject destitution.

Chapter 1. Society in Pre-Partition India

Socio-political upheavals, cultural background and economic circumstances have as much impact on the psychological make-up of a person as genealogy. We are all, in different ways, a synthesis of the impact of history on our individual and specific circumstances and the cumulative result of biological evolution.

We were brought up in the tumultuous times of World War II and the upheaval attendant upon the final phases of the struggle for Indian independence and partition of India. The families of both of my parents had lived in a kasbah called Dewa-Sharif.[1] Our local saint was Hajji Waris Ali Shah, most of whose adherents have adopted the surname Warsi after his first name. He was a Sufi who, in true traditions of the school of thought, preached love, tolerance and non-discrimination in religion, cast, creed or sect. He had as many Hindu followers as he had Muslims ones. During one of his many pilgrimages to Mecca he detoured to England, and was received by Queen Victoria.[2] She thanked him for taking such good care of the souls of her subjects. She also offered him estates. He declined the gift and told her that Allah provided for all his needs.

Dewa has two *melas* (festivals/fairs) every year. They have, over the years, taken on the character of gala events in which religious rites take a back seat. Until the very last day the period is devoted to cultural events, recitation of poetry — devotional and secular, a peculiarly rural re-enactment of Maha Bharat[3] and the legend of Aalha/Udhal, a folk poetical rendering of an ancient Indian battle, acclaimed

---

1 An Indian term denoting a size between a village and a town, it is very different from the Moroccan variety. Dewa is believed to be named after Dewka Rani, a princess of antiquity. Sharif, an adjective that denotes piety/gentility etc., is attached to the name of a place where a notable saint had been born/lived /preached etc.

2 This is mentioned in his biographies.

3 Indian classic, a history of war between cousins, one good the other bad. Aalha-Udal is a folk song.

Mushairas,[1] (recitation of new works of poetry), where one had the pleasure and edification of listening to such great masters as Josh Malihabadi and Jigar Muradabadi,[2] along with many lesser lights. People went into virtual trances, especially towards the early morning hours. Sports and athletic contests in which national teams participate are held as well.

There was, of course, a stupendous street market in which one could buy practically anything made in India, and most of the imports too, including all kinds of arts and crafts, machinery, jewellery, cosmetics, dresses, and books. For miles around the village, the area was transformed into a veritable tent megapolis; about a million people attended the festivals. Restaurants catered to all kinds of tastes representing all the regions.

You could also find itinerant preachers admonishing listeners, though they usually did not attract many in the audience. Devotees of all faiths visited the shrine every day of the festival, bringing flower garlands and more material offerings too. Some prayed directly to the saint; this was an adaptation of Hindu mores. Others begged the saint to intercede with God and or the Prophet of Islam for them.

Conspicuous in their dress and mode of speech were tempters and temptresses, inviting visitors to more earthly pleasures. Young and old, boys and girls, met un-chaperoned. Many a rendezvous and tryst were arranged and many a romance made and broken.

On the last day, devotional frenzy would gradually build up and reach new heights. People would flock to the shrine in ever-greater numbers. They would pray in the style, language and mode of their own particular creed. In immediate juxtaposition one could hear incantations of Ram, Bhagwan, Allah, Muhammad and Ali.[3] Some would offer Namaz, the five-times-a-day Muslim prayers. Free food and scented sweet drinks would be distributed. Stronger drinks would be on offer but more surreptitiously. Qawwali,[4] the particular devotional recitation of the Sufi school, would start about 9:00 p.m.

The more popular of the festivals is in mid-October and nights can be chilly. People would be well wrapped up, as most of the devotees would find room only under the open skies. The climax would be a ceremony called the "Qul." About 4:30 a.m., well before sunrise, a procession of devotees with earthenware pots full of drinks and food on their heads, would enter the arena and make its sinuous way to the dais seating the Qawwals (reciters of devotional poetry). The tempo of

---

1 A cultural gathering to hear recitation of new poetry.
2 Leading Urdu poets of the twentieth century.
3 Ali, the fourth caliph of the prophet of Islam, is regarded as the patron saint. His name exercises equal fascination on the minds of Sufi oriented Muslims and Hindus.
4 It is difficult to accurately describe Qawwali. Roughly the lead singer would recite one verse, repeat it several times in ever-louder tones, with accompaniment of hand clapping by his entourage, who would occasionally be joined by the crowd. Farsi poems would be frequently interspersed with the Urdu ones.

Qawwali (recitation) would suddenly increase. Many in the audience would go into ecstatic trance; some would even swoon to impress their ladyloves. Women and children would watch the proceedings from behind a *chilman*.[1]

Tradition would have it that scholars from Arabia and Iran arrived in India and presented themselves to the Moghal court; and the king, after adequate authentication of their scholarship, bestowed large land holdings on them. Dewa was one of the places so favored. A neighboring village is named Jahangirabad after the Emperor Jehangir, who visited the place on his way east and bestowed the estate and the title of Raja on one of his retainers.

The area was dotted with smaller villages around it. Another "holy" village, Bansa Shareef, was about ten miles away. It was widely believed that the shrine was inhabited by *churails*, mythical half woman–half she-devil creatures. Actually the less affluent families used to abandon their "insane" females at the shrine. At the time women were much accorded less value and were controlled by men more than they are now. All kinds of frustrations, not getting married, not being able to marry a man of their choice, unhappiness in marriage and eclampsia[2] related to pregnancy were very common.

The railway station was eight miles away in the city called Barabanki, which was the district headquarters as well. It was an hour's uncomfortable "ekka"[3] ride. The route passed by an impenetrable forest infested by highwaymen. It was not safe to pass by the way after dark. Lucknow was only twenty-eight miles away, but that was a long distance in those days. It took about an hour by a slow train. People did not travel unless they had to for weddings and other family affairs. Telephone service was rare, telegrams were usually meant to announce tragic news, and letters took a long time to get to their destinations. The times were very different and much less complicated.

Most of the Muslims in our village supported the Muslim League, though the well-known members of the Qidwai[4] family, who had large estates not too far from Dewa in two villages called Rasouli and Masouli, were firm Indian National Congress votaries. The family was also distinguished in the educational attainments and political stature of its members.

The environs of Barabanki and Lucknow merit special mention. Lucknow was the seat of the Nawabs of Oudh, who ruled under the Moghals. Oudh comprised several districts and was merged with the surrounding districts by the British into the United Provinces (UP). Lucknow became the seat of the provincial gov-

---

1 A *chilman* is a bamboo strip latticework curtain.
2 A once nearly incurable affliction attendant upon pregnancy sometimes damaged the brain permanently.
3 Ekka was a one horse carriage with a square, canopied platform on two wheels, upon which one had to squat.
4 A well-known Muslim family of the sub-continent, they count many academics, governors, diplomats and scientists in their ranks. Indian National Congress was a secular party. Muslim League claimed to represent all Muslims. They are mentioned in detail later in the narrative.

ernment. The Nawabs functioned as viceroys till they became semi-independent, when the Moghal rule lost its vigor. The later Nawabs had developed indolence, self-indulgence and sloth into an art form. The affluent among the populace adopted the ways of the rulers. The name of the last Nawab Wajid Ali Shah became synonymous with luxury, dissolution and dissipation.

Administration, such as it was, was in the hands of the ever loyal Hindu business and warrior class. Even the latter were not much of warriors in the waning days of the Nawabs. It is reported that when the British forces were approaching the outskirts of Lucknow, two notable citizens with responsibility for defense of the town were playing chess. The scene is well depicted in a Bollywood[1] movie "Shatranj Ke Khilari," roughly translated as The Chess Players.

Culture appears to run parallel to moral and political decay in all societies. Music, poetry, dance, etiquette, ostentatious mode of dress for male and female, games like falconry, pigeon fancying, cock fighting, sedentary sports, musical evenings, Mushaira and other such pursuits were the norm of the period. All outdoor sports, hunting, and horse riding were shunned. Kite flying was the extent the common folk went to by way of rigorous past time. People attended concerts in houses of pleasure every evening and frittered away their inheritance at the altar of the goddesses of beauty. Another Bollywood movie, "Umrao Jan" with the delectable actress Rekha, shows the times very well.

But they produced sublime poetry and literature.

There was a great deal of inbreeding among the few score or so "Ashraf"[2] or families of gentlefolk. If they could not find a match in the immediate vicinity of Dewa, a net would be cast to kasbahs and villages further afield. Mohona, Fatehpur and Lucknow were given reluctant consideration. Even a distance of fifty miles was supposed to be an impediment. The better families were mostly of the Sunni persuasion but had amiable relations with Shias. Hindus and Muslims had adopted each other's customs and traditions.

Farsi had been the court language in the times of the Moghals. Urdu[3] developed as a common medium of communication to enable soldiers from different regions who spoke different languages to talk to each other. It is therefore, a purely Indian language and not a Muslim language by any stretch of the imagination. From its very inception, the language has been the vehicle for immortal literature produced by Hindus, Muslims and Sikhs, and not only secular odes to love, beauty and their beloved ladies, but some of the best devotional poetry eulogizing the Prophet of Islam has been written by non-Muslims. The first British

---

1 The Indian film industry, based in Bombay, is actually larger than Hollywood and has been nick-named Bollywood to rhyme with Hollywood.

2 Ashraf in local usage in the region meant descendents of the prophet's favorite daughter Fatima and Imam Ali, his cousin and fourth Caliph.

3 The word Urdu is of Turkish origin and literally means "Lashkar" — troops,

arrivals[1] and their progeny through native spouses made a considerable contribution to Urdu literature. Hindu detractors and misguided and ill-informed Muslims, for their own chauvinistic reasons, have appropriated it as a Muslim trait.[2] They have done a great disservice to the language.

Sufis had mesmerized the populace, and their teachings naturally had a basis in Islam colored deeply with mysticism. Many later Nawabs of Oudh adopted the Shia creed. Ashura, on the 10th of Moharram, the day the prophet of Islam's grandson Imam Hussein and his family were ambushed by the army of Yazid,[3] was observed with due solemnity. In Dewa, as in many other places, a Hindu feudal landowner traditionally led the procession from sunrise to sunset. When I saw him he was a venerable old man who never left his house throughout the year except to lead the procession on the 10th of Moharram.

Society was very feudal; landlords consorted with landlords and peasants with peasants. Religion did not come into the equation. Hindus followed their religion, Muslims theirs, but they had developed a common ground in matters devotional under the aegis of the Sufis. I never came across or heard of a dispute on grounds of religion in the society where I spent my early years. Muslim children and youth actually enjoyed the colorful Hindu festivals more than they did their own rather drab ones. The free atmosphere of Holi and Deewali[4] lent a helping hand to numerous *amours*. Like all forbidden fruit, Muslim and Hindu boys and girls thought that the others were more desirable. Certain Muslim festivals, which are now condemned by the more traditional as heretical, are borrowed from Hindu practice. Shab-e-Barat, a celebration of the Prophet's birthday during which Muslims used to clean their homes and light numerous oil lamps, could easily be taken for the Hindu Holi when the latter washed their homes and emblazoned the whole town with tiny oil lamps. Hindu youths enjoyed Muslim festivals as their own, and took care not to ring temple bells at the time of Muslim prayers. When passing a mosque drums would be muffled. "Ashraf" Muslims did not eat beef, except for making kebabs.

That was the time of communal frenzy in the sub-continent. We never had Hindu–Muslim riots in our town, but there were rumors galore and attendant tension in the air. When the rumors were more credible, there was near panic in town. We firmly closed our bedroom doors. Sometimes we even barricaded our rooms at night. One such occasion was when Gandhi Ji was assassinated and some miscreants spread the word that the assassin was a Muslim. We feared the

---

1 It is also part of our folklore and is described well in *White Moghals* by William Dalrymple.

2 *The Politics of Language, Urdu / Hindi: An Artificial Divide* by Abdul Jamil Khan

3 The dominant faction of Muhammad's tribe, led by Muaviya, who had tactically accepted Islam, rebelled against the fourth caliph. After the caliph was assassinated, Muaviya took over and breaking his word to hand over the caliphate to Hussein, the younger son of the fourth caliph, nominated his own son Yazid to the throne.

4 Holi is a festival of colors and Deevali (abbreviation of Deepavali — of the Deeps, candles) that of lights.

worst. But an hour or two later it was announced on the radio that the assassin was named Nathu Ram Godse, a member of the fanatic Hindu Mahasabha. The fascist organization was banned soon after.

But people were politically aware. In 1948–49 there were simultaneous strikes by All India Students, teachers, postal workers and many other trade unions. Unions, most of them controlled by leftists, were certainly effective in curbing overt hatred among adherents of different religions. During an annual fete in our college (high school in India is to the tenth grade; this was an intermediate college with classes from third to twelfth grade), a Hindu inspector of police beat up a Muslim student for a seeming slight and fled. When he was brought back on orders of the district magistrate[1], the whole body of students, led by a Hindu boy, nearly killed him.

1 A relic of colonial times, the office combined administrative, judicial and security powers.

To be fair, many British men had tried to nativize themselves in the early days. They used to frequent concerts of dancing and singing girls where the Indian elite sent their children to learn etiquette and manners and polish their diction. They counted several notable Urdu and Farsi poets among their ranks. Some tried to make the best of both the worlds by sending their children to England. A poignant tale of one such family is told in Dalrymple's *White Moghals*.

But the trend was effectively quashed by the advent of steamships which cut England-to-India voyage to two weeks. To keep their British employees from liaisons with local women, the East India Company dispatched hordes of girls from Britain.

With the defeat of Napoleon in Europe, the French were demoralized. They had lost their home base. They left the field to the British. The Nizams and the Maratha Peshwas (regional rulers, the former Muslims and the latter Hindus) were still considerable powers, but they were apprehensive of Tippu Sultan, the Muslim ruler of Mysore, who had defeated the British several times. The triad of the Nizam and Peshwa and the British ganged up on Tippu. He went down fighting. Subsequently the British imposed humiliating terms on the Nizam and the Peshwa and started taking on the airs of conquerors.

Muslims felt the loss of suzerainty acutely. Hindus had to give up their fond hopes of supplanting Muslims in the country. The feeling of deprivation was, however, not directly related to religion, as was made perfectly evident by Hindu rulers and public joining hands with their Muslim compatriots when the leaderless soldiers raised the flag of rebellion in1857. Used to the paternalistic behavior of the erstwhile Indian army commanders, they had been alienated by the supercilious attitude of the British officers who had not paid any attention to their complaints.

All the soldiers, native rulers, men of religion and the populace swore allegiance to and accepted the leadership of Bahadur Shah Zafar. It was technically not a rebellion. Bahadur Shah, as he was to assert in his trial later, had simply withdrawn the charter he had bestowed on the East India Company. Some historians claim that he was virtually forced into the leadership role. He, in fact, never had any control. Princes openly flouted the orders of the non-royal commander in chief he had appointed.[1] The whole campaign was terribly disorganized and ad hoc. Communications were poor, supplies uncertain. Indians still performed beyond expectations. As in any other war and revolution, unarmed British civilians were subjected to atrocities,

Despite all the handicaps Indian forces very well could have succeeded in ridding India of the English, except that the North West region, mainly the Punjab, came to the rescue of the foreigners. The province had had more upheavals than the lands in the plains of the Ganges. It had a new dominant religion, Sikhism, derived in part from both Islam and Hinduism, which for reasons of state had been suppressed by the Moghals. Sikhs bore a historical hatred of the Muslims. Ranjeet Singh, a Sikh chief who had acquired a large territory comprising much of current Pakistan plus Afghanistan, had converted the famous Badshahi Mosque in Lahore into stables for his cavalry horses. In fact Sikhs had vowed to carry a knife, wear an iron bangle, a pair of ceremonial shorts, a special comb in hair and not to remove any body hair till they had avenged their gurus (literally teacher, but in this context roughly equivalent of prophets).

With their back to the wall, or rather the sea, the British fought ferociously. As it happens they won and wreaked terrible vengeance on Indians, killing a dozen or more sons of Bahadur Shah in cold blood after luring them out of their hideouts with solemn promises of mercy. They hanged people on trees for miles and miles, looting, pillaging and murdering, burning whole neighborhoods and demolishing villages and towns. Survivors were pauperized and reduced to beggary, stealing and prostitution.[2]

Supporters were suitably rewarded, given large landholdings and titles. The ancestors of the current feudal lords in Pakistan were among the chief beneficiaries.

Indians, Hindus and Muslims alike, except for those in the Punjab, Deccan and Madras went into national mourning. Madras was the first province to come under British control and had been socialized into accepting the British as overlords. The Nizams (Nawabs) of Deccan had supported the British.

---

1 During the campaign Bahadur Shah banned the slaughter of cows during the Muslim festival of sacrifice and revived the Moghal tradition of paying homage to Hindu sensibilities.

2 An estimated one million Indians were killed and untold millions wounded.

The British, after quenching their thirst for blood, moderated their stance. The crown took over from East India Company, a conglomerate of British feudal/industrial/mercantile interests. The British government now directly ruled India and Victoria became its Empress. The rulers, more cautious now, made special efforts to develop a comprador class, and started giving subordinate administrative, judicial, police and non-commissioned officer jobs in the army to Indians. The occasional senior job that an Indian got was based not on merit but on the genealogy of their sponsors. Some favored and few enterprising Indians went to England for higher education.

The British had introduced a colonial administrative service in early nineteenth century. It was in part based on Moghal administration. In order to create a comprador class they made the tax collector's job hereditary, thus creating a landowner class, which supplanted the rebellious Muslims especially in Bengal. They were later to invent the Indian civil service, whose competitive examinations were held in London. The British exclusively manned the service. It was only in the early twentieth century that even the progeny of toadies were allowed into these services. The lynchpin of the service was the deputy commissioner/district magistrate who controlled, administered and held court in a district. They were trained to keep away from the natives and socialized in exclusive "whites only" clubs.

But the British did develop an adequate railway, road transport system, telegraph and postal communications.[1] They also established universities, medical, law and technical colleges and such services as the national Geological Survey, Meteorological Department, banking and financial services, the Scientific Research Council, etc. The Moghals had neglected some of these innovations and others could not have been conceptualized in earlier days. Some historians, forgetting that foreign rule demoralizes the people and engenders an inferiority complex, claim that if the Indians had won in 1857 and reinstalled the Moghals on the throne, India would have been left behind in science, education and public services. They should remember that China, perhaps a worse victim of warlordism than India, forged far ahead after breaking the shackles of a foreign overlord.

That the British bequeathed a representative government to India is a carefully nurtured myth. For nearly ninety years after the British victory at Plassey in 1757, there was no legislature. The 1853 Charter Act established a Legislative council. But to call it a representative body would be a cruel joke on Indians. All the members were appointed. It comprised the Governor General, his executive council, a number of bureaucrats and judges. Even this feeble attempt at forming

---

1 They had initially adopted the Moghal "Harkara" message carrier system. Sarai, wayside inns, were built every fifteen to twenty miles on well-maintained roads. The railway and telegraph system was to facilitate the transfer of raw material to ships for transport to industrial mills in England and to reduce turnover time.

a legislative body was vitiated by the complete control the executive exercised over all the legislative functions.

Post World War I saw the advent of another Government of India Act, which introduced the principle of diarchy. In theory, the executive was to share law and policymaking powers with a bicameral legislature. A majority of the seats in both houses were to be filled by elected representatives. But suffrage was restricted to the elite, few in number, who could be, and were, easily manipulated. And if this assuredly supine body were to raise its head, it could simply be dissolved.

In 1935 yet another Government of India act was promulgated. It proposed to transfer some political authority to provincial legislature, but the governors retained wide discretionary powers to dissolve the legislature and dismiss the cabinet under section 93 A. Elections were held, again under a restricted franchise; the Indian National Congress won and formed ministries in several provinces. Under the act the upper house at the center was exempted from dissolution. The act was never implemented at the central level. India till independence had never had a functioning legislature.

At the local government level, rural and urban municipal boards were introduced at the end of the nineteenth and the beginning of the twentieth centuries. But till 1918, only 0.6% of the rural population was enfranchised. Over 90% of the board chairmen were appointed. Further, except in Bengal and Bombay, the District Officer could override them. The Montague–Chelmsford act of 1919 did envisage Punchayats (village councils) throughout the country. The electoral base was to be expanded, the Chairmen were to be elected and the councils would be independent of local bureaucrats. But again only Bengal achieved a complete system of local government. In the Punjab, only one in twenty-five villages had a Punchayat. Other areas now comprising Pakistan had even less representation.

A few Indian reformers and men of letters, labeled collaborators at the time, performed monumental services by developing educational institutions. Aligarh Muslim and Benarus Hindu University come to mind instantly. Muslims, but for Sir Syed Ahmad Khan, the founder of Aligarh Muslim University, would have lagged much farther behind Hindus than they, in the event, did. The students of Aligarh University formed the backbone of the Muslim intelligentsia and spearheaded the Pakistan movement. They formed the core of the civil service of Pakistan in the initial years. But Aligarh and a few other institutions could not quite overcome the general sloth and lack of vision. Even as late as the 1920s my Nana's (mother's father) brothers did not bother to acquire an English education.

The British did not encourage industry. They did not want Indians to use their raw material to make finished product to compete with the mills in Lancashire. It is a part of Indian folklore that the colonists had the hands of Dhaka muslin weavers cut off, as their own textiles could not compete with latter's superior produce. The rulers actively destroyed other Indian manufactories as well. India had a well-developed heavy metal industry. The ships of the British Navy during Napoleonic wars were built in India. In the seventeenth and eighteenth centuries, the country produced more steel than all the European countries put together.[1] The two large industrial houses, Birla and Tata, together with many small to medium textile, leather and small machine cottage industries spearheaded by Gujerati and other business oriented communities, to a degree, compensated for this wanton destruction of local enterprise.

After the dust had settled post 1857, Indians started off by appealing to the generosity and good nature of the rulers, presenting respectful memorials to the viceroy and pledging or renewing a pledge of fealty to the crown and begging for relief from this or that, or a favor in allocations of jobs/representation etc. The Agha Khan, in his current incarnation entirely a product of British colonial policy, led the Muslim delegations. Other members of Muslim delegations were also drawn from the feudal families most loyal to the Empire. Hindu delegations were similarly constituted from among the elite.

The Khan is a descendant of the Shia Fatimids, who ruled Egypt for a long time. They were overthrown by the Sunnis, exiled, and were living a life of penury in Iranian Baluchistan bordering the Indian province of the same name. They are a deviant sect of Shias in that they accept only seven Imams.[2] A farsighted British administrator had brought over the grandfather of the current head of the community and his followers to India. The leader of the group was given the title His Highness the Prince Agha Khan.

With rising numbers of educated professionals whose ranks were dominated by barristers, the Indians raised the ante, asking for more and more representation. They still intended to remain loyal subjects but wanted more rights and recognition of their services. Their highest expectation was that, in due course, they would obtain dominion status like the former "white" colonies like Canada, Australia and New Zealand. They still subscribed to the view that Muslims and Hindus were one nation. The majority of Muslims had converted to Islam from Hinduism, some in living memory. If the argument that a religion was to be the sole determinant of nationality was taken to its logical conclusion, a convert should lose his birth nationality and be awarded the nationality of the country of his/her new faith.[3]

But the latent divide between the Hindus and Muslim had started becoming more apparent and wider. Muslims demanded fixed quotas in services and Hin-

---

1 *Globalization and Uneven Development* by Thomas Sebastian.

2 The seventh Imam was Ishmael; hence they are also called Ishmaelis. Even moderate Muslims have reservations in accepting them as a legitimate sect of the faith. Please see the book *The Agha Khans* by Sirit Bose.

3 The concept of Muslim Ummah—international brotherhood—does not even confer the status of a national on the person born in most Muslim countries.

dus were reluctant to concede the demand. It came to a head in 1905 when Bengal was divided into two units because, according to the viceroy, Lord Curzon, it was too big and unwieldy to administer properly. The division was approximately along the same lines as that in 1947. Hindus protested vehemently. The unity of Bengal was sacrosanct to them. One of their main arguments was that Muslims were recent converts from the lower social classes, would not be able to manage without their Hindu compatriots, and would fall prey to the machinations of the British. The independence movement would be retarded. The more rational and sophisticated among them talked of economic disruption, the loss of Calcutta the main center of educational, industrial and cultural activity, to the less developed eastern region. From all accounts it would appear that Muslims from the province had welcomed partition. Hindus were, in any case, much the more powerful element of the province and backed by the national movement, forced the British to rescind the partition in 1911.

The first definitive step towards eventual independence, although he had no such intention, was actually taken by a liberal Englishman Alan Octavian Hume, an obscure member of the civil service, who founded the Indian National Congress (INC) in 1885 and became its first president. It was very much an upper class body, presided over by the luminaries of Indian social, cultural, professional, economic and political elite. The second president of INC was a venerable Parsi (follower of Zoroastrianism) gentleman Dada Bhoy Nauroji. He was later to be known as the grand old man of Indian politics. As a result of the efforts of this forum, the rulers did concede limited representation to the Indians, but it was based on highly restricted franchise. Only the educated or the wealthy could vote. This in effect meant the ardent supporters of the Empire.

Muslim landowners, apprehensive of their fate under a nationalist organization like INC, founded the Muslim league (ML) in Dhaka in 1906. Nawab Salimullah of Dhaka presided over the first session. Agha Khan was prominent among those present and was to be its president for a long time in later years.

One of the youngest (and arguably the brightest) of the entrants into the ranks of the nationalists was a young barrister, M.A. Jinnah. For a while he served as Dada Bhoy's secretary. Sharp as a needle, unshakable in resolve, confident to the point of arrogance, he rose rapidly in INC ranks. He also reached dizzying heights in his profession. His biographers have related numerous incidents in his life, highlighting his courage, integrity, determination and skill as an attorney and a debater. One Secretary of State for India ruefully described how Jinnah had tied him and the Viceroy into knots.[1] He advocated secular politics and constitutional methods and firmly believed in Hindu–Muslim unity. Separation of religion and government was an article of faith for him.

---

1 *Jinnah, Pakistan and Islamic Identity* by Akbar S. Ahmad.

He was successful in impressing both communities. He was the only person ever to play a leading role in annual sessions of both congress and Muslim league, held simultaneously in Lucknow in 1916 and engineered a deal between the INC and ML on minority rights-separate electorate, a larger number of seats in the assemblies than their population would merit; for example in the UP Muslims would be so favored as non-Muslims would be in the Punjab. Gokhle, a leading light of INC and Sarojni Naido, another leading congress luminary, poetess and a member of India's first post independence cabinet, hailed him as an ambassador of Hindu–Muslim unity.

Jinnah married a Parsi lady, Ruttee Dinshaw. She was twenty years his junior and the daughter of a close friend. The friend, a titled luminary, filed a case in the courts accusing Jinnah of abducting his daughter. The lady, in a celebrated appearance in the court, denied the charge and famously declared that if anything, she had abducted Jinnah!

But he was wholly cerebral. His speeches were logical, substantive, and legalistic, and mesmerized those who could understand him, including judges, witnesses and opposing counsel. He spoke no Indian language, dominated the legislature, and overwhelmed the British and Indian members alike with incisive arguments. His ready wit was celebrated. But he found it difficult to relate with the common man and could never become a populist.

Now Gandhi, wearing the halo of his success in South Africa, appeared on the scene. He managed to convince, persuade, and if all else failed, browbeat the Congress leaders into accepting his thesis that without recourse to religion, they would not be able to engage illiterate peasants who constituted eighty five percent of the population of the country, and would not be able to force the government to concede any of their demands. He started mixing religion with politics and had the Gita (Hindu holy book), the Koran and the Bible recited in public meetings and advocated populist, extra-legal and unconstitutional methods. He freely used Hindu imagery in public meetings calling for Ram Raj. Hindu and Muslim elitists objected to this irredentism. He was eventually to qualify his statements claiming that by Ram Raj he meant Insaf (justice) Raj, but it was to be too late. His detractors ran away with it, proclaiming that the recitation of the Koran and the Bible in his meetings was a "dikhava" — a pretence, and merely a subterfuge to obscure the hidden and real agenda of Hindu Raj.

Gandhi too believed in Hindu–Muslim unity and took up the cause of Turkish caliphate which was close to the heart of Muslim India, vigorously supporting the campaign launched by the famous Ali brothers, Mohammad and Shaukat, in the process garnering Muslim support for the Congress. But he precipitately ditched the Ali brothers once Turkey abolished the Caliphate. That led to a bitter fall out.

Jinnah would have none of it. He vehemently objected to introduction of religion in public affairs, predicting that it would actually lead to parochial politics and dissension between communities and was a certain recipe for disaster. He disdained non-cooperation, civil disobedience, boycotts and strikes. Gandhi sidelined him easily and when he rose to dispute Gandhi's program in an annual session of the Congress of 1921, he was hooted down. Shaukat, the brawnier of the two brothers, threatened to lynch him.[1] Gandhi did not move a finger to admonish the unruly crowd. Jinnah left town by the next train, repeating his dire warnings that religion and politics were not compatible and would end in great disruption. He was, tragically, to be proved to be too right.

Jinnah had lost support among Muslims too. For their class and parochial interests, feudal lords and obscurantists of the creed, supported by the colonial power, were successful in marginalizing him. The clerics even called him "Kafir"(infidel), apostate etc. Prominent nationalist Muslims like Maulana Azad were acolytes of Gandhi. From the perspective of the rulers, Jinnah was a great threat to their paramount. They could not countenance a pillar of secularism and the most effective votary of Hindu–Muslim unity.

The Indian National Congress, blindly following Gandhi and for their own narrow interests, played into imperial hands. In late 1920s, a Congress committee, headed by Moti Lal, the future Prime Minister's father, assigned the task of re-evaluating Hindu–Muslim representation in future independent India, he repudiated the agreement Jinnah had painstakingly worked out and which had found general acceptance among both communities.

Jinnah gamely carried on till the early thirties when, finally disillusioned and frustrated and disgusted, he went into voluntary exile in England and established a lucrative law practice. The Muslim League, in the hands of feudal lords, split into many factions, and for practical purposes disintegrated.

Gandhi[2] grew from strength to strength, totally dominating the Congress, manipulating its leaders at will, ordering agitations, and withdrawing the call when things got out of hand. Subhash Chandra Bose, a popular young secularist firebrand from Bengal, darling of Indian youth, accepted by Hindu and Muslim alike, affectionately known as *Netaji* (Mr. Leader), was elected to a second term as Congress President against Gandhi's wishes. He was the last one to be able to do so. He advocated a militant movement, violent protests and guerilla insurgency against the British. Gandhi forbade leading congressmen from joining the executive council. Bose was forced to resign.

Jinnah's predictions came true. The nightmare of reincarnation of a Hindu theocratic state began to loom large on Muslim perception. Gandhi could not

---

1 The Ali brothers eventually apologized for their behavior.
2 Gandhi was the first practitioner of the idea of non-violent resistance in political movements enunciated by the Russian writer Leo Tolstoy. INC leader Maulana Hasrat Mohani was the first one to demand independence.

combat it; he could not swim against the tide of revitalized Hindu obscurantism. Among his close associates Nehru disdained overt religiosity; Patel, a rightwing rival to Nehru, was comfortable with it. Maulana Azad, the only Muslim in the highest counsels of the congress, was flabbergasted.

The Muslims were alienated. But they had no credible leader. Feudal lords whether Muslim or Hindu were scared out of their wits as the Congress planned to confiscate their lands, even though Gandhi, true to character, was ambiguous, preaching that the landowners should act as trustees of the land and should use it for the benefit of their peasants.

Nehru had always had an irresistible appeal for the young, and the passionate. Muslim youth started drifting towards the Congress. With no viable alternative, more mature Muslims also started having second thoughts. If the congress were eventually going to rule, they would be better off supporting it. If Hindu zealots got the upper hand, because Muslims had withheld support from the congress, they would be much worse off.

An overview of the social/economic conditions of Muslims of India is pertinent at this point. Muslim rulers had concentrated on North India — Delhi UP, Bihar and Bengal. There was an outpost in the South, the princely state of Hyderabad, with a Muslim ruler. Hyder Ali, at one time a minor officer in Hyderabad army, had joined the army of a Hindu chieftain of Mysore and had risen to the rank of army commander and later became its ruler. He and his son Tippu had defeated the British in four battles. There were other less notable Muslim states in the South. Muslims who had emigrated from Arabia, Central Asia and Iran had been the beneficiaries of the king's largesse and constituted the Empire's elite.

Muslims had a higher share of jobs, property and land in Northern India than their percentage in the population would merit. The British, as a matter of policy, promoted the minority at the cost of the majority. With nine percent of the population in the UP, the Muslims held twenty four percent of junior civilian and seventy percent of police jobs. A majority of the Muslim League leadership hailed from these areas. During the period of Muslim rule, a considerable proportion of Hindus had accepted the faith in order to escape the burden and stigma of belonging to lower and untouchable classes. Upper class Hindus never forgot that aliens had elevated the erstwhile dregs of the society to a level equal to them-in-law. Meanwhile the progeny of immigrant Muslims, forgetting the egalitarian teaching of their religion, had adopted the mores and norms of the Hindu upper class.

Muslims in the majority provinces — Bengal, Punjab Sindh, NWFP and Baluchistan — had been largely excluded from education, jobs, trade and commerce. They lived in slums outside all major cities. When non-Muslims left during the cataclysm of independence, schools, colleges, Hospitals and offices were nearly completely denuded of staff. Businesses and industries collapsed. What Muslim majority provinces in West Pakistan did have in abundance were feudal lords and their landless peasants. In contrast, in East Pakistan most landowners were Hindus elevated to the status by the British for purposes of tax collection and suppression of the erstwhile Muslim ruling class. The office was eventually made hereditary.[1]

Members of the Muslim elite from the minority provinces, fearful of being swamped by the Congress and losing their privileged status in society, sent a delegation comprising the Agha Khan and Nawabzada Liaquat Ali to England to beg Jinnah to return and save them. Jinnah disparaging the Congress for, in his opinion, its muddled approach, and feeling that Muslims at the end of the day would get the short end of the stick, decided to heed their appeal. His detractors would have it that he was motivated by the prospect of avenging the slights he had suffered at the hands of the Congress leadership. He was not very young and it would be his last chance of making history. He tarried in England long enough to settle his affairs, and returned to India to, it would seem, effortlessly take over the Muslim league.

It was in actual fact far from easy. The feudal leadership in the western Muslim majority provinces did not actually accept his leadership till the League led by him, had won an overwhelming majority of Muslim seats in the elections held in 1945-46, just a year before independence and partition. Punjab leaders[2] had openly defied, ridiculed and belittled him. They flouted his directives and concocted coalitions based on non-Muslims capitalist/professional class and Muslim landlords. Only Bengal had a League led government headed by Jinnah's nominee, Khwaja Nazimuddin. There too, Moulvi Fazal Haq and H.S. Suharwardy were ever ready to go their separate ways.

The British government had, in the meanwhile, been forced to cede some authority to the Indians. Provincial elections were held in 1936. The Congress won nearly all general and most of the Muslim seats. The Muslim League, except in the UP, did poorly even in the seats assigned to the community. This was a major setback. Jinnah simply had not had time to put the Muslim League's machinery in working order and gather mass support to force the feudal interests to follow him. He was further handicapped by poorly motivated feudal class assistants, disgruntled rank and file, and empty coffers. The Indian national Congress had a track record, dynamic leadership, superb organization and funds in plenty. Its legislators formed a government in eight provinces and entered into coalition in

---

1 Hindus left, and East Pakistan was able to enact land reforms and redistribute land in the same time frame, India did. Land reforms continue to elude Pakistan. This has created a wide fault line between the socio-economic systems of the two wings of the country.

2 A local leader, Mian Shafi, had set the Punjab ML against the 1916 INC-ML pact on safeguards of minority rights.

Punjab and Sindh with nationalist Muslims who were mostly landowners, and loudly proclaimed that there were only two parties in India, the British and the congress. Jinnah, with a stiff upper lip, rebutted that there was a third party, the Muslims of India.

Jinnah, highly secular, sporting a lifestyle of an upper class Englishman, Muslim in name only — he drank alcohol and relished ham[1] — had to play the communal card. But he did not stoop to demagoguery, and never claimed that he was a warrior on a white charger, staking his life to save Islam. For a long time he only demanded that the legitimate rights of the Muslims be guaranteed in an independent India. He worked tirelessly to organize the party, and in spite of failing health, toured the whole country on campaigns of mass contact. By sheer force of personality, tenacity and acclaimed integrity, he overcame the setback, which would have shattered a lesser man. People listened to him, even though he could not adequately articulate a sentence in any Indian language. They braved weather, walked miles, and stood under the ferocious Indian summer sun, just to get a glimpse of him. I read in one of his biographies that once while he was visiting Madras, people in the city heard that he was in the area. They came in the thousands to see him. He sent word that he was busy. The crowd held firm. He came out, furious at being disobeyed, and in biting tones upbraided the crowd that they were undisciplined worthless, ignorant, no good "mochi-walas" (cobblers — untouchables in India). Not understanding a word, the crowd clapped wildly and, screaming "Qaid-e-Azam Zindabad" (long live the great leader), melted away.

He could not have succeeded in the task without the unstinting help and devotion of the students of Aligarh Muslim University, who with unsurpassed dedication visited practically every place in India they could find a Muslim in. Other Muslims students from Lahore and the rest of India also pitched in, but their role was marginal.

All this would probably not have amounted to much. The Congress was much stronger and nationalist Muslims of high stature and highly respected Maulanas (clerics) with vast followings were supporting it. But the fates played into Jinnah's hands. It was only in UP that the Muslim league had managed to win a significant number of seats in the state assembly. Its leaders made an offer to state Congress leaders to join in a coalition government. The local INC leaders were amenable to the request. But Nehru demanded that the Muslim league leaders dissolve the party and join the Congress before being considered for cabinet posts. This was too much to stomach even for the feudal lords who led the party in the UP. Maulana Azad opines that if Nehru had not spurned the advances, the Muslim League would, most likely, have collapsed.[2]

---

1 *Jinnah of Pakistan* by Stanley Wolpert.
2 *India Wins Freedom* by Maulana A.K Azad.

Some Congress functionaries, intoxicated with unaccustomed power, behaved abominably to Muslims. Senior leaders officially condemned this, but the mischief of a few had done the damage. Jinnah appointed an enquiry committee under the Raja of Pirpur which documented instances of discrimination against the Muslims, and the Muslim League workers skillfully exploited this exhibition of blatant high handedness. They argued that a party which could behave so badly with Muslims when it only had the form of power would certainly make life impossible, if they had its substance. Muslims left the congress in droves. They demanded the dismissal of the provincial governments.

But the fates smiled on Jinnah again. World War II was looming on the horizon. The British, on the verge of declaring war, asked the Congress for cooperation. The Congress leaders demanded status of an equal partner for India in the war effort and an unequivocal pledge of independence after hostilities were over. The British viceroy in India was agreeable but Churchill, an arch imperialist, was now head of the national government in Britain. He declared that he had not become the Prime Minister of His Majesty the King in order to preside over the dissolution of the Empire and rejected the demand out of hand. Congress ministries resigned in a huff, and the party gave a call for non-cooperation. The viceroy ordered the arrest of all leading Congress leaders.

Jinnah took full advantage of the now uncontested field. He proclaimed Friday, December 22, 1939, a day of deliverance, offered unconditional cooperation to the government (which would pay handsome dividends later), and set about courting Muslims with renewed vigor. He had no problem fusing principle with pragmatism. He was staunchly anti-fascist. So was Nehru. But the latter had misjudged the will of the British. If the Congress had followed the lead of Subhash Bose and had developed a guerrilla force, it might have been able to bend the British to their will. But *ahimsa* (non-violence) is no match for guns when the wielder of the gun is prepared and determined to use it ruthlessly.

CHAPTER 3. NEGOTIATIONS FOR TRANSFER OF POWER AND PARTITION

In the early days of World War II, activism was in a state of suspended ani-
mation on the political front in India. Nearly the whole of the Congress leadership was in jail and their followers were lying low. British forces had suffered
reverses everywhere; they had been driven out of Europe and thrown out of their
far Eastern possession. France lay supine, and northern and Eastern Europe were
crushed under the heels of Nazi Germany. Japan had dislodged the Dutch from
Indonesia and the French from Indochina. Hitler had signed a non-aggression
pact with Russia. But determined censorship laws kept India in the dark.

Subhash Bose[1] escaped from the prison in Bengal and had made his way to
Germany, where he met Hitler and in exchange for a promise of independence of
India had pledged his support for the Axis powers. He had gone on to Japan and
made a similar deal with the Japanese leaders and had subsequently organized
an Indian National Army from the ranks of Indian prisoners of war. The Japanese
were at the doorsteps of Bengal. The British, according to most independent observers, had let the province slide into the grip of a massive famine. Millions died
of starvation.

Alienation of Indians to the British had reached new heights and was exhibited whenever it could be. Josh Maleehabadi, by popular acclamation hailed as
Shari-e-Inqilab — Poet of the revolution, announced that he had written a new
poem and invited people for a public recitation. Tens of thousands flocked to the
poet's home in Lucknow. Not many among them understood plain Urdu, much

---

1 Subhas Bose advocated militant resistance to the Raj. Elected to the presidentship of the Congress,
he antagonized Gandhi and got elected to a second term against the latter's wishes. He was the
last one to be able to do so. Gandhi forbade leading members of the party to serve in the executive
committee. Frustrated, Bose resigned.

less the highly stylized poetry, but they went wild with passion when the poet declaimed the opening line. "Salam ai Tajdaar-e — Germany ai Fateh-e-Azam" — "I salute thee, holder of Germany's crown and conqueror of the world." The police expeditiously whisked the poet away to jail.

Public opinion in the US was either neutral or sympathetic to the Nazi creed. Hitler was actually quite popular among the "red necks" or unsophisticated rural population, and many Americans were of German descent. A majority of Americans hoped that the Europeans would cut each other up. Thousands of Japanese immigrants lived peacefully and productively in the United States. Churchill and Roosevelt were apprehensive that Germany would become a real world power and rival their position in the increasingly global economy. Between them, they managed to entangle the United States in the war.[1]

With a massive infusion of American arms and men into Europe, and with startling resistance of Russians, whom Hitler, casting aside all considerations of the solemn non-aggression treaty, had attacked preemptively, the tide began to turn in favor of the Allies. Churchill, who presided over a national Government, realizing that Britain would no longer have the will or the strength to hold on, acceded to the demand of his labor party colleagues to settle the "India" question. Loud mutterings that the 1943 famine in Bengal was contrived were frequently heard.[2]

A cabinet mission was sent to India to negotiate with the leaders of public opinion in the country. Congress leaders were released for the parleys. Jinnah had, in the mean while, taken full advantage of the absence of congress leaders from the scene, and had consolidated his hold on the Muslim imagination. Reeling under relentless pressure from their own rank and file, leaders in Muslim majority provinces, who had for long evaded Jinnah's reach, had to accept his dicta. In any case the Congress had vowed to abolish the feudal system. It was an existential issue for the feudal landowners. Jinnah now negotiated from a position of strength. The Congress had to concede the status of sole spokesman of the Muslims of India to him. Protracted negotiations followed. Jinnah achieved his long sought after aim of parity between Muslims and Hindus in a federal India.

The cabinet mission presented a plan with a federal government in charge of defense, foreign affairs, communication and currency. The country would be divided into three wings, (a) the present Pakistan plus Indian Punjab and Kashmir, (b) Bangladesh plus Indian Bengal and Assam, (c) the rest of India. Provinces

---

1 Churchill had a US ship torpedoed in the mid-Atlantic and a US airplane shot down off the coast of Spain and put the blame on Nazi forces. Roosevelt, in his turn, seemingly ignored intelligence of the impending assault on Pearl Harbor, leaving the ships in port (albeit with most of the crewmen safely ashore), which the Japanese shot like sitting ducks. He thus won a propaganda victory and was able to garner public support for participation in the conflict and to persuade the US Congress to declare war.

2 It was widely believed in India that, apprehensive that Bengal might fall to Japan, the colonists deliberately created problems in the food supply so the former would be blamed for it.

had to stay in their wings for the initial ten years. After that period a referendum could be held to determine if the constituents units wanted to stay in the wings or coalesce with other units. The Congress objected to the denial of choice to provinces to opt out but after a lot of wrangling signed on to the proposal. The Muslim League did too.

A federal cabinet was to be formed. The Muslim League stuck to its assertion that it represented all the Muslims of India and should be allowed to nominate all Muslim members of the cabinet. Represent as it did a considerable number of Muslims, the Congress would not accept that and forego claim to its secular-nationalist status. The Viceroy went ahead with cabinet making, with the understanding that if and when the Muslim League changed its mind, it would be offered at least two major portfolios. The League, left out in the cold, agreed to join under the face-saving formula that they would be able to nominate a non-Muslim member of the cabinet.

The League wanted the Home (control over police and security agencies) and Defense ministries. Patel would not relinquish the Home Ministry. Nehru had given Defense to a Sikh leader, Sirdar Baldev Singh, whose support was critical, as other Sikh leaders especially Master Tara Singh, were flirting with Jinnah. Being a novice at governance, Patel urged his party to offer the Finance portfolio to the League. Nehru and the rest of the congress high command, equally innocent of administrative experience, went along.

Jinnah nominated Liaquat to head the League part of the cabinet. Unsure of his skills in finance, he demurred, but was reassured by two Muslim finance officials, Ghulam Muhammad and Chaudhury Mohammad Ali. Liaquat stunned the nations industrialists by presenting a truly "progressive" budget, levying high taxes on capitalists, most of whom were Hindus. The Congress was the political wing of Indian capital, bank rolled by it and beholden to it. They howled in anguish. Liaquat relented a bit, but put the onus of concessions to the capitalist class squarely on Congress's, especially Nehru's, head. Patel, woefully moaned, that he could not even appoint a peon without Liaquat's approval.

Congress leaders floundered and finally came to the conclusion that they could not coexist with the Muslim League ministers. And post independence, if Jinnah deigned to consider an office, independence would not be worth the trouble. That presumably made Nehru, the Congress president declare to a press conference that the sovereign constituent assembly of India would not be bound by any pre-existing agreements and would frame a constitution based on the will of the majority. This was a flagrant denial of the letter and the spirit of the tripartite acceptance of the cabinet mission plan.

Jinnah took the bait, fell into the trap or as some would have it, acting in character, pounced on the blunder of his opponent. He issued a statement that a party which, when not even wielding real power, could so blatantly repudiate agreements that had been so solemnly concluded, obviously could not be trusted to abide by them when it had the actual reins of government in their hands. He withdrew his acceptance of the cabinet mission plan. Reacting to the Congress's demand that it being the majority party, all power be handed over to it, Jinnah gave a call for direct action and exhorted his followers to observe a day of peaceful protests. Muslims all over India took out processions. In Calcutta, there was widespread rioting. Suharwardy, the Chief Minister of the province, a Muslim League nominee, was widely accused of presiding over the mayhem, or at least not taking effective measures to control the situation. But Jinnah had impressively exhibited his street power, exulting that it was not the Congress alone which could mobilize the masses.

The viceroy Lord Wavell, former commander in chief of the British Indian Army, a man of undoubted integrity and respected by all parties, was mindful of the support Jinnah had given the British in their hour of peril. He flew to London to present the case for partition of India.

The labor party had won the 1945 general elections in Britain, and Atlee was the new Prime Minister. Several members of his cabinet had close ties with Nehru. The Congress, accusing him of favoring the League, had demanded Wavell's head. Atlee told Wavell that he accepted the idea of partition of India, but did not think the latter should preside over it. According to impartial observers, the dismissal was patently unfair. The viceroy was managing quite well. Churchill, now the leader of the opposition, asked Atlee not to show disrespect to a war hero. But the latter wouldn't budge.

Atlee chose a new viceroy, Lord Mountbatten, a member of the British royal family, admiral of the royal navy, former head of the allied forces in South Asia, and as some would have it, Nehru's nominee.[1] Mountbatten had met Nehru in Singapore during the final stages of the war and been impressed by him. His wife had fallen in love with Nehru. Her husband was quite "understanding."[2]

Mountbatten's partiality was to cross all bounds of integrity. He showed all the plans to Nehru before making them public and let the latter change them at will. He retained a Hindu Civil servant V.P. Menon as his political secretary. Menon was in Patel's pocket and divulged state secrets to his boss on a regular basis.[3]

It turned out to be a singularly poor and tragic choice. The man had no experience in civil administration. He was arrogant, vain, and overly conscious of his

---

1 There is of course no documentary evidence that Atlee was swayed by Nehru's opinion, but it stands to reason that he would listen to his cabinet colleagues.

2 She was to have a lengthy affair with Nehru, as shown by her posthumously-released correspondence. The liaison would have grave and deleterious effect on Jinnah and Muslim league. Please refer to *Mission with Mountbatten* by his military aide Alan Campbell Johnson.

3 Ibid.

royal connection. He had little foresight or insight. He was much more concerned with his place in history than the fate of Indians.

On arrival in Delhi, declaring that in the first instance he simply wanted to get acquainted with them, he invited Gandhi, Nehru and Jinnah for informal talks. Jinnah famously told him that he would agree to a discussion only on the condition that the he be regarded as the sole representative of the Muslims of India.[1] Mountbatten told Jinnah that the meeting was only to give both an opportunity to get to know each other better. They developed immediate antipathy. The meeting lasted over an hour; Jinnah would only respond in monosyllables. Mountbatten told his assistants that he would rather have several meetings with Gandhi and Nehru than one with Jinnah.

Lengthy negotiations ensued again. Mountbatten had to concede the demand for partition of India, but he told Jinnah that if the country could be divided, provinces could be too and if Jinnah would not agree with the idea, he would simply hand over power to the congress and be done with it. Conscious of his fast deteriorating health, and certain that his assistants would not be to able to withstand the combined onslaught of the British and the congress, he agreed to a "moth eaten Pakistan"[2].

Now, the small man that he was, having been thwarted in his designs to inaugurate a united independent India, Mountbatten decided to leave a veritable mess. Transfer of power was planned for June 1948. In March 1947 he advised the British government to bring the date forward to August 1947, otherwise, he claimed, the situation would get out of control. Civil war might break out. The loyalties of Indian soldiers would be sorely tried. British soldiers, too few and too tired, would not be able to cope with the situation. The cabinet had no choice but to accept his plan. He chose August 15, 1947, the date he had accepted surrender of the Japanese army two years earlier, as the date of transfer of power into Indian and Pakistani hands.

Mountbatten, willful, unmindful, unaware, and not caring much for the consequences, delayed announcement of the boundary commission awards till two days after Independence.[3] On Independence Day hundreds of thousands did not know which country their home was in. Officials had no information either.

Such intricate business as dividing a country which had been one political entity for centuries would tax the skill of an experienced and seasoned administrator. Mountbatten, devoid of any such attributes, set unrealistic deadlines and proceeded with haphazard, disjointed and disorganized partition of the country, government and assets. He charged a boundary commission, the leader of which was unfamiliar with topography, with demarcating a line of control between

---

1 Ibid.

2 Jinnah, on being shown a map of the future Pakistan, with Hindu majority areas, hived off the Punjab and Bengal, so described the country.

3 Please see *Jinnah, Pakistan and Islamic Identity* by Akbar S. Ahmad and *The Sole Spokesman* by Ayesha Jalal.

India and Pakistan. The man had at best a rough outline of districts, few maps, and no statistics of the majority–minority areas. And he had only a few weeks. It was truly a scuttle.

Mountbatten still harbored ambitions of staying on as the governor general of both countries. Nehru, cognizant of the advantages of keeping on the right side of the British government which still controlled all the levers of authority, readily offered the job to him. Jinnah rejected the feelers, claiming that his people wanted him to be the first Governor General of Pakistan. Mountbatten threat-ened Jinnah that it would have an adverse effect on Pakistan, but Jinnah would not budge. He sought advice from the British prime minister, who urged him to stay on as Governor General of India alone.

Whether Jinnah had spurned the advances of Mountbatten because of vanity and arrogance or, as he told his confidants, because he wanted, right at the begin-ning, to claim an unquestioned independent status for Pakistan, one will never know for certain. The fact that he was terminally ill may have been the determin-ing factor in his decision. Whatever the reason, it was to have a far reaching and grievous effect on Pakistan's fortunes.

Patel and Nehru (and, I suspect, Gandhi) were confident that Pakistan would collapse soon. There would be no other rational reason for Gandhi to change his stance abruptly and acquiesce to the idea of partition which previously he had vowed would happen only over his dead body. Patel is on record making a pub-lic speech that it would be only a matter of days, weeks, or at the most months, before Pakistan would collapse; they would go down on their knees to be taken back into the Indian Union.

Only Azad, among the top Congress leaders, remained steadfast in opposing partition. Azad and Nehru were very close. Nehru probably did not take Azad into his confidence. Being acutely conscious of the latter's sensibilities and lack of guile, he also may have wanted to spare his friend the Machiavellian designs of Patel. Azad had been the president of the Congress from 1940 to 1946. He would have been the automatic choice for the office of the first Prime Minister of India. But that was, under the circumstances, untenable. Muslims had got Pakistan. One of them could not be the PM of India too; such was the overwhelming senti-ment. The party machine wanted Patel to succeed to the office. Azad offered to resign, but told Gandhi that he would not, till he was given solemn assurance that Nehru would follow him.

To hasten the collapse, Nehru and Patel withheld Pakistan's share of the joint assets. Mountbatten aided and abetted them. The patently lame excuse they gave was that Pakistan would use the funds to wage more effective aggression in Kashmir. And collapse it would — it did not even have funds to pay salary to government servants — if the Nizam of Hyderabad had not come to the rescue. Reputedly the Bill Gates of his time, he gave Pakistan two hundred million rupees (equivalent to about $150 million at today's value). Once Pakistan became a going concern, Gandhi went on a hunger strike to force India to hand over Pakistan's share of assets to the country.

I would not like to give an impression that I am attempting to belittle Gandhi Ji or imputing immoral motives to him. He had put his life on the line and toured the riot torn provinces of Bihar and Bengal, alone, without any protection whatsoever. In the immediate aftermath of partition he had gone on a hunger strike to force a reluctant Patel to offer security services protection to the Muslims of Delhi. He had undertaken a fast unto death so the wretched of the wretched, the untouchables, would be conceded equal legal status. Finally he was assassinated for favoring Muslims in 1948. All I am saying is that he was a pragmatic politician who would sacrifice friend and foe alike for what he considered a "higher" cause.

Post partition, starving refugees in untold millions, physically and mentally battered, destitute, and possessing only the clothes they wore, often carrying disabled elders and sick children on their backs, flooded into devastated towns and villages of the "moth eaten" land of the faithful. Millions more, in no better shape, moved to the other side.

India had a functioning government and was blessed with more geographic depth to accommodate the refugees. Pakistan was bereft of any infrastructure, with its administration in complete chaos, and businesses, industry, schools, and hospitals paralyzed. The law and order situation was fast deteriorating. British police and other civil service officers, from provincial governors and heads of the secretariat down, lacked direction and focus. Further, they were incensed that Jinnah had rejected Mountbatten's overtures to be asked to become the Governor General of Pakistan. The ones lower in hierarchy openly and gleefully witnessed the collapse of normal life.

India under Britain had two administrative divisions. Most of the country was ruled directly by Britain. About one third of the country comprising princely states was ruled through hereditary princes. The fiction of the princes having ceded certain discretionary rights to the paramount power was maintained. A British resident was, on paper, an "ambassador" from the mother country, but in effect supervised the state administration. The treaty agreements included a provision that if and when the British crown surrendered its paramount status, the ceded powers would revert to the princes. The Deputy Commissioner of the area supervised smaller states. If a small to middling ruler did not toe the line, he was easily replaced by a more amenable relative or the state could be taken over by the Court of Wards.[1]

There were literally hundreds of states ranging in size from Hyderabad, which was slightly bigger than France with its own currency, police and armed forces, to virtually those of the size of a village. Kashmir was the second largest state. In

---

[1] My Nana (mother's father) worked for the system and was highly respected by the rulers.

addition there were tiny Portuguese and French possessions, which did not fall in the equation of British-Indian negotiations.

The Independence of India act passed by the British parliament contained the provision that major rulers could a) remain independent b) accede to India c) accede to Pakistan. The legislation provided that the desires of the population were to be taken into account. The legally valid claims that unfettered sovereignty had been restored to the states were thrown overboard by the British government. Mountbatten did go through the charade of calling a Durbar of the native rulers and affirming that Her Majesty's government would stand by them, but advised that reality on the ground dictated that they strike a deal with one of the succeeding governments.

Most of the states, surrounded by Indian or Pakistani territory acceded to India or Pakistan. Hyderabad and Junagarh, both with a Muslim prince and largely Hindu population, decided to opt for independence. The Hindu Raja of Kashmir with Muslim majority among his subjects was wavering, and was negotiating with India as well as Pakistan. He could not make up his mind, and signed a standstill agreement with both Dominions. The dominant political party in Kashmir, with its fiery leader Sheikh Abdullah, favored India. In the event the Raja's mind was made for him. Muslim Mujahids, drawn from the ranks of zealots and tribal elements, reinforced by irregular elements of Pakistan army, decided to force the issue. They marched into Kashmir.

The joint force easily reached the capital, Sirinagar and the trained members of the expedition captured the electric supply station and cut off power to the city. The Mujahids fell upon the city, looting and pillaging. Both overlooked the airport and failed to secure the only link India had with the state. The land link with India was closed due to winter conditions.

The Raja, now desperate, asked India for help. Nehru was uncertain of the legal position. Mountbatten advised Nehru to demand accession of the state to India as the condition of support. The Rajah agreed. Indian troops were airlifted to Sirinagar and easily overcame the Mujahideen. Thus started the festering sore that has bled and debilitated both countries ever since. Pundit Nehru accused Pakistan of aggression and took the case to the UN Security Council. The council did demand that Pakistan withdraw its forces, but mandated a plebiscite to ascertain the opinion of the public. It also sent UN peacekeeping force to keep the combatants apart at the cease-fire line.

Lahore had been the capital of the since the Sikh ruled Punjab.[1] The Sikhs had deluded themselves into believing that the city would go to India. Though only 40% of the population, non-Muslims controlled 90% of education and health, 86% of industry and commerce and 75% of agriculture of the province. The Sikhs

---

1 After the fall of the Moghal Empire, the Punjab and much of what is current Pakistan (barring Sindh and Baluchistan), had fallen to the Sikhs. Please refer to *The Other Side of Silence* by Urvashi Batalia

had nearly as many holy sites in the western as in the eastern districts of the province. They would have been better off, many adherents of the creed came to believe later, if they had joined hands with the Muslims.[1]

Non-Muslims could not move to Indian Punjab overnight. Muslims could not go to Pakistan immediately, either. There was no one to advise them, much less to help them. People trickled to the other side in caravans which were pounced on by gangs on either side who murdered, raped and abducted women and children — for the greater glory of their religion. The military "genius" Mountbatten had not taken time to organize escorts of soldiers for the caravans. About a million lives were lost, over ten million displaced, women in the hundreds of thousands were abducted, raped and often burnt alive after the outrage. Dozens of trains with all the passengers dead, often cut into pieces, driven by a British conductor, would arrive in Lahore (Pakistan) or Amritsar (India), triggering further massacres.

Indian and Pakistani leaders could only look on helplessly, the liberal ones repentant that they had not come to an agreement with each other, the zealots swearing vengeance. There was not a word of apology from Mountbatten for the largest carnage in human history perpetrated by civilians because of his stupendous mistakes and mindless haste in partitioning India.

There was conflagration in other places too. Delhi was aflame. With no protection and little escort, at the very risk of their lives, Nehru and Maulana Azad and other ministers toured all precincts of Delhi. The Maulana made a memorable speech[2] to the Muslims who had sought shelter in the Red Fort. Bihar, parts of UP and Bengal exhibited examples of unprecedented bestiality.

India was passing through its own period of turmoil. Besides the constant threat of the Hindu–Muslim tension breaking into open warfare, all too often provoked by rumors of cow slaughter spread by miscreants, the authorities had to deal with *sharnarthees* — refugees — from Pakistan who, though concentrated mostly in the Indian Punjab and Delhi, had also spread all over northern India in substantial numbers. They were a generally enterprising lot and quickly established stalls of food, groceries and general merchandise on footpaths and in parks. Residents and shopkeepers of the posh area, Aminabad Park in Lucknow, were not happy with the situation. Out of sympathy with the displaced persons they refrained from protesting, initially, but gradually became vociferous in their complaints. The park was the pride of the city. People used to have picnics and children played there in the evenings and on Sundays. It was dotted by Qulfi and *lassi* shops.[3]

---

1 During later insurgencies in India they would join hands with Muslim Kashmiri rebels.
2 Please refer to his collected speeches.
3 A delicious ice cream and yogurt drink, very refreshing in the sultry heat of Indian summers.

There were linguistic and cultural problems too. People in UP addressed each other as Aap.[1] Sindhis were used to calling each other "Sain." We called beggars Sain. Among the Punjabis "Tusi" was a mark of respect. With us it sounded like a corrupted version of "Tum," an expression indicative of familiarity. Many a quarrel, sometimes ugly, would erupt between the natives and newcomers on such seemingly trivial issues.

The loss of wartime jobs had led to severe unemployment. At one point there were all India students, teachers, and trade union strikes simultaneously. Municipal and Civil services had been pushed to the breaking point. Refugees from Pakistan were living in Railway stations, parks and footpaths. Shantytowns had mushroomed in the outskirts of all cities. Governments, federal and provincial, were unable to cope. As though Hindu–Muslim conflicts were not enough, there were Muslim sectarian Shia–Sunni, Hindu upper and lower caste, immigrants and native, rich and poor, worker and capitalist conflicts.

There were bizarre incidents too. Pundit Nehru, triumphant after a non-aligned conference in Bandung, Indonesia, arrived in Lucknow and was greeted by black-flag-waving crowds of refugees. This was a novel experience for him. Visibly upset, he asked UP chief minister Panth to explain. The man, terrified out of his wits, expostulated that they were demonstrating against the UP government for not being able to provide jobs and shelter.

Expecting the usual mass adulation when he started to speak in the public meeting the next day, he was instead met by unruly crowds chanting antigovernment slogans and again waving black flags. It must have been a shock to a person who had emulated Jinnah and called his admirers uncouth rustics during a countryside tour.[2]

The whole scene was clearly visible from the balcony of the house facing the Park where I was staying. He started, "I went to Indonesia," only to be interrupted with hoots and catcalls. Annoyed, he turned to Panth, who gave him the excuse that the mike was not working. Workers scrambled to sort out the mike. He started again. The crowd erupted again. Now Panth blamed the gaslights hanging in front, obscuring public view of him. People could not see Pundit Ji. The lights were removed. The clamor did not diminish.

At this point Nehru lost his composure completely. Shouting at the top of his voice, he asked if they could not hear or see him, or was it an exhibition of insolence. He went on, targeting refugees, teachers, students, policemen and trade unions in turn, threatening to have refugees who had despoiled Lucknow's historic gardens and parks thrown across the Gomti (a local river), and to close

---

1 People in the north of India addressed elders and those they were not familiar with as "aap"; it denotes high regard. "Tum" is you.

2 On a motor tour of Indian Punjab some peasants stopped his car and asked him to make a speech. Incensed, he shouted rude remarks. The crowd responded with, "Pundit Nehru ki Jai" — long live Nehru. I read it in a newspaper in 1950.

schools and factories. The teachers had turned into gangsters, students had not learnt that they had won independence, workers that they were no longer serving the Raj and policemen had been very good at arresting him and clearing the way for the white masters but were unable to get him from the airport to the governor's house without harassment.

The police launched into the crowd, only to be told not to behave like fascist animals. He was working day and night to enhance the image of the country internationally. He was doing his job, and did not want expression of gratitude. He went on ranting and raving. Total silenced ensued. He smiled enigmatically and started again "I went to Indonesia" and the public terrified out of their wits, wouldn't even clap and applaud, when he regaled them with description of international meetings and events where he was feted and India so highly regarded.

While analyzing the early post independence period, one must not overlook the fact that the public and private persona of most of the people and some of the leaders were at a wide variance with each other. The first Indian president, Rajendra Prasad, though he had sworn to uphold and defend the Indian constitution, which was and remains secular in spirit and word, and though he was by convention bound to follow the prime minister's advice, decided to go to the consecration ceremony of the rebuilt Somnath Mandir against the express and public advice of Nehru. He covered himself with the fig leaf that he would attend the ceremony as a private citizen. He was, however, accorded the full state protocol.

There was overt discrimination against Muslims in jobs, school admissions and award of private and government contracts. If a member of the family had migrated to Pakistan the property of all members was confiscated. Muslims could not rent houses in choice localities. They were taunted and asked openly as to why did they not go to their beloved Pakistan? It was a Hindu Raj now. They better conform as the Hindus had done to Muslims norms when the latter had ruled India. In the famed Bollywood movie Garam Hava, the incomparable Balraj Sahni plays the lead role of a Muslim whose elder brother has left for Pakistan. The house they lived in was held in the name of the departed head of the family was taken over by the government and they were forced to leave. A poignant scene depicts the fate of the family. The mother hides herself in a chicken coop in a futile attempt to escape the government functionaries.

Independent India ushered in a rather radical change in the school system. In the ninth grade one could opt for Science, Arts (humanities) or Crafts (trades) groups. I chose the Science group, which did not have history, geography or drawing, all the subjects I detested. My school was highly competitive and strived to get one of its students among the top sixteen positions in the UP Education board examination once about every three to four years.[1] Our teachers gave free coaching to a select group of students. My mathematics teacher nominated me to

---

1 About 165,000 students took the 10th grade examination every year.

the group. He was a tall and fair Kashmiri Brahmin, immaculately clad in a *kurta* and *dhoti*[1] and sported a *tilak* (caste mark) on his forehead, but did not have a bit of communal prejudice. He advised me that I should learn Hindi because, given the prevailing linguistic chauvinism, answers/essays written in the national language would be given higher marks than would attempts in English. I had been brought up in an English medium of instruction. I protested; this was not fair. My teacher, as good a philosopher as any I have met, told me that life was not fair.

I was elated to be included in the select group. But it was not to be. In the first week of May 1951 we, along with the families of my Nana's brothers, embarked on a long and circuitous journey to Pakistan.

We alighted from the train at Muna Bao, the last station on the Indian side, tired but exhilarated by the idea of finally being within reach of the land of the pure and unlimited promise. We were herded into an open flat-bed truck, which drove us to the still open border. Fortunately it was only a short journey. We were off loaded on the Indian side and walked across to the Pakistani soil amid loud slogans of "Allah o Akbar" (God is Great) and "Pakistan Zindabad" (long live Pakistan). Pakistani truck drivers were there to greet us. We eventually arrived at a railway station named Khokrapar, which was a veritable tent town. We were lucky enough to find room under a huge water tank, which was a great relief in the harsh desert summer. We had to camp in the open air for several days waiting for the once-a-week special train to our next stop.

Quetta was unlike any city we had lived in before. It was cold even in May; the temperature would not go above the mid-sixties at midday and would drop to forties at night. We were, of course, comparing it to what we were used to in the UP province of India, over 110° during day time and in the 80's at night. The city was clean; the roads were actually washed and swept twice a day. Fruits and groceries were much cheaper than they were in India. But the most astounding difference was in the price of fruits. In India grapes were a delicacy. Only the rich could eat them, or apples for that matter, every day. They were offered wrapped in cotton wool at the fruit stalls. In Quetta they were dumped unceremoniously on carts as potatoes were in India, for about sixteenth of the price. We gorged ourselves on grapes and apples and developed indigestion.

The first house we rented had a surprisingly low rent. We were soon to discover the reason why. Among Indian Muslims when people move to a new accommodation, whether bought, built or rented, they have a gathering in which poems praising the Prophet of Islam are recited. It is called Meelad Sharif. Neighbors always join in and bring offerings of sweets. At the end of the proceedings Koranic verses are recited over the sweets. This is called Fateha. At the end of the

---

1 A waist-length shirt and intricately bound loin cloth was the typical dress of Brahmins, the priestly and academic class of Indians.

Fateha there is a bit of socialization and small talk and sweets are distributed to all.

Well, we had a very colorful party and the ladies of the neighborhood sang lustily and in good voice and tune. They were well made up and good looking, too. It turned out that my father had stumbled upon a *mohalla*[1] of singing and dancing women. To my dismay, we moved again within a few days to a drab and ugly location where no female could be sighted for all the gold in the world. It was a terrible letdown.

---

1 Popularly known as a red light district.

CHAPTER 4. EARLY POST-PARTITION: DIVERGENT PATHS

Right from day one of independence, India and Pakistan marched on different paths. The early divergence was predictable, I would venture to use the term pre-determined by the history, character, and to a minor extent by the belief system of the elite of the two communities.

The ruling class in Pakistan clung to the historic memory of primacy, disdain of commerce, and secular learning. Paying lip service to the nebulous concept of an international community of Muslim nations, the "Ummah,"[1] they nevertheless embraced the West, which they felt was the most certain means to secure their class interest. The general public was deluded by calls to unite under the banner of Islam. When India threatened to send its army to quell disturbances in Hyderabad, many Muslims believed that Turkey, which had been defeated in World War I, lost its Empire, escaped dismemberment by the skin of its teeth, abolished the Caliphate in 1924, would come to the aid of the Nizam, and that its armed forces will vanquish the Indian forces in two hours.

For Muslims left behind in India, the task of reconciliation of loyalty to India with the extra-national allegiance to the holy land was very onerous. A majority retained a passion for Pakistan too and would root for the country's team in field hockey and cricket matches between the two countries. This annoyed the Hindus terribly and gave invaluable ammunition to the fascist Hindu political parties and the narrow-minded Hindu officials an excuse to discriminate against

---

1 Ummah, referred to earlier, as well, is a nebulous concept indicating that all Muslims of the world belong to one community.

them in security related jobs. The unkindest cut was that they covertly, some-times even overtly, supported Pakistan in the Kashmir conflict.[1]

The basic teaching, that Islam was universal and all lands were God's cre-ation, was too esoteric a concept for the unsophisticated. Indian Muslims were bereft of cohesion once more. Moulvis stressed the hereafter at the expense of the here and now, adversely affecting initiative and diligence. They disparaged the process of assimilation, adherence to divines, and Mazar (tomb) veneration and unabashedly tried to subvert the composite Hindu–Muslim culture evolved over centuries. In fact I think, but for the tranquilizing visits to shrines and devotional music, many more Muslims would have fallen victim to the schizophrenic milieu they lived in.

Pakistan, no doubt suffered from relative lack of organization, resources and industry. Of much greater long-term significance was the fact that the core leadership of Muslim league minus Jinnah, a few expatriates and East Pakistanis, came from the feudal class and would naturally do whatever they could to retain and secure their privileges. They, in collusion with Mullahs and the bureaucrats who stood to lose their colonial status in a democratic dispensation, were able to subvert the political process.

Hindu upper class, on the other hand, had honed its diplomatic finesse, com-mercial expertise, and administrative, academic, and legal skills during a millen-nium long "foreign" rule. They were not hamstrung by anachronistic ideology.

India abolished the feudal system, bid goodbye to Mountbatten in 1948, ap-pointed an Indian Governor General and adapted a constitution, secular in lan-guage and intent in 1950. It overhauled the education system, initiated higher scientific and technological learning, put tariffs and other barriers to give the nascent industry a period of growth unhampered by foreign competition and molded the economy along socialist-welfare state lines. It enunciated a moral, anti colonialist and egalitarian stance in foreign policy, all this and much more within three years of independence. Under the auspices of Patel, India took over Hyderabad, Junagarh and Goa, thus wiping the colonial slate clean. By taking the Kashmir dispute to the UNO, Nehru upheld the rule and sanctity of law and went a long way to hold back the fascist element in India. It also kept his (and India's) image untarnished.

Nehru and Liaquat exchanged state visits in 1950, during which the public on either side welcomed them with equal enthusiasm. They agreed to substantive and goodwill measures, which included exchange of property and protection of minorities in each dominion. It became evident that if the governments, the zeal-ots and messianic maniacs did not incite them, the public was prepared to forgive and forget the dark days of partition.

---

1 The saving grace was the stellar performance of a Muslim non-commissioned officer Abdul Hameed who won the highest gallantry awards in the 1965 war with Pakistan.

In fact, the only blemish on India's performance thus far, but it was a big blot and did not bode well for the future, was failure to prevent Gandhi's assassination, though it gave Nehru a good reason to ban the fascist-communalist Hindu Mahasabha and its militant wing.

Jinnah had given a clarion call to his nation, that Pakistan would be a democracy, with equal rights for all citizens, regardless of creed or caste. Religion and state would stay in their own spheres, with non-interference in other's space. In a speech to the constituent assembly on September 11, 1947 he went to the extent of declaring that in times to come, Hindus would cease to be Hindus and Muslims would cease to be Muslims, in the political sense of the term.

With unprecedented zeal, sincerity and good fellowship, Pakistanis, the public and officials alike, setting aside all the ethnic, sectarian and linguistic fault lines, worked day and night to restore a semblance of order out of the shambles that they had inherited. Sindhis, Baluchis, Pathans and Bengalis received refugees bereft of worldly possessions with open arms. Export of jute from the Eastern Wing and cotton from the Western wing, roughly in proportion of two to one, earned the much-needed foreign exchange. After the initial tribulations, Pakistan's economy also received a timely shot in the arm from the financial bonanza of the Korean War.

In September 1948 the country suffered an early and overwhelming setback in the death of Jinnah. In sharp contrast to the Congress where Gandhi, though exercising decisive influence at critical times, could and often did fall back to Nehru, Patel and Azad, he had occupied a unique position in the Pakistan movement. The Muslim League before independence would have literally fallen on its face without Jinnah, he was Gandhi, Nehru, Patel and Azad all rolled into one. He used the League's Executive Committee only tactically to bide his time, weigh the pros and cons of a decision before announcing it. Many a time he was able to force the hand of his opponents to a hasty announcement.

His implacable will, incisive mind, supreme self-confidence and a character seemingly without a blemish, at least in the eyes of his followers who by 1946 counted nearly all the Muslims of India, endowed him with dictatorial powers in his party. He had a track record. He had quit politics rather than compromise on principles. He had defied Gandhi and Ali brothers and declared that introduction of religion in politics was a sure recipe for disaster. Earlier in his political career he had valiantly carried the flag of Hindu–Muslim amity. He had disdainfully declined the offer of a knighthood by the British government. Muslims made much of this gesture of self-respect.[1] They would have placed him on a higher pedestal if they could find one.

---

1 Gandhi had accepted a much lower honor for helping with recruitment of Indian soldiers during World War I.

It was not that Muslims were totally bereft of talent. But they suffered from a serious divide in the ranks. Azad, Qidwai, Khan brothers of NWFP, and the majority of Muslim clerics had lost credibility, in Muslim eyes, by association with the Congress. Mullahs opposed Pakistan. Jinnah had to function as the ideologue, chief executive and political leader all in one. The poet philosopher Iqbal, highly venerated and acceptable to all Muslims and many Hindus, in a supreme gesture of self-denial, had accepted Jinnah as his leader.

After he had been persuaded to return from England, Jinnah took charge of the League. He was lucky to outlive such stalwarts of feudal politics and his implacable foes as Sir Fazli and Sir Sikander Hayat, both of the Punjab. Eventually he was able to sideline the Muslim grandees who did not toe the line. He excluded such stalwarts as Sir Khizar Hayat of the Punjab and H.S. Suharwardy and Moulvi Fazal Haq of Bengal from core leadership of the League. He elevated people one could justifiably describe as yes-men into position of authority. He ridiculed a man of such stature as Maulana Azad into virtual nonentity among the Muslims. He treated religious scholars of Islam with haughty disdain, and reduced them to irrelevance in political affairs.

He had been seriously sick with tuberculosis for a long time and as one of his biographers[1] put it, he lived on will power, whisky and cigarettes, in that order. It was a highly and successfully kept secret. Mountbatten was to concede ruefully that had he known of the state of the health of Jinnah, he would have postponed independence and left India united.

Jinnah had worked indefatiguably for many years and continued doing so post-independence. He presided over the deliberations of the Pakistan Constituent Assembly, cabinet meetings, civilian and military state functions, inaugural ceremonies of all kinds and took all major policy decisions. In addition he undertook tours of the country. While addressing the Military brass in Quetta Staff College, he told the officers in no uncertain language that Civilian authority would always remain supreme in the country. He cashiered Ayub Khan for insubordination and would have dismissed him but for a plea of mercy on him by Miss Jinnah at whose feet Ayub had fallen upon, and pledged exemplary behavior forever.

He tried, according to his lights, to imbue the disparate ethnic, sectarian and linguistic groups in his charge, with a spirit of one nation. He overrode the objections of Sindhis and ordained separation of Karachi from the province and its designation as federal capital to be administered directly by the central Government

In fact, Jinnah made only one ill-considered move. This was his unequivocal and uncompromising declaration that Urdu and only Urdu will be the State language of Pakistan. Jinnah could not be accused of favoring one nationality or

---

1 *Jinnah of Pakistan* by Stanley Wolpert.

linguistic group, over another. He wanted to mold multilingual Pakistanis into one cohesive nation. Being entirely cerebral, he overlooked the need, passionate attachment and love people have for their own mother tongue. And he was in a hurry too, to take all the critical decisions before he passed on.

After Jinnah passed on, the threads of body politic started unraveling, slowly at first, precipitously as time went on. Liaquat, the designated heir, had been in the shadow of the great leader for too long. He was no Nehru with a well-defined persona and national constituency. He arranged the election of Nazimuddin, a well meaning though ineffective person from East Pakistan, to the office of Governor General. He made ambitious attempts to enhance his stature by addressing public meetings all over the country. He reiterated Jinnah's declaration in a public meeting that only Urdu would be the State language of Pakistan. The public exhibited their displeasure with vociferous protest and black flags. What people would take supinely from Jinnah, they would from no one else. Irrational insistence on solo status of Urdu was the first nail in the coffin of united Pakistan[1].

Liaquat could not persuade the disparate elements in the constituent assembly to frame a constitution. By presenting an objective principles resolution, which declared Pakistan an Islamic state, he conceded even the secular character of the state. That put paid to Jinnah's dream of a secular dispensation. Liaquat was a hereditary feudal lord and a conformist Muslim as well. Islam ordains inviolability of private property, however acquired, as do all other faiths. The Pakistan movement had more slogans than substance of an egalitarian society. Preservation of the holdings of the Muslim feudal class was devilishly camouflaged by shrill cries of Islam in danger. Liaquat shared the aversion of the West for communism and the Soviet Union with other Muslims.

In a foreign policy blunder, which was to have far reaching consequences, he turned down the invitation to visit the Soviet Union. The country had, forsaking its secular tenets, ordered a very reluctant Communist Party of India (CPI) to support the Pakistan movement.[2] Liaquat went to the USA instead, incurring long-term hostility of the leaders of the Soviet Union who were justifiably expecting more equitable treatment.

With time Liaquat got a firmer grip on the government. He had the advantage of recognition as a national leader. Other leaders had provincial constituencies. Suharwardy was still groping his way in the Punjab and had substantial rivals like Fazal Haq and Maulana Bhashani in his home province. Association with Gandhi had tainted him and made him suspect in most West Pakistani eyes.

---

1 As noted in the chapter on the student movement, the government gave in and accepted Urdu and Bengali as national languages with equal status after several students had been killed in a language riot in Dhaka, but it was too late.

2 Stalin ordered the Communist Party of India to support the Pakistan movement because it, according to him, represented self-determination for nationalities.

At a critical juncture Liaquat was distracted by an unfortunate development, the so-called Rawalpindi conspiracy in 1951, hatched by some disgruntled senior officers, in their opinion, less than zealous stand of Pakistan Government on Kashmir dispute. According to the Government of Pakistan, it was co-sponsored by the Communist party of Pakistan (CPP) and their fellow travelers. CPP categorically denied the charge, claiming that the government used the conspiracy as an excuse to neutralize it, reportedly at the advice of the CIA.[1]

CPI had been the most militant and fiercely anti-British component of the whole spectrum of the independence movement of India. They had joined hands with the Congress and other parties under the umbrella of the nationalist coalition and generally toed Gandhi's line. They were a little uneasy and ambivalent over the Soviet/German non-aggression pact, but were able to gloss over it by calling it a pragmatic and practical necessity. But they lost valuable political capital by seemingly unprincipled approval of a fascist system, which, except for a few Muslims and Hindus on the lunatic fringe, was derided by the whole spectrum of public opinion in India.

Once Hitler attacked the Soviet Union, CPI declared the war they had not too long ago derided as fascist-imperialist conflict, a people's war. But they had to pay a heavy price for supporting the colonial masters. They were accused of supporting anti-national interests and were effectively marginalized by the Congress. It is a tribute to the resilience of the CPI organization that they rebounded, regrouped, not only to survive but also to thrive in independent India. Even the great Soviet-Chinese schism, ideological on the surface but in reality nationally chauvinistic in nature, did not quite extinguish the flame of class struggle.

Communist stalwarts and staunch fellow travelers willingly accepted army commissions. One of them, Faiz was the leading leftist-revolutionary poet of Urdu. He taught English in a college and was to be the Chief Editor of the leading publishing house, Progressive Newspapers of Pakistan and a recipient of the Lenin peace prize. He was, as is the wont of academics, bohemian in his habits and did not quite fit the image of an officer in a spit and polish army.

CPI sent a few party stalwarts to organize CPP as most of the communists in what became Pakistan were non-Muslims and had migrated to India. Communist or not they were at the risk of being physically eliminated. But the party shared the general disarray of the society. Members openly flouted the directives of the Secretary General Sajjad Zaheer, claiming that he had been foisted on them. A railway trade union leader in Punjab launched a strike against specific advice of the party chief who had told the man that workers had not attained the degree of political maturity to withstand the inevitable government onslaught. He

---

1 I met several stalwarts of the party during my stay in Pakistan between 1983 and 1991. With one voice they asserted that there was no conspiracy, only drunken boasts by a few disgruntled army officers who knew Sajjad Zaheer, the secretary general of the party.

was proven right. The government was easily able to crush the union into virtual oblivion.

In any event, the conspiracy was such an amateurish affair; more akin to a school prank than a serious attempt to wrest power from an entrenched regime. Key members, in their cups, confided detailed plans to fellow officers, many of whom were in the intelligence wing of the Army. The conspirators were apprehended. Liaquat made a great speech on Pakistan Radio, castigating ideological foes of the nation, pledging his life to the integrity of the country and complimenting security services for the good job they had done. Widely acclaimed for the superb handling of what could have turned out to be a nasty and destabilizing affair, he was finally recognized as his own man. The nation closed ranks behind him.

The conspirators, armed forces officers and their civilian comrades were tried and awarded exemplary sentences. Civilians, Faiz among them, spent years in jail. For Urdu literature it was a boon. He wrote some of his best poetry while incarcerated. Among the Indian nationals caught in the net was Sajjad Zaheer Secretary General of CPP, a leading light of Progressive Writers Association of India and scion of a leading nationalist Muslim family of India. Another was Hasan Nasir, scion of an aristocratic family from Hyderabad Deccan, who had been recruited to the communist Party while a student in Cambridge, England. The government availed itself of the opportunity to ban the CPP.

Liaquat's words turned out to be prophetic. He did give his life for the nation. Empowered by his successful handling of the conspiracy, he had become a great threat to the feudal/bureaucratic cabal. He could generally overcome the opposition on routine issues, but not on basic conflict of giving seats to East Pakistan in the parliament commensurate with their numbers. He had permitted H.S. Suharwardy to return to Pakistan perhaps with an idea of an alliance with him against the feudal interest. Next only to Jinnah in intellectual weight, scion of an ancient Sufi house of eminent scholars, Suharwardy could serve as a counter weight to the parasitical reactionaries. He had earned the displeasure of Jinnah for the temerity on a few occasions to oppose the big leader who had forbidden the latter in Pakistan, ostensibly for not having attended the proceedings of the constituent assembly for several months. He had stayed behind in India and accompanied Gandhi into tours of areas worst affected by communal riots. Returning to Pakistan in 1949, he launched a political party which soon attracted wide attention and following in both wings of the country.

Now Liaquat had finally achieved the status Nehru enjoyed after Patel died, and could overwhelm the feudal-bureaucratic cabal. The cabal could not countenance hara-kiri. In an election based on adult franchise, East Pakistanis would have a majority of seats. With their help Liaquat would be able to command a big enough majority to pass a democratic constitution, divert expenditure to social services, and God forbid abolish the feudal system. He had to be removed.

On October 16th, 1951, he was gunned down just as he had started addressing a mammoth gathering in Rawalpindi. It was reported later that a demented former soldier who was unhappy with his Kashmir policy had acted alone. The assassin was beaten to death on the spot by the enraged public, or so was claimed by Government officials. He was thus kept, in the most effective way, from divulging names of co-conspirators. An official enquiry came to no definite conclusions.

On Liaquat's death, Khwaja Nazimuddin was persuaded to step down from the office of the Governor General, and takeover as the Prime Minister on the ostensible grounds that a person of his standing, hailing moreover from the majority province, was needed at the helm in such parlous times. It was not Khwaja's stature, but his weak personality, which was so enticing. The office of Governor General had all the reserve powers of the British crown vested in it, but only Jinnah had the stature and the nerve to use them. At his death it had become ceremonial, as it was meant to be. Ghulam Muhammad, finance minister under Liaquat, took over as GG. He was the godfather of bureaucrats of Pakistan. A shrewd operator, his claim to fame was the anti-capitalist budget he had helped Liaquat draft during the term of the interim the Congress/League coalition Government of 1945.

Khwaja Sahib's tenure as PM was marred by intense factional infighting among the ruling Muslim League power brokers. The Anti-Qadiani[1] movement, aided and abetted by Mullahs and surreptitiously supported by detractors of Khwaja Nazim, broke out. Agitation in the Punjab, initiated by *agents provocateurs* under the sway of the cabal, was strongly supported by a leading cleric Maulana Maududi. It resulted in loss of lives of scores of hundreds of people and could only be controlled by an imposition of martial law in Lahore, which gave the Pakistani Army the first taste of authority over civilians.

Khwaja Nazim was not in full control of his cabinet. According to Shahab,[2] even a cabinet-secretary level person like Iskander Mirza could interrupt the Prime Minister, rudely and with impunity. Khwaja Sahib was short and rotund. Soon a concerted campaign of ridicule, the most potent weapon of undermining a person, was launched against him. His eating habits, the enormous amount of food he allegedly consumed, were given common currency. His detractors stooped to spread rumors that he would regurgitate food after a full meal and eat again.

---

1 Qadianis, so called after Qadian, the birthplace of the founder of the sect, believe in all the basic tenets of Islam but do not subscribe to the belief that Muhammad was the last prophet. They are also called Ahmadis after the last name of their prophet, Ghulam Ahmad. Current scholarship would have it that the British inspired the faith to divide Muslims. This view is supported by the fact that Qadianis do not accept the concept of Jihad. This was ostensibly a campaign to declare the sect as non-Muslims. The army had to be called in and that gave it a taste of power.

2 *Shahab Nama* by Q.U. Shahab, a senior civil servant of Pakistan.

He had frequent confrontations with Ghulam Muhammad who was in cahoots with the cabal[1]. He subverted the democratic process by using his reserve powers to sack the cabinet and co-opted the army into civilian administration by giving the army commander Ayub Khan simultaneous charge as defense minister, thus setting a precedent that all coup leaders since have followed. The Governor General, by convention, could not sack the Prime Minister, unless the latter lost a vote of confidence or was defeated on a major legislation like the budget and refused to resign. This Prime Minister had just successfully piloted the annual budget bill through the assembly.

Ghulam Muhammad recalled Pakistan's ambassador to the USA, Muhammad Ali Bogra to take over as Prime Minister. The man had no constituency or public standing. His only qualification was that he hailed from East Pakistan. Ghulam Muhammad was from the Western wing, so he balanced the ticket, on paper. He functioned more as a personal assistant than as head of the government.

When the assembly tried to assert its inherent powers, Ghulam Muhammad decided to give up even the pretence of abiding by the rules/traditions of separation of executive and legislative branches of the government and sacked the assembly. The speaker of the assembly Moulvi Tamizuddin Khan, a highly respected legislator of high integrity, filed a suit against the dissolution of the assembly in Sindh High court, which found the Governor General in contravention of the laws of the country. The government appealed to the Supreme Court, which found a legal subterfuge to uphold the Governor General's decision. That was the blow from which democracy and the judiciary in the country never recovered.[2]

Pakistan had hitherto never had national elections. Denial of due number of seats to the majority of the population living in East Pakistan had always been the stumbling block. The real apprehension of the ruling West Pakistani junta was that East Pakistanis will not only try to redress their under representation in civil and military services, but also cut back on the defense budget, promote industrialization and development of the capitalist-bourgeoisie class, which will sound the death knell of the feudal-tribal system.

The national assembly had been a holdover from pre-independence days. To test the waters, it was decided to hold elections in East Pakistan. Power brokers were optimistic that with a bit of slogan mongering, rigging, official coercion and meddling, a malleable assembly would be elected. They had reckoned without the intense feeling of alienation, and political awareness of East Pakistanis. The opposition agreed to a coalition of all parties under the leadership of a triumvirate of H.S. Suharwardy, Moulvi Fazal Haq and Maulani Bhashani, all stalwarts

---

1 Bureaucrats with the feudal landowners and army as junior partners controlled all levers of power.

2 In 2007, after he was asked by Musharraf to resign, the Chief Justice of the Supreme Court put up a lot of resistance but was "dysfunctionalized" by the dictator. He was reinstated after an intense struggle. Musharraf, not sure if the court will declare him eligible to contest the office of the President, preempted the court by suspending the constitution and imposing emergency

of the independence movement. It was a debacle for the ruling party. Out of three hundred ten seats on offer, the ruling Muslim League could win only nine. All the outgoing cabinet ministers lost, the Chief Minister losing to a college student. The ruling junta was, however, able to promote one faction at the cost of another. The coalition partners fell out.

The country had to have an elected central legislative-constituent assembly. They could not risk another humiliation in an all country election under adult franchise. They chose members of the provincial assemblies as the Electoral College. It was an indirect election. Its representative character of the assembly thus elected, was at best dubious.

Ghulam Muhammad died. He had reportedly been suffering from G.P.I.[1] He had to be kept in the office, Mafia style, till his last breath so the power brokers could take decisions in his name without falling out among themselves. The cabal chose to replace him with Iskander Mirza[2], a past master of the art of divide and rule, trained by colonial bureaucrats themselves.

Mirza manipulated members of the new national assembly like puppets on a string. He even managed to entice Suharwardy and many others with the lure of office and power. A new political grouping christened the Republican Party was concocted. Even Dr. Khan Sahib, an icon of Pakhtoon nationalism and secular politics, who had been the pro Congress Chief Minister of the Frontier province in 1947 and had taken on Jinnah himself, joined the new group.

Under the pretext that neither of the two wings would be able to dominate over the other, all the provinces of the Western wing were merged into one unit. Members of the smaller provinces were forced to vote in favor of the unholy union, some literally at gunpoint. Despairing of the hope of ever attaining their rightful goal of commanding a majority of seats in the central assembly proportionate to their population, East Pakistan leaders capitulated and agreed to parity between the two wings. The assembly was able to pass a constitution in 1956. Pakistan was to be an Islamic republic with a parliamentary system of government. Iskander Mirza, the Governor General, was elected the first President of the country.

Now the stage was set for the first general elections, based on adult franchise. All political parties started campaigning in earnest. Qayyum Khan, a veteran League leader led a procession tens of miles long, of trucks, bullock carts, motorcycles, buses, and tractors. It was a carnival making its serpentine way from one end of West Pakistan to nearly the other. People were euphoric. They will be able to face up to the rivals from birth, India that had had a democratic dispensation all along. The press was rejuvenated. All shades of opinion from radical left to

---

1 General Paralysis/Insane, the terminal stage of syphilis.
2 He had been a senior officer in the colonial army and had transferred to the political department of civil service, which administered tribal areas. He traced his lineage to Mir Jafar of Bengal who had betrayed his ruler in a battle with East India Company in 1757.

fanatic right had their unfettered say. Suharwardy, Bhashani and Fazal Haq addressed mammoth crowds in East Pakistan.

Suharwardy commanded a following in smaller provinces of West Pakistan as well. He was accepted in the Punjabi heartland too. The cabal was apprehensive that if they lost Punjab to an East Pakistani leader, they were well and truly lost. Religious parties were conspicuous by the lack of support they could command. The army was still unsure of its credibility in the political domain. Maulana Bhashani, also known as the "red" Mullah because of his radical views, combined in his person a peasant leader, a practicing "Pir" — living saint — with a huge following and a populist politician, would command substantial support in East Pakistan. The party had a considerable following in smaller provinces of West Pakistan and urban areas of the Punjab. The redoubtable Hasan Nasir, Secretary General of CPP, was in charge of the central office. Moulvi Fazal Haq was a populist par excellence and a cleric/attorney as well and had had the largest following in Bengal till overwhelmed by Jinnah.

People, though, had a feeling that the cabal was looking for an excuse to subvert the nascent democratic process. They still clung to a forlorn hope and cheered the speakers when they made a good point and were duly respectful to men of national stature. They were, by and large, well informed. Holy cows like religion and Kashmir were freely argued over. The inordinate amount of funds spent on maintaining a disproportionately huge armed forces establishment at the cost of health, education, creation of jobs and public welfare, was openly discussed.

The power brokers could, however, not countenance the possibility of losing even a tiny measure of control. They set about creating chaos as a pretext to unconstitutional takeover. Police informers, gangsters, smugglers, petty thieves and all the antisocial elements got into the act. Mullahs played the most infamous role. They claimed that secular leaders would subvert the very basis of Pakistan, which was "there is no God but God." Bureaucrats used their power, authority and patronage unscrupulously to disrupt public life. Landowners used their considerable muscle. Frequent fist fights were staged in assemblies. The deputy speaker of East Pakistan assembly was killed when he got in the way of a chair thrown at a member of the assembly.

# Chapter 5. Education and Socio-Economic Conditions in Pakistan, 1951 to 1957

## Sandeman High School, Quetta, 1951–1952

Quetta had been a beautiful town. A shallow *nallah* separated a meticulously organized cantonment area from the town.[1] But it had been devastated. Even in 1951, four years after independence, at least half the houses retained obvious signs of arson. Nearly every house had the characteristic Hindu cult sign-phonetically called "OM" — which looks like inverted Swastika of Nazis.[2] In pre-partition days, non-Muslims lived in towns; Muslims, as in all other provinces of the new country, lived in shantytowns outside municipal limits.

In the Punjab, local Muslims had captured most of the property of fleeing non-Muslims. The rest had fallen in the hands of Muslim refugees from the Indian Punjab, who were ethnically and linguistically the same as the local population. Punjabis were the great beneficiaries in Baluchistan as well. In the NWFP, the local Pathans initially looted, and subsequently took over all the evacuee property, as the homes and businesses of non-Muslims who had fled to India, were called. In Sindh Urdu-speaking immigrants grabbed the lion's share. Local Sindhis were left high and dry, harboring resentment[3] which is very much alive to this day.

Baluchis, who constitute the majority of the population, have always been under the firm control of the tribal chiefs and took up arms only when ordered to

---

1 A drainage stream, which can vary enormously on size. This one was 10 feet wide and 8 deep.
2 Fanatic Hindu parties in India actually support Hitler-Nazis. In fact the two signs claim a common Aryan heritage. Please refer to *Temptations of the West* by Pankaj Mishra.
3 Dealt with at length in the chapter Pakistan 1983–91.

do so by the Sirdars.[1] Their resentment over exploitation of the natural resources of the province, incited largely by tribal chiefs who were unhappy because Punjabis ruled over their region, developed into a latent insurgency, which erupted into a violent form every few years. Ayub took mild punitive measures against them. Bhutto initially gave them considerable leeway, but resorted to coercive measures soon after, reportedly at the behest of the Shah of Iran, who was apprehensive that his own restive Baluchis would join hands with their Pakistani brethren. Zia followed suit with his own atrocities. It was relatively quiet during the quasi-democratic dispensation between the Zia and Musharraf dictatorships. The latter emulated Bhutto in the ferocity of his assault on the unfortunate province.

The school I was admitted to was a far cry from the posh school I had left in India. The building was good enough, but the students looked like denizens of a reformatory. One of my classmates had the dubious distinction of making the most wanted list with his picture-posters adorning the drab walls of every police station. The milieu was medieval. Even the most hardened criminal would bow his head before his teacher. I remember my Urdu teacher mercilessly caning a ferocious student, twice his size, in my class. With a few exceptions the teachers were uniformly kind. If any teacher got out of line, the Head Master who belonged to the "old school," would straighten out his subordinate in no uncertain manner. The standard of teaching and the caliber of students were far lower. A peculiarly archaic version of Urdu I was not familiar with was used as the medium of instruction. One question sticks to memory. The plural of "Dukan" (shop) was not the usual "Dukanain," but the Arabic "Dakakeen".[2]

In the half yearly examinations I failed in all the subjects except English.

Most of the students were Punjabi speaking, who though physically well endowed were no match in ferocity to the indigenous Baluchi, Pathan or Hazara students.[3] Hazara is a Shia-Pathan tribe originally from Afghanistan, where they still live in the north. They have Mongol features and initially I had taken them for Nepalese Gorkhas. Hazaras who lived in the south of the Afghanistan had fled the ethnic-sectarian atrocities to Quetta in late nineteenth and early twentieth century. I had felt acutely uncomfortable in the school. I was a sickly boy. That didn't matter so much in India. Nearly all my fellow students were puny. Here physical build was at a premium. And like the Britain of mid nineteenth century intellectualism was disdained. All the emphasis was on sports and fashion.

---

1 It has since changed much for the worse. Zia's Jihad bestowed guns and heroin on it. An influx of Afghan refugees, ethnically similar to Quetta Pathans, tilted the ethnic balance against Baluchis.

2 Usual plural would be "Dukanain" but an Arabized version was being taught.

3 Hazaras have snub noses like those of the Nepalese. They follow the Shia creed of Islam and had fled religious persecution in Afghanistan in the nineteenth century. They were persecuted again by Taliban in the 1990s.

## Government College, Quetta 1952–1954

I had this terrible desire or I should say longing to be popular, looked up to and be a highly respected citizen. Public speaking was highly regarded only among the intellectually inclined. They were scarce. This was all that could be well within my reach. But I was terribly shy, and spoke very fast, almost unintelligibly. My first experience of public speaking, though over five decades ago, is still fresh in my mind. It was an unmitigated disaster. I walked to the dais, put my hands on the rostrum and started my peroration. After a minute or two, the speech which I had memorized and rehearsed innumerable times, went clean out my mind. I started stuttering. My trembling hands, with which I held on to the rostrum for dear life, caused it to shudder on the dais. Both were both made of wood, and produced a sound like early thunder. I was myself not conscious of the noise at the time. I heard of it later from my friends. The audience became hysterical. They had never witnessed a scene like that before. The presiding officer tried to calm them down, in vain.

I was distraught and ready to give up. If I could not hold my own even in an intellectual field, I was a lost cause. I decided to put myself through more trials of public speaking. But a sage once said that you cannot produce a melodious voice out of a harsh one, however much you practice. I did not have to go through the agony of the first stage fright, but never could master the art. I did not have the gift.

My intense desire to be famous led me to the meetings of the student wing of a fundamentalist organization called Jamaat e Islami (JI). It was founded by and led at the time by an outstanding scholar and prolific writer, Maulana Maududi. Maulana Sahib had a small, but an intensely loyal following in Pakistan and was respected even more in the Middle East and counted the Saudi Royal family among his admirers.

Pakistan had not yet become the most allied of the allies of the US-that was to come later, and had actually recognized the communist government in China. The clerics, vociferous in castigation of the infidel USSR and China, were subdued in their reaction to the Korean War, which was actually a great economic boon to Pakistan in that its exports got a good market. Nasser's takeover of Egypt in 1951 presented a dilemma to conservative cadres. While they could not openly condemn it till Nasser came down heavily on Akhwan ul Muslimoon,[1] they were uneasy with his nationalist, anti-imperialist stance. Maududi's incitement of anti-Qadiani movement in Punjab in 1953 was to have a far-reaching effect.[2]

---

1 Muslim Brotherhood.
2 Qadianis referred to earlier. The campaign reflected collusion between establishment and religion.

## University of Karachi: 1954-1957

I was accepted in the three years BSC honors course at the University of Karachi. I chose chemistry as my major. I was not terribly keen on chemistry but had somehow to while away time till I could get into a medical college that was two years away. Early on in the university I did attend classes conscientiously.

Before arrival in Karachi I had spent all my time in small provincial towns and was socially naïve and unsophisticated. I believed going to a restaurant for a cup of tea was a sign of dissipation. It was actually not such an outlandish concept, nor a sign of mental backwardness. In India people had spacious houses with plenty of room for entertainment. Only cosmopolitan cities like Lucknow boasted of a large number of teahouses.

Karachi had had an unprecedented influx of refugees and was bursting at the seams. Pre-independence, it was a small well-ordered city with a population of about 150,000. It had plentiful water supply, good sanitary service and clean air. Roads were wide and well laid out. Trams and buses provided effective local transport. Numerous parks dotted the city. There was little ethnic strife. Under a gentlemen's agreement, the Mayor's office rotated between Muslim, Hindu and Parsee communities. Muslims, except for a few rich landowners in the fashionable seashore locality of Clifton, lived in ramshackle dwellings outside the town.

In 1954, just seven years after independence, the population had already risen to about three million. Mansions of Hindus and Sikhs had been inundated with an over flowing mass of humanity. Municipal services had even stopped pretending that they could cope. Water was brought in tankers, I think twice a week. Long lines would form hours before a tanker was scheduled to arrive. If the sanctity of the line were violated, frequent fistfights would break out, even among the delicately nurtured. Prefabricated toilets were set out in rows outside the Jhuggis.[1] Starting at early hours of the morning, long lines would form there too. There were open gutters everywhere. It stank to high heaven. But nobody was particularly put out by the smell. It was more like a vast refugee/displaced persons camp than a city. When it rained, the "roof" of the Jhuggis dripped capriciously. But the huts were very cheap, could be erected in hours and did provide shelter.

Hundreds of thousands lived in apartments. Several families would share tiny quarters with a family of five or six or more people in a room. But compared to Jhuggi dwellers, these were the lucky ones. Still others lived in public parks, corridors of government offices and footpaths. Adversity brings out fellow feeling in people. A newly arrived family was sure to find shelter with the extended family, friends or with erstwhile neighbors or even with people of the same town back home in India

---

1 A Sindhi name for a primitive hut fabricated with a skeleton of bamboo poles and covered with straw mats.

Unlike the Punjab, Sindh had not been traumatized by a communal holocaust. Riots started only a year after partition. Sindhis continued to maintain good relations with their Hindu compatriots. One of the reasons for the nostalgia Muslim Sindhis have for the Hindu ones is that, again unlike the Punjab which had an influx of ethnically identical refugees, Sindh faced an avalanche of culturally and linguistically very different immigrants. To make matters even worse from their perspective, the newcomers took over all aspects of life in Karachi and other large cities of Sindh.

More than half of the college and university students held a full time job as well. They would generally make a token appearance in the office, and then slip away to their classes. Practically everyone from tenth grade upwards had a part-time job. I tutored fifth and sixth graders.

The three years I spent in Karachi University were the most formative years of my life. I got exposed to political activism and developed a passion for reading. My first mentor was a classmate in Chemistry Department, Sibghat U. Kadri. He was a veteran of the student movement in Pakistan.

Sibghat left for England in 1959 after he had managed to get a two-year degree in five years. He had spent most of his time on political activities, and had been elected General Secretary of the Students Union in 1957. In England he worked for the BBC for a while, was active in the Labor party and the local communist party, qualified as Barrister-at-law, and in due course developed a good legal practice. His crowning achievement was appointment as Queens Counsel (QC).[1]

Besides indulging in radical politics, I developed the habit of reading during those years. It took some effort, though. The first book I managed to read was *Moulin Rouge*, a novel based on the life of the French artist Henri de Toulouse Lautrec, after several frustrating attempts. The second was *Hot Water* by P.G. Wodehouse. I found PG is a humorist beyond compare. I also read tomes on history, politics, international relations, and literary classics of French, Russian, English and others European masters, books on philosophy, especially by Bertrand Russell, Urdu novels, and *Arabian Nights*. The university librarian used to marvel at my consumption of books, and at times would admonish me that I should pay more heed to the subjects for which I had enrolled in the university.

---

1 Highly regarded barristers in the UK.

## CHAPTER 6. NEHRU AND AYUB YEARS

## INDIA UNDER NEHRU

In India, an enlightened and liberal leadership of immensely popular veterans of the war of independence had concentrated on building a nation. They had earned a lot of political capital by land reforms. The reforms were on the whole effective, though many loopholes like exemption of self-cultivated lands and orchards from government acquisition had been left in the legislation. Rajputs[1] were the main beneficiaries. This specially occurred in UP and Bihar, where the erstwhile warrior class dominated the countryside.

There were a few tragicomic episodes. The descendents of Wajid Ali Shah, the last Nawab of Oudh,[2] which had been incorporated by the British in the UP state in 1856, with a promise to restore the territory to his progeny, took out pathetic processions demanding that the head of their clan be restored to the throne. The claimants were legally in the right. The government of India had inherited all the obligations of the departing regime. The Queen was still the head of the state of both countries. But history supersedes law.

The country was beset with all kinds of problems. Unemployment, poverty, hunger, lack of clean water, inadequate shelter, a poorly maintained infrastructure and socio-economic inequities were issues of enormous proportions. An avalanche of demoralized refugees had been driven out of their home and hearth in what became Pakistan. They had lost their loved ones. Young women had been

---

1 The warrior, ruling class Rajput — progeny of the Raj — are known by different names like Thakur, Rana, etc. They came to a working arrangement with Muslim rulers, especially with the Moghals, with whom they intermarried.

2 The Nawab of Oudh was the last word in decadent living. East India Company, which ruled India as agents—on paper—of the Moghal king, removed this Nawab and exiled him to Calcutta.

abducted, and fathers had been forced to witness the rape of daughters. They wanted to avenge all the wrongs committed on them by the gangsters in the land of their fathers on the Muslims left in India.

The twenty million Indian[1] Muslims had, in popular perception, lost all rights in the country of their ancestors. They would have shared the fate of the Jews in Germany, but for the fact that India had a liberal, secular, and democratic leadership, which passionately believed in justice, fair play, and reason. The Indian National Congress (INC) leadership counted such Muslim stalwarts as Maulana Azad and Rafi Qidwai among its top ranks. Patel who was not exactly sympathetic to Muslims, did not allow Nehru a free hand, but was kept in check by the liberal members of the cabinet.

Muslims in India were frequently subjected to such taunts as "why don't you go to Pakistan" or undergo "Shuddhi"[2] (re-conversion to Hinduism), even in the cities which had never seen a communal riot. Riot ridden towns treated their Muslims in a much worse fashion. These insults were hurled at students too, but never in the hearing of teachers. There was no doubt that there were communalists among the teachers too, but except in rare instances and that too covertly, they never ignored their implicit duty that, *in loco parentis*, they had a responsibility to all students in their charge. The police were less restrained and would often look the other way if a Muslim were being harassed.

Nehru had shrewdly, idealistically if you will, steered India clear out of sphere of influence of Americans and Soviets alike. India was the world's largest democracy and inheritor of an ancient history and vibrant culture. Both superpowers had been clamoring for India's affections. Neither could afford to let go. Nehru had also imposed tariffs and controls on imports to protect the Indian bourgeoisie, which was to be the biggest beneficiary of freedom from foreign competition. Abolition of *zamindari* also had removed an entrenched rival of industry from the corridors of power.

Nehru was one of the primary proponents of non-alignment. That was an anathema to Dulles, the US secretary of state and *eminence grise* of the country's conservative establishment. But he dared not say it openly. Nehru went from triumph to triumph. He consorted with Tito, Nasser, Soekarno and Zhou-en-Lai. A grand conference of non-aligned nations was held in Bandung. Punch Shila, five principles of non-alignment movement, struggle against colonialism, peaceful coexistence, self-determination, non-interference in internal affairs, and economic emancipation of the workers were enunciated as the guiding principles. Nehru

---

1 India in 1947 had a population of 400 million out which 100 million were Muslims. Pakistan had 80 million Muslims, while India kept 20 million of them.

2 Hinduism does not accept converts. On the theory that nearly all Indian Muslims had converted to Islam from the untouchable class of Hinduism, they were offered this opportunity and would revert to that class.

castigated Britain, France and Israel on its invasion of Egypt while Pakistan's response was muted.

Contrary to common belief, Nehru had not neglected domestic issues. Indians owe their large presence in international finance and industry to his far sightedness. The computer/internet centers in the Indian cities of Hyderabad and Bangalore control the information services of the United States. This was all built on the foundations of All India Institutes of Technology. There are five such institutes. Admission in anyone of them is more highly prized than that in one of the Ivy League schools in the US.

Nehru fumbled in one cabinet appointment. He had given the ministry of defense to a respected crony, Krishna Menon. Menon had spent lonely and forlorn years in the UK and was embittered by anonymity, while less mentally endowed politicians basked in the glow of public adoration in India. He earned his keep in London by cooking Indian-style desserts[1] and selling them to Indian students. Nehru had initially appointed him High Commissioner of India to Britain. This was appropriate reward to a person who had been disdained by the British establishment. In the early years, Menon had represented India's case on Kashmir to the Security Council of the UNO and had made himself wholly unpopular in a very short period of time. He snubbed journalists, financiers and diplomats with equal facility. Nehru had brought him back home to mend fences with the international community.

At the ministry, the unquestioning obedience of military officers seemed to give him more scope for un-orthodox behavior. Further, he appeared to harbor unmitigated aversion for the men in uniform. He transferred senior officers at a whim and took to promoting them out of turn, with scant consultation with the chiefs of services. In one widely reported incident he shouted forty senior generals out of his office. There was uproar in the parliament. Opposition leaders demanded Menon's head. Nehru was hard put to defend him. He resorted to a declaration that civilian authority would always reign supreme in India. As though not entirely content with treating the senior brass shabbily, he had refrigeration and washing machine manufacturing machinery installed in ordnance factories.

In a Machiavellian move Nehru had got rid of all the senior ministers from the cabinet under the Kamraj plan[2] when the border dispute with China blew up in his face. Ostensible cause of the dispute was the border, which the British, in their imperial arrogance and ignorance, had arbitrarily drawn along a line named

---

1 During the late 1960sI visited a restaurant founded by Menon in London located near the Indian High Commission. It displayed a large portrait of the man. The owner told me that Menon made *gulab jamun*, a syrupy and very sweet Indian dessert.

2 The plan attributed to Kamraj, the then Congress President, proposed that senior ministers resume party organizational work, which the junior functionaries were not able to do well. Nehru asked for the resignation of the entire cabinet and then proceeded to reappoint his favorites.

McMahon[1] after the perpetrator of the deed, without any regard for historical, cultural or linguistic considerations. The Chinese were too weak at the time to do anything about it. India and China had conducted low-level and unsuccessful negotiations to sort out the dispute. The area was desolate, high up in the mountains, with air so low in oxygen that for a person of the plains it was difficult to take a few steps without getting short of breath. Only nomads, grazing sheep and goats could subsist there.

Nehru and Chinese PM Zhou-en-Lai were two pillars of non-aligned movement. India had willingly courted disapproval of the US government, which had consistently vetoed all moves to replace Taiwan with the government of the mainland in the UNO, by vigorously supporting China's rightful claim to a seat in the General Assembly and the Security Council. Whenever a delegation from either country visited the other, the public made frequent, enthusiastic and vociferous demonstration of goodwill with slogans such as Hindi Chini Bhai Bhai — Chinese and Indians are brothers. Passions grew to a crescendo when the prime ministers exchanged visits.

China, seemingly out of the blue and peremptorily, demanded that India withdraw immediately to a line the former had decided was the correct border. India rejected the ultimatum. China responded by swarming over the border. They met surprisingly little resistance. Indians fled,[2] leaving their arms, ammunition and even their uniforms behind. With Indian forces melting away from their path, the Chinese pushed on deep into Indian Territory.

A wide spread international uproar ensued. The Soviet Union and other communist bloc leaders adopted a posture of studied neutrality. The US was the great beneficiary of the conflict. India had to climb down from its lofty moral pedestal and look up to rather than down on the West. President Kennedy, a great admirer of Nehru, offered moral and material assistance, and expeditiously air freighted massive supplies.[3]

Indian Armed forces were the other great beneficiaries of the border war. The new defense chief bent over backwards to cater to all their desires. Resources were lavished on them. The Soviet Union, which had hitherto been the main supplier of armaments, offered manufacturing technology in addition to making up all the losses incurred in the border war. Americans and other Western powers, though desirous of not being outdone, did not dare go quite as far, did ship substantial arms supplies. Indian armed forces also managed to develop a working relationship with the American brass.

---

1 The British and the French had carved out countries across Africa and the Middle East. The border between Afghanistan and Pakistan, called the Durand Line, is similarly disputed. Please refer to the book *Empire's Workshop* by Greg Grandin.

2 The Pakistani press gleefully and derisively reported that Hindu *banyas* — a term for petty shopkeepers — had left their *dhotis* — loin cloths — behind.

3 He and his brother Robert had visited him in India in 1951 and had behaved like traditional Indian "*chelas*" — disciples — do with the *guru*, the master.

Ayub, under tremendous pressure from the hawks in his administration to allow his troops into Kashmir, was hard put to restrain them and did so at Kennedy's behest. In return the American President did, reportedly, manage to get Nehru to renew his pledge to permit a plebiscite in Kashmir. If Ayub had occupied Kashmir there would be more monuments to him in Pakistan than there are to Jinnah. But he was no Nasser and could not defy the US President as the former had done over Aswan dam.

It would appear that Nehru did want to keep his word given to Kennedy re plebiscite in Kashmir. After the border situation with China had cooled down, he did send veteran Kashmiri leader Sheikh Abdullah to Pakistan. Sheikh conferred with the country's leaders, and even managed a visit to a Pakistani held part of Kashmir where the public enthusiastically welcomed him.[1]

Nehru was distraught. His meticulously built edifice of non-alignment was in shambles. His reputation had been tarnished. India was in parlous state and he had to go, beggars bowl in hand, to the hitherto despised Imperialist Western powers. He accepted all the blame for the debacle, and offered to resign. No one, not even the opposition would countenance his departure. They asked for Menon's head and got it. Pundit Nehru never got over the debacle, mentally or physically.

The Chinese and Russian factions of the Indian communist party, which had developed a *modus vivendi*, suffered another setback. The latter were the worse losers.

The Chinese, after a decent interval, as though disappointed that the other team would not play ball, withdrew to what they claimed was their side of the border. The Chinese seem to be satisfied with making their point, without actually overstepping. They were to make a similar unilateral withdrawal from their incursion into Vietnam.

## AYUB — MIDDLE TO FINAL YEARS

Ayub was beset at home by charges of nepotism, corruption of army officers[2] and under siege for letting go of the golden opportunity of taking over Kashmir while India was down and out. He was, nevertheless, confident that he would have a walkover in the 1964 elections as he had in 1960. All his possible opponents were pygmies, as he told his confidants. The Basic Democracy system[3] was, anyway, his surefire safety net.

---

1 But it soon became a moot point. Kennedy was assassinated in 1963. His successor was indifferent. Nehru was to die soon after and in 1964 his pledge was cremated along with his body and sprinkled all over India.

2 In the later period of his rule army officers had started raking it in. Corruption of the armed forces was to reach its zenith in Musharraf's time. Please refer to *Military Inc.* by Ayesha Siddiqa.

3 As explained in an earlier chapter, ordinary voters would elect 80,000 basic democrats who would function as the electoral college for national, provincial assemblies and local government offices as well for the president's office.

But a rude awakening awaited him. The opposition happened to hit on a dream candidate. Bhashani proposed the name of Miss Fatima Jinnah, favorite sister, confidante and long time companion of the founding father of the nation. The public venerated and loved her in equal measure. She was affectionately called Madar-e-Millat (mother of the nation). Disdainful of Ayub, she had never bothered to keep the opinion to herself that Ayub was an ingrate of the first order and had subverted her brother's legacy of a democratic Pakistan. A delegation of the opposition leaders waited on her. But she despised the opposition leaders almost as much and summarily dismissed them, telling them that if they had not perversely and ineptly dragged the country to the current deplorable state, they would not be begging her at her age to contest an election.

But she had reckoned without the wily "red" mullah — Maulana Bhashani,[1] who was perhaps the only person in the ranks of the opposition for whom she had some respect. He went to see Miss Jinnah alone. He is reported to have told her that he agreed with her that Ayub was beneath notice, but the latter would surely lead the country off a precipice. He played on the elderly lady's heart strings, telling her that "Tumhara Bhai Pakistan Banaya, Tumhara Marzi Hai Usko Bachao Ya Na Bachaao" — your brother made Pakistan, it is up to you to save it or not. Not a procrastinator, Miss Jinnah agreed to don the mantle of the savior instantly.

The news spread like a proverbial wild fire. The public came out on the streets in untold numbers. They relived the heydays of 1946 elections, admittedly vicariously, when they had beaten all odds and predictions and followed Jinnah to an unprecedented victory for the Muslim League and Pakistan. The opposition set aside all their differences and got busy with sorting out logistics and organizational problems of arranging public appearances for the candidate. They found willing and ready volunteers and funds for the campaign poured in.

Ayub was visibly shaken. He was hamstrung. He dare not publicly go on the offensive and engage in slandering the revered mother of the nation. Privately though he was reported to froth at the mouth at the mention of her name. He was reduced to moaning that he would, till death, retain the highest respect for Madar-e-Millat and was sorry that she had permitted her name to be used by the unscrupulous opposition etc.

Miss Jinnah addressed mammoth crowds in all the major cities of the country. Ancient tribal leaders, who would never leave their homes except to go to a mosque, came out of retirement to greet her, shedding tears of joy, that their sister had come calling. When she flew to Dhaka airport, East Pakistanis set aside all the resentment at being treated like a poor relation by the West. Her motorcade could not leave the airport and she had to be flown on a helicopter to

---

1 Bhashani was a living *Pir* — a holy man, a leftist, and pragmatic politician all in one. He is credited with getting part of Assam province, where he had a large following, to vote for Pakistan in 1947.

Paltan Maidan, the time-hallowed public meeting ground in Dhaka. The size of the crowd exceeded even the ones her brother used to address. She addressed the crowds in English. Few in the audience understood more than a sentence or two. They nevertheless hung on her words, cheered and shouted themselves hoarse. Old and frail though she was, she made stops in all major towns of the country.

The ensuing campaign, initially for electing Basic Democrats, was reminiscent of pre-independence days. Nearly all candidates had to pledge allegiance to her. They would, literally, have been lynched if any had expressed support for Ayub in Karachi, East Pakistan, Baluchistan or the NWFP.

In an election based on universal franchise, Ayub would have lost his shirt. But Electoral College was restricted to 80,000 Basic Democrats. Though an overwhelming majority of the candidates had pledged support to Miss Jinnah, they were now vulnerable to all the repressive and coercive forces under the command of government functionaries. Some were not averse to favors, bribes and other blandishments. The establishment also resorted to large-scale rigging, and ballot stuffing. The election was widely regarded at home and abroad as tainted and the desired result obtained fraudulently.

In spite of all the chicanery, they could not keep Miss Jinnah winning in Karachi and Dhaka divisions. Pakistanis had united on one platform for the last time and were robbed of victory. Bhashani's words were destined to be prophetic. Pakistan could not be saved. Ayub's victory, brazenly dishonest as it was, would slowly but surely lead to the dismemberment of Pakistan. Ayub's son Gohar, later to be speaker of the national assembly under another dictator Zia, incensed at the *lèse majesté* of Karachites in not voting for his father, unleashed a reign of terror on the helpless populace. He personally led a group of armed marauders looting, pillaging, maiming and killing. Scores were killed, hundreds injured. Police looked on as uninterested onlookers, as they would in later years too.

Ayub had lost what little legitimacy he had. He was despised not only as a usurper, but also as a person more dishonest, unscrupulous and corrupt than the politicians he had overthrown. He desperately needed to regain a semblance of self-respect and hit upon a reckless plan. He will wrest control of Kashmir from Indian hands and will go down in history as Ahmad Shah Abdali who had saved Delhi for Muslims from the infidel Marathas[1]. Egged on by fawning sycophants, he deluded himself into believing that the Indian Army would melt away against the might of the *ghazis*[2] (holy victors; those who die are *shaheeds*, martyrs). Had they not fled with tails between their legs before the Chinese, who though possessed of stronger spines were nevertheless infidels, with no hope of eternal bliss? Kashmiris would rise in exemplary unison to welcome their Pakistani liberators.

---

1 In the declining years of the Moghal Empire, Marathas had surrounded Delhi. The king asked for help from the Afghan king who came to the rescue and defeated the invading force.
2 Muslims who survive a war are called *ghazi*; the dead ones are martyrs. When Muslims fight each other, the fallen on both sides are so honored.

Indian Prime Minister Shastri was new. He would surely lose his nerve and sue for peace.

All these spurious arguments were presented to him most cogently by the latter day Machiavelli, Z.A. Bhutto, his foreign minister and are in the domain of public knowledge.[1] Ayub, however, decided to test the waters before taking a plunge. He ordered his army to challenge the Indians across Runn of Kutch, an impenetrable swamp and an area of little importance on Pakistani Sindh/Indian Rajhastan border. Pakistan controlled the high ground. Indians fell back. Bhutto claimed vindication. Had he not told them that the Indian army could not stand and fight? The staff officers twirled their moustaches. Emboldened by the victory Ayub let his "volunteers" — paramilitary personnel out of uniform — loose to infiltrate the Vale of Kashmir across the line of control.[2]

With his back to the wall, Indian Prime Minister Shastri gave an ultimatum. Cease and desist or we will attack across the international border. Ayub, kept in a state of delusion by Bhutto that the Indians would respect the international border, had left the Lahore border relatively undefended. The Indians actually marched into outskirts of the city. Surprised at finding no resistance and fearing an ambush, Indian troops halted in their tracks.[3] In the event, Pakistan rushed re-inforcements to Lahore. The city did not fall though BBC announced that it had.[4]

Pitched battles followed with grievous loss of life and material on both sides. Both sides claimed victory. The number of planes that either side claimed they had brought down came to at least three times as many as both possessed together. Both awarded medals for gallantry and outstanding valor etc. In Pakistan many streets were named after "Shaheeds." East Pakistani members of the armed forces, though scantily represented in the services, exhibited outstanding feats of valor.

But in the end, it all came to nothing. Within two weeks of start of hostilities, both sides ran out of bullets. Both countries were set back by years in economic development. India, with a much larger industrial base, came out much less damaged. A cease-fire was mandated by the UNO Security Council and accepted by India and Pakistan. There were renewed calls for ascertaining the wishes of Kashmiris.

East Pakistanis were never very worked up about Kashmir, which they correctly perceived as a lifeline for the outsized army. The obscene expenditure on defense establishment benefited only those West Pakistanis whose relatives were

---

1 Much later he was to disclaim all responsibility, but Ayub continued to call it Bhutto's misadventure.

2 The boundary between India- and Pakistan- controlled parts of Kashmir is called the line of control because it is disputed.

3 The Indian army chief had taken bets; the losers would have to treat him to drinks in the Lahore Gymkhana. Gymkhana was a colonial institution, a whites only club in pre-independence India.

4 Indian soldiers had "captured" a Lahore bus and had shown it to a credulous BBC reporter. They had to retract the statement an hour later.

members of the armed forces and the contractors and suppliers at best. They felt that if Kashmir were ever to come into possession of Pakistan, its population would suffer the same fate they themselves and other second class citizens of the country did.

One sorry fall out of the war was that Pakistan had provided India with a good excuse to whittle away at Kashmir's autonomy and added to the misery of its people who had kept their counsel through the duration of the war. Another side effect, which was to have far reaching consequences, was that East Pakistanis loudly voiced the opinion that through the duration of the war, they had been left undefended, at the mercy of India. The fact is well documented that the two wings had lost all communication with each other for the duration of active hostilities. They scorned the patently spurious thesis of Pakistan army top brass that East Pakistan would be defended on the plains of West Pakistan. What was perhaps worse was that the blunder gave a new lease of life to orthodoxy in the country. People took to attending prayer meetings in ever-greater numbers.

The UN Security Council assigned the role of mediator/arbitrator in the dispute to Kosygin, the Soviet Prime Minister. The country had always favored India. The fact that the US had acquiesced to the proposal indicated that they did not care much for Pakistan either. Ayub had in fact demurred. Johnson, it is believed, told him to fall in line or else. Kosygin collected the two parties in Tashkent, a city in Soviet Central Asia, which had once been the pride and leading center of Muslim scholastic and intellectual attainments. He coaxed, coerced and brow beat the two parties, Pakistan more often, to agree to and sign an agreement to return to pre-war borders. There was nary a mention of a plebiscite to determine the preferences of the Kashmiris for which purpose Pakistan had gone to war. Ayub returned empty handed. It was a clear victory for Indian diplomacy. Scattered riots followed the agreement signed in January 1966. Two students died as a result of police firing in Lahore.

The war was to lead to disastrous consequences for Pakistan. It gave a credible excuse to two demagogues to oppose Ayub, Bhutto on the Western side and Mujib in the Eastern wing. Bhutto had started distancing himself from Ayub immediately on return from Tashkent. He was entirely a creation of Ayub. But that did not stop him from castigating his mentor. Mujib was handed a live and burning issue he could and did use to inflame public opinion in the Eastern Wing.

Bhutto resigned from office. Ayub dissuaded him. In due course, when he felt sure of his footing, he sacked his foreign minister. Nobody paid any attention to Bhutto. He assiduously courted audiences. The public, when it did deign to react to his strident statements that Ayub had betrayed the trust, reminded him that he was a) fully a party to the cease-fire agreement, b) it was his job as foreign minister to advise the President on diplomatic tangles, c) till lately he had fawned on

Ayub, calling him uncle. etc. His one imaginative move as foreign minister had been the opening to China. But Ayub, to Bhutto's consternation, had claimed all the credit for the diplomatic coup. Finding no support at home Bhutto went to what appeared to be a well deserved oblivion in England. He was frequently seen drowning his sorrows in a bottle and exhorting any Pakistani who would listen to him to return with him to Pakistan to launch a revolution. Tariq Ali[1] describes a meeting with him in Paris. Ali very sensibly and as matter of principle declined the invitation.

Things were comparatively quiet in the Western wing of the country. People had been, by and large, taken in by the fables of the Pakistani Armed forces working near miracles. They tended to blame not Ayub but Russia and America for forcing him to accept the cease-fire. The more deluded ones claimed that the two countries had kept the Pakistani flag from flying on the Red Fort in Delhi.

From the perspective of the integrity of the country, a somewhat different and worse situation obtained in East Pakistan. Mujib had been a bit more successful in exploiting the "abandonment" of Bengal.[2] He had a track record as a student leader, had been active in the language campaign and had served as General Secretary of East Pakistan Awami League. The political field had been depleted due to depredations of Martial law and he appeared to be the most prominent survivor. The issue coupled with the already existing sense of general alienation, and the fiction deliberately given currency that all West Pakistanis lived a life of plenty, even luxury, had the potential of becoming a highly combustible mixture.

Matter of fact is that, though East Pakistani complaints were legitimate, social services were ignored in the West too. An ordinary mortal was as disempowered in the West as he was in the East. Further, India was simply not in a position to divert its armed forces to open a second front. Shastri had abjectly apologized when in the early days of Indo/Pak hostilities the Chinese Government, probably at the instance of Pakistan, had claimed that Indian soldiers had intruded into their territory and abducted some animals.

Ayub's regime was tottering. The huge outlay of resources on the war had negated all the economic gains of the previous seven years. People could not live on jingoistic slogans. They wanted jobs, food and shelter, education, health care and clean water.

They had waited for long years for a sign that some day they will get out of the grind of poverty. They dreamed of an equitable society when a mill worker will have livable wages and peasants would be able to throw off the yoke of serf-

1 *Street Fighting Years* by Tariq Ali.
2 They resented being called East Pakistanis rather than Bengalis and sympathized with residents of the North Western Frontier Province, who objected to retention of the colonial name for their area and had demanded that the province be named Pukhtoonistan. Punjabis lived in the Punjab. The province Sindhis lived in was called Sindh. Baluchis called their province Baluchistan. Why not Pukhtoonistan for Pakhtoons?

dom. The statement by an economist Mahboob-ul-Haq that twenty-two families owned all the wealth of the country was given wide currency.

Ayub's martial law had denuded Pakistan of all credible leaders who commanded respect in both wings. Especially tragic was the loss of Suharwardy, arguably the ablest Muslim politician after Jinnah. Scion of a highly educated Sufi family, he was at home among the intellectuals, politicians, students, peasants, feudal lords, trade union workers, leftists, moderates and liberals alike. An outstanding orator and parliamentarian, he was also an able administrator who had bested British bureaucrats when they were still ruling India.[1] He had been on the verge of an outright victory in the scheduled 1959 elections. On being released from jail where he had been incarcerated under martial law on trumped up charges, he had opted to live in exile in Beirut, Lebanon. His retirement and death, coupled with the passing from the scene of other stalwarts of Independence movement, left the field in East Pakistan to mediocrities like Sheikh Mujib, whose only competition was Bhashani. The Maulana was mercurial in temperament and had in the initial years of his regime persuaded himself of the virtues of Ayub.

Ayub resorted to desperate measures. His Government announced, with great fanfare, that they had un-earthed a conspiracy against Pakistan. Pakistan establishment had long been used to equate the country with the clique in power. This, latest in the line of conspiracies, had been blown out of proportion by the fevered brains of military intelligence agencies. It incriminated a few junior Bengali officers in the army and the civil service and Mujib who was most probably attracted more by free whisky than any idea of a coup. The participants had divulged their grandiose plans while in their cups. It was named Agartala, after the town where the whole thing was supposed to start. It was incredible, even from Pakistan military intelligence standards. Bengali officers accounted for less than one percent and were not trusted with key positions. The conspirators were tried in a Kangaroo court and duly sentenced to long terms of jail sentence. Mujib became an authentic hero.

During his exile Bhutto made frequent trips to Paris and had had detailed discussions with J.A. Rahim, at the time serving as the ambassador of Pakistan to France. Rahim was a senior and exceptionally talented civil servant. He was Bhutto's mentor, guide and philosopher and had helped Bhutto navigate through the minefield of bureaucratic establishment when Ayub had taken the latter into his cabinet, and was to become the secretary general of the party Bhutto founded and wrote its constitution.

Fed up of the life of an exile in London, Bhutto returned to Pakistan and started a furious campaign to gather support and did manage to attract a few

---

1 Q.U. Shahab, a senior civil servant, in his book *Shahab Nama*, describes how Suhrawardy while serving as a minister in Nazim's pre-independence ministry in Bengal had out maneuvered the top British civil servant by acting in the name of the chief minister.

left wing intellectuals and lawyers. But they were political nonentities. Then he struck a gold mine. A student leader, whom the Intelligence agents running the communist party in Pakistan had managed to run out of Karachi, threw his support behind Bhutto. Leftist and progressive elements,[1] veterans of innumerable insurgencies against the Ayub dictatorship, though weakened by the internecine warfare of Soviet/China ideological divide, were as a group still a force to reckon with. But Bhutto was still not able to catch the imagination of the people of Pakistan at large.

Ayub came to his rescue and put him in jail. Each incarceration that Nehru, Gandhi and Azad suffered added to the halos around their heads. The glamour associated with prison *yatra*[2] was dimmed but not quite faded. Putting Bhutto behind bars was quite unnecessary. He was widely despised for his perceived penchant for opportunism. But Ayub was clutching at straws to distract public attention from his predicament. He succeeded only too well. But in the process he managed to create a hero in the Western Wing too. The public mind accepted the fiction that Bhutto must have been telling the truth that Ayub did not listen to the latter's advice and caved in under American-Soviet pressure.

Ayub's minions now came up with an extremely outlandish idea. They advised him to celebrate ten years of his rule, dubbing it a "decade of development." Accepted wisdom is that you lie low when the object of hate, not dance on a rooftop.

The catalyst to the upheaval was a scuffle between the police and students in Lahore. The students had apprehended a purse-snatcher and the police wanted to let him go. That incident led to a conflagration. Demonstrations, processions and public protests broke out all over the country. In Karachi, Dacca and Lahore, administration fell apart completely. East Pakistan had already been simmering. The unrest had reverberated to the Western wing. Led by students, both exploded simultaneously. There was a spate of student/industrial workers strikes and other disturbances.

Ayub addressed the nation on national TV, a nascent medium in the country at the time. He looked like a dog which had been kicked by its master. "You dog, Ayub, shame, shame," was actually a popular refrain.

Ayub had to withdraw all cases against Mujib, release him and invite him and Bhutto to an all parties conference with a view to forming a national government. Shrewder of the two, Bhutto declined the invitation. The conference ended in expected failure, but Mujib had gained "face." Bhutto could finally put behind him the record of public and private sycophancy to Ayub. His minions were able to claim that Bhutto had genuinely believed in Ayub's sincerity and

---

1 The "Left" in Pakistan has been fragmented since Ayub took over. They had, aping other communist parties, split into Russian and Chinese factions.
2 In pre-independence days leaders were literally graded according to the number of years spent in jails.

integrity, but Tashkent had opened his eyes and he had promptly cut his links with the regime.

# CHAPTER 7. MEDICAL EDUCATION AND SURGICAL TRAINING, 1957–1972

I was admitted into Dow Medical College in Karachi. Dow Medical had been in the vanguard of the progressive movement of Pakistan. It stood out among the colleges even in the politically vibrant city of Karachi and provided key leaders, who became legends in their time.[1] The college had sustained a well-organized radical leftist student organization, the National Students Federation (NSF), which dominated student politics of the city. Student wing of fundamentalist Jamaat e Islami (party of Islam) played very much a second fiddle, as did all other right wing groups.

Unlike students of medical schools in Europe and North America, we did not devote our entire time and attention to studies. Most of us studied in the last three months of the year. We did not have multiple choice questions or regular tests. Essay type examinations gave us an opportunity to cram the year's work in the last few months.

Like all adolescent boys in repressed societies, where boys and girls are strictly segregated, I had "fallen in love" with many girls of all classes, shapes, looks, in the extended family, among the neighbors, in college and at the university. Approaching a girl directly was not socially accepted. None of my infatuations came to fruition. Now a classmate smote me. I felt that this was finally it.[2] I thought she was the most beautiful girl in the world. Her eyes were the most captivating. She was from a conventional, conservative, conformist middle class background, though not from a fundamentalist family. I would have given my right arm to be able to tell her so, but never had the courage. She was from all accounts aware of my passion.

---

1 Sarwar, Hashmi and Sher Afzal to name only three.
2 I actually feel the same way now, after these long years.

I got feedback that the goddess of my dreams did not hold with people who wasted their time in frivolous activities. We were here to study etc. That was rich. I was by far the better student. I argued coherently, intelligently, rationally and objectively with myself that I had laid my heart at the wrong feet. But the flame wouldn't go out. Many years later I got word that if I was serious, I should get my parents to approach her parents. I wanted her to tell me so directly. She wouldn't. I would agree to an arranged marriage, but not with the object of my abiding passion.

Soon after, union elections were announced. I tried to drown my grief in student politics. Our main candidate lost.[1] Though I had missed a whole semester of the first year, yet the idea of slowing down my political work did not even cross my mind. In fact my involvement escalated and I started visiting different campuses, learning political theory, hawking our official mouth piece called Talib-e-Ilm[2] on the streets, inside campuses etc and actively sought higher rank in the hierarchy.

In October 1958, the Martial Law regime of Ayub had proscribed student unions. Waiting on how events would turn, we were all lying low. This gave me respite too. I managed to put in about three months of work, and passed the second year examination.

In the third year, the professor of the main subject Pharmacology was a good teacher, but he was widely believed to be member of an American sponsored right wing Organization called Moral Rearmament Association, (MRA). It was an anathema to us. The professor had other ugly traits as well. He would actively discriminate against leftist students and was very good to sycophants. He wanted responses to examination questions exactly as he taught us. In fact, he failed an outstanding student because he quoted a textbook which the professor did not follow.[3]

Pharmacology did not have as big a curriculum as other subjects like pathology. I spent the usual three months poring over books at the tail end of the year. The day the result was to be announced, I was trying to distract myself by playing chess rather nervously. I expected to pass, but one is never quite sure of examination results. Suddenly, Sher Afzal, our undisputed leader, trailed by a few friends, burst into the room; he was all exited and embraced me. Others did too, announcing that I had stood second in the examination. I was flabbergasted and told them not to play such sick jokes. They took me to the notice board where the list of successful candidates was posted. I had, indeed, placed second. But I still found it difficult to believe. So did my classmates. Only my political cronies rejoiced. For one of their rank to get a position was unheard of. The same evening they took me

---

1 I have described it in the chapter on student movement.
2 Idiomatic translation would be seeker of knowledge. The term was made notorious by Afghan Taliban.
3 I. A. Jokhio, later to be professor of Orthopedic Surgery at Dow Medical College.

to a restaurant in a horse drawn carriage[1] and gave me a sumptuous dinner. I felt invincible. And plunged myself deeper into student politics.

The students union organized a fete in aid of the lending library. The official college library was fairly well stocked, but would not let students borrow text-books. I was assigned the task of publishing the souvenir of the event. It would give me an opportunity to present myself as an effective worker, organizer and a leader. Dr. Taffazul Husain, Head of the Department of Pathology, was the Chair-man of the Fete Organizing committee. I had to see him frequently. In those pa-ternalistic days, one was generally kept standing in the presence of a professor, but he would always invite me to take a chair. On one occasion he told me that the work I was doing was very worthy, but I should not neglect my studies. I promised to attend to my academic work as soon as the Fete was over.

In due course election dates were announced. NSF held party caucuses. I was nominated for the office of General Secretary. The election was hotly contested. My party and I lost rather badly. We found ourselves at a loose end and were depressed. I did not want to revert to the humdrum routine of classes, labora-tories and hospital work. We launched protests as a way of getting at the Ayub military government and ended up by getting arrested.[2] After the dust had settled down I tried to catch up with my studies, but it was too much of an uphill task. I had missed too many classes and laboratory work. But I got down to the task and tried to emulate the dedication to books I had shown in 1951-52 while in the tenth grade.

I heard that my father was not well and took a train home. One of my old classmates spied me at the railway station in Quetta. My fame had reached the town and terribly excited, my friend called to everyone in sight around to an-nounce that I was one of those who had taken on the military government. A crowd of admirers escorted me home.

I had not had time to inform my family that I was on my way. On seeing me, my mother, who had nerves of steel, broke down. I too cried in her arms. I must not neglect my sister. She was rather proud of all the attention paid to me and basked in reflected glory. I decided there and then that I could not smash all the hopes my mother had in a bright future for me and that the days of my playing truant were over. My mother had had a very bitter and sad life. I owed a lot to her. She had sacrificed what little comfort she could have had for me. Her only hope for fulfillment and meaning in life lay in my future success.

The news soon spread all over town that I was visiting, and I was treated as a minor celebrity wherever I went. In a small town everyone knows everybody else. My adventure was particularly exciting. One of my college friends, now the editor of the local English daily, wanted to write a piece about me, but I asked

1 It was a one-horse carriage more elaborate than Tonga and Ekka described in chapter one. It was called Victoria after the English Queen of the name.
2 Described in the chapter on student movement.

him not to; I did not want the provincial education department to learn about my activities because they would surely cancel my scholarship.[1]

Finally examination time arrived. It was an adventure. I had, somehow, managed the theory papers fairly well. Oral examination was another story. My reputation had preceded me to the examination halls. Junior teachers, who had only a few years on us, were sympathetic. They would put in a word with the examiners to go easy on me. The examiners, of course, knew of our conflict with the authorities, and aside from a few who would be in the ranks of the neo-cons now, all despised the military regime.

I managed to pass in all subjects but pathology, which I cleared in the supplementary examinations held three months later. Professor Husain, incensed by a particularly inept response I had given to a question from the external examiner had, in fact, walked out of the room.

I got down to my books in real earnest in my final year. But recovery from neglect of three years would not be easy. Coaching and training for the final year examination begins in the third year. Students are introduced to internal medicine and surgery in that year. They have lectures in the subjects and attend clinics and operating sessions. It is the first exposure to patients. They are expected to learn to do a History and Physical and learn how would they manage and treat the patient on their own.

Pre-examinations period was tense, stressful, but exciting. Part of the oral examination consisted of identification of instruments. Adeeb Rizvi, now one of the best-known physicians in Pakistan was, at the time, a senior Resident (Resident Medical Officer or RMO) in one of the professorial units in Surgery. I had known him through our mutual radical affiliations. He paid special attention to me in the sessions. I still failed in surgery and had to take the supplementary examination, which I passed without too much difficulty.

Now I was poised to take a decision which would affect the rest of my professional life. I opted for surgery because I was very impressed by Adeeb Rizvi. I have mentioned Adeeb a few times already, but it will bear repetition. After spending months in jail during the 1950s, he had returned to the pursuit of a medical career with a vengeance, as it were. His hard work and dedication borders on the obsessional. He embodies the saying that genius is 90% perspiration and 10% inspiration.

At this juncture one of my classmates, Arshad Husain, offered me a deal. I should try surgery for six months. He would take medicine; we will swap jobs at midyear, in the process completing the whole requirement for registration with the General Medical Council of Great Britain.[2] When the time came, neither of us was quite willing to go through with the swap. He was happy where he was.

---

1 I was on a merit scholarship from Baluchistan, which was enough to pay for most of my expenses.
2 Practically everyone at the time in Pakistani medical schools planned to go to England. In order to get senior training jobs, one had to have full registration (license) with GMC.

I had developed a little interest in surgery. This was mainly due to the professor I was working under, Col. Saeed Ahmad of blessed memory. His was a many-faceted personality. He worked day and night, was highly unorthodox in his techniques, had a passion for reconstructive surgery and created a special ward for repairing cut noses.[1] Col. Ahmad was rather temperamental and when in a bad mood, which he usually was at the beginning of the day, could argue you to the brink of exasperation. After he had several surgical procedures under his belt, no one could be more charming.

After working for Col. Ahmad for a year, I left for a six-month stint as a demonstrator in the department of Anatomy. When his RMO left, Col. Sahib was kind enough to recommend my appointment in his surgical unit. Unlike most professors of his time in Pakistan — later ones did not particularly distinguish themselves either — he was keen on research and publication of the work he did. Since he did not have much by the way of secretarial assistance, it fell upon the RMO to take dictation for his articles. I used to be irked by it, as were my predecessors. But the training was a blessing. I owe whatever little facility I have in writing to Col. Ahmad.

In 1965, I proceeded to England and got a job in Orthopedics and Casualty.[2] My first six months in the country were rather uneventful. I had the usual problems adjusting to an alien milieu. Initially I had great difficulty in understanding the local English accent, though I was in Guildford in the south of England where they were supposed to speak the Queen's English.[3] I had a few interesting experiences in the casualty department. On one occasion a drunk wanted to see for himself if the insides of an Indian looked the same as that of a white person. When the Sister (Head Nurse) remonstrated with him, he said, "Your blue uniform does not frighten me."[4]

Junior staff in the hospital had two social groups, the native and foreigners, with little contact between them outside of work. White doctors, even though they had a monopoly on all the prized jobs, resented us; without the doctors from the subcontinent they could have pushed the department of health harder for better conditions of work and higher salaries. What cut them to the quick was that the nurses were partial to brown skin and would rather go out with an Indian doctor than with a white one. Indians treated them with much greater courtesy. That must have been a part of the equation.

---

1 This is the favorite form of mutilation that jilted lovers of ladies of pleasure practice on the latter.
2 The six-month appointment was split into three months in Orthopedics and three in Emergency Room.
3 Also called Home Counties, denizens of the region around London thought they were a cut above their countrymen in the north.
4 In those days a Sister would wear a dark blue uniform, her immediate assistant a lighter blue and so on.

Initially I had great difficulty in differentiating one person from another.[1] In those days England was very formal and conservative. During my first hospital dinner, I lit my pipe after the meal was over. The white doctor sitting next to me was horrified. The toast to the Queen had not been offered yet. My chief at the head of the table had noticed the transgression too; he got up hurriedly and raising his glass said, "To the Queen!" We all followed him. You did not talk to people unless formally introduced first. Once on a railway train I started a conversation with a fellow passenger. He was taken aback. You must be new, he said. I said, indeed I was and what part of England he hailed from. The color on his face rose to rich magenta. Then he controlled himself and in a grave voice told me that he would give me a piece of advice; never to call anyone English, unless I was a hundred percent sure. He was Irish and to be called an Englishman was a mortal insult![2]

Shops closed at five in the evening on weekdays and at noon on Saturdays. On Sundays you could not even buy cigarettes. Oxford Street in London would close its doors at 12 sharp on Saturdays. Only the pubs would open in the evening, but they too would shut their doors at 11:00 p.m. The British were sticklers for traditions of all kinds. In the bars, the tender would ring a bell at ten minutes to closing time for last orders. You had absolutely to leave by the appointed time.

Medical education, training and practice in Pakistan and the UK were very different from each other. In Pakistan, sophisticated laboratory tests were not ready at hand and doctors had to depend much more on clinical diagnosis, based on History and physical examination. We also tended to treat symptoms empirically,[3] without proper diagnosis. Once I had prescribed, as was standard practice back home was, an antibiotic to a patient who had developed high fever after surgery. My registrar[4] gave me an object lesson. He asked me why had I started the patient on antibiotics. I told him, "He had high temperature." He let a barrage of questions loose on me — if I had bothered to find the underlying cause, if all the fevers could be treated with antibiotics, if I would treat malaria the same way, if I had even looked at the dressings to see if the incision was inflamed, etc. I was dumb struck. He relented and told me that he was a foreigner like me. Our work was scrutinized with greater vigilance. We had to be more careful than the natives had to be.

---

1 Indians used to get terribly upset when Englishmen used to claim that all natives looked alike. We thought that the rulers were insufferably arrogant. But during my first few weeks in the UK, all the white men looked the same to me too! I told my chief of this observation. He was not amused.

2 I had heard of the animus Irish people bore to the English, but did not know that they despised the latter as much as Indian nationalists did.

3 For example you give a painkiller for back pain without bothering to find out the cause of the problem.

4 A senior resident trainee, though not quite as exalted as a chief resident in the American system, gave on hand training to junior trainees.

The other lesson I learnt during my six months in Guildford was the real value of record keeping. Only Col. Saeed Ahmad, among all the professors in the hospitals in Karachi, had insisted that meticulous records be kept. In fact we used to have chart rounds. But we had attributed it to a strange streak in the chief.

I was in a hurry. I wanted to obtain the FRCS (Fellow of the Royal College of Surgeons) diploma, complete my training, and go back home. There was an eight-week gap between the end of my job in Guildford and start of the part one FRCS course. I started applying for a *locum* (short term job). I had never worked in Obstetrics and Gynecology and had had awkward moments in the casualty department (since renamed accident and emergency, in the UK) when I was asked to perform an internal examination on a female.[1] To my surprise I was called for an interview[2] in one such department in Leeds in the north of England, for a job as locum Senior House Officer (SHO). Such was the demand of doctors, but still to my greater surprise I was offered the job. Under normal circumstances, one had to train in the specialty for one year before being considered for this level of appointment.

When I arrived in the hospital one evening a few days later, I found all the junior doctors in the department holding a caucus in the doctors' lounge. The Registrar asked me if I had had any experience in the specialty. On being told that I had none, he enquired of me how on earth was I to supervise the junior doctors and take independent call in the Casualty Department. I told him that his chief had given me the job and the question was better directed that way. At that, he subsided. To be fair, their discomfiture was justified. With me out of the equation, he would have to share the calls with the other SHO; it would be one in two, quite a heavier burden than one in three.

It was decided that I would be second on call with the other SHO and do all minor operative procedures during the day for others as recompense. I ended up doing the D&Cs for all the doctors.[3] It was a very large department so I did about a dozen such procedures each day five days a week for six weeks. I am sure I set something of a record, as a busy practitioner does not get to do more than half a dozen a week.

On my first day at work the ward Sister asked me to do history and physical (H&P) on a patient. I was trying to decide what questions I would ask her. Correctly diagnosing my predicament, one of the Junior House officers, a charming young Hindu lady from India, took pity on me and offered to do my work. The relief was immense. I asked her if I could do anything for her. She said, "Well, you could draw some blood and start a few intravenous lines." I could kiss her, and would have, but she was married and her husband worked in the same hospital.

---

1 In Pakistan, very few male doctors would be inclined or even be allowed to examine a female patient internally.

2 This was a reflection of the acute shortage of doctors the UK suffered from at the time.

3 D&C is a diagnostic as well as a therapeutic treatment procedure.

Civilization has its drawbacks. I had to be nice to him. We actually became good friends. I took to calling my benefactress "Bhoji."[1] The couple followed the Jain religion, an ancient and pacifist faith in India. The adherents of the religion are strict vegetarians. They don't even eat eggs. Any form of life has supreme sanctity for them. In India the more devout ones go around with masks on their faces, lest they inhale an insect. They do not wear shoes either so as not to crush a worm underneath.

The eighteen-week long primary FRCS course offered by the Royal College of Surgeons in London was an ambitious financial undertaking. After several sessions with friends in similar circumstances, we came to the conclusion that we would just be able to make it. We decided to take the plunge and started looking for cheap lodgings and found a place in a rather dubious neighborhood. A notorious maximum-security jail was at a stone's throw. The owner was an obsequious Pakistani.

The premises were shabby and poorly maintained. Wallpaper was peeling off all the visible surfaces. Tiles were missing from the floors. Carpets were dirty, windows ill fitting, stairs hazardous, and sinks dysfunctional. But it was cheap. The owner's wife would give us breakfast and supper. It was a good twenty minutes brisk walk from the house to the tube station (subway) and with a change of train midway, it took another half hour to the Royal College of Surgeons. For us, used to the tropical weather back home, it was terribly cold, and at times snowy weather. The London City Corporation was not very good at plowing roads or sprinkling salt on the roads, which used to get quite slippery.

About one hundred fifty doctors were enrolled in the course. Most were non-British. Lectures and laboratory sessions started at 8:00 a.m. and lasted till 5:00 p.m. We studied till late at night, and got up early. Weekends were also spent poring over books. Once in a while we would go to a restaurant near Warren Street which sold cheap biryani.[2] We did not have any spare funds to fritter away on a good time. The ones with regular girlfriends were forced into abstinence. Things got a bit better as spring approached, but then the examination was around the corner.

We had a solitary South Asian girl in our class who looked, at least to me, more like a fashion model than a doctor. I took her for a Hindu girl. One tends to romanticize objects that are out of easy reach.[3] She actually turned out to be a Muslim from Pakistan. Nearly all my friends and others in the course tried to attract the attention of this lady. I too was terribly attracted to her. But I hid my passion in a cloak of strong reserve. That was to be my undoing, literally She took me for a strong, silent type. We inevitably came across each other. At times we

---

1 A friend's or elder brother's wife. The relationship is strictly platonic.
2 A highly spiced rice dish.
3 I remember Muslim boys thought all Hindu girls were beautiful while Hindu boys found all Muslim girls enchanting.

talked about our future plans, careers and ambitions. I had earned a reputation as an intellectual. Doctors from my college tended to look up to me. The ones with me were rather more under my influence.

I did not pass the examination. She did. I was very depressed. She encouraged me. There would be other examinations. It was not the end of the world. I felt almost happy at my failure. If I had been successful, she would not commiserate with me.

We had about a week before proceeding to our new jobs. Our group, which now included her, did the rounds at all of the tourist spots including the Tower of London, Hampstead and Buckingham palaces, and Kew Gardens.

During our wanderings, she and I would often fall back and indulge in private conversation. She talked of the future, our hopes and aspirations. I dwelt on art, poetry literature, politics and current affairs, in a conscious effort to impress her. There was plenty to keep me riveted to her. I could not, for the life of me, see what she found in me. She could only have been taken in by my intellectual pretensions. I do not have the looks girls write home to their mothers about.

She had not had time to apply for a job. At the end of the all too short holiday, I asked her if she would like to apply for a job in the Swansea, Wales, hospital where I was going. In those days, this kind of offer amounted to a proposal of marriage, or at any rate as near as one could get to, without saying so in so many words. To my utter surprise, and under the circumstances, profound elation, she agreed. The next day we took a train to Swansea. The following day we called on the Medical Superintendent, who sure enough gave her a locum in Orthopedic Surgery.

I thought our idyll would continue. But she had other ideas. She exhorted me to resume study for the primary FRCS examination immediately. She even bought a watch for me to time my essays. I would have preferred to gaze into her eyes, hold her hand and tell her how good life was. But girls are pragmatic. And in the state of mind I was in, I would have pursued a doctorate in nuclear physics, if she had asked it of me.

I started studying again. When they learnt that I was preparing for the primary FRCS examinations, other hospital staff members gave me full consideration, as did my consultants (chiefs of service). I went to London to have another shot at the examination. To keep my spirits up, she would call me at least once a day. This time I passed. She deserved most of the credit and I told her so. She graciously accepted the tribute. As an award for good behavior and for passing the examination she agreed to spend a weekend with me in London. She stayed with some cousins forty-five minutes train ride from the city. I bunked with a friend and told him I had to leave early to be at the Royal College. We met at a cinema showing "Moghal-e-Azam" and saw it twice in one day. My friend was very acute. He slyly remarked that he had never seen anyone so happy after a full day of lectures. The next day we saw "Ganga Jumna" twice again.[1]

Welsh people are nearly as laid back as Indians. If it was their concept of punctuality, consistency and good fellowship, you could not tell the two apart. Once I had to catch a train to London from the station seven miles away. The taxi driver was late. I scolded him. He said, "I will be back in a minute," and took about five. I was more annoyed and told him off. He laughed and asked me to hold my horses, and drove like a maniac. On arriving at the station, he screeched to a stop, barely avoiding a truck, and with a twinkle in his eye advised me to keep the money to purchase the ticket ready in hand. I ran to the station. A man in uniform asked me if I was the doctor for the London train, gave me the ticket, took the money from me and pointed to the train. I boarded the train and it took off immediately. I asked the guard what was all that about. He smiled; the taxi driver had called the stationmaster and asked him to hold the train for me. Next time, he went on, I should make sure to get another taxi driver; this one was surely crazy as a coon.

I had formally proposed marriage to my ladylove before she left for her new job. She had agreed but said she would like to put it off till both of us passed the final FRCS examinations. It had to be a proper wedding. She did not want to make it seem as though we were eloping. I did write to my mother, who wanted to know more about her but did not say no. My sister was very excited. The news soon spread through the very active Pak-Indian grapevine and I was inundated by calls of enquiry, felicitations and dire warnings.

I had to get a job in General Surgery, which was deemed essential training for the final FRCS. Paying court to her had distracted me from my work. But with the primary FRCS under my belt, I did not think it would be too hard. I had two consultants, one a very polite and urbane Englishman who never complained of my work. The other was a Scot, very gruff, blunt and did not mince words. I naturally gave the Englishman's name as a referee. I hardly got any interviews. And when I did get called to one, I was not offered a job. In one of the interviews, one board member whom I had come across in two previous interviews took pity on me and took the highly unusual step of showing me the Englishman's quite unflattering description of me.[2]

I went, cap in hand, to the Scottish gentleman. He told me that I was no good and should take up another profession. I couldn't be quite retarded as I had managed to pass the primary examination. After he had exhausted himself with the tirade, I asked him sheepishly, "Sir, what am I going to do?" This started him off again. But the verve, the enthusiasm and the passion were missing. He told me

---

1 Indian movies often run three hours long. We must have set some kind of record holding hands for six hours, two days in running.

2 I know it is not fair to generalize, but I have since not been quite able to trust Englishmen.

that if I promised to work hard in my next job, he would get me one. At my next interview I was offered a job in General Surgery under a well-known consultant who was an honorary tutor at the Royal College of Surgeons.

My new hospital was in a small village called Aberdare, in Glamorgan County, Wales. It had been a busy mining town. Unemployment had soared after the mines ran out of coal. People subsisted on welfare. The train station had been closed "temporarily" a year before. If you did not drive, you could only get in and out of town by an infrequent bus service. I did not have a car. Luckily the village market was within walking distance. It boasted of a few grocery and general merchandise stores and three eating-places. By way of exotica, there was a Chinese takeaway. We did not have many pubs either. A cinema house opened its doors on weekends.

The major city Cardiff was forty minutes drive away. One of its cinemas exhibited an Indian movie on Sunday afternoons. We used to take a bus to the city. On one occasion the bus was a few minutes late. I told the driver that we did not often get to see an Indian movie and would miss a good bit of it because of him. He asked us what cinema house we wanted to go to. We told him. He drove like a bat out of hell and omitted to stop on any bus stops on the way as well. The other passengers protested. He would only say that the doctor was from India and did not get to see an Indian movie very often. "There is little else for him to entertain his girlfriend with. I will drop you on the way back." He stopped the bus with a flourish right in front of the cinema house, right on time.

There was not too much work in the hospital. I alternated calls with a Doctor Sen Gupta from West Bengal. He was a very nice man and had a subtle sense of humor. He offered to wash the dishes if I would cook. I called around asking my friend's wives for recipes and technique. In my first attempt, I remember I made beef curry and boiled rice. It was passable. Over confident, the next venture resulted in a barely eatable concoction. I called Sen Gupta. He said we would invite guests. I did not understand. He would not explain and called all the native doctors. They came and ate up all the curry with obvious relish. Sen Gupta, who had been in the UK for much longer, told me that he had learned early on that the natives did not have a sense of smell or taste!

By now our "honeymoon" was over. We had started quarrelling over the most trivial things. She was used to having her way, I to mine. I am a feminist and a liberal. I am, nevertheless, too much of a product of the East to contemplate a domineering wife with equanimity.

We decided to take eight weeks off to attend a prep course for final FRCS. The London FRCS was based on ancient practices. The patients presented for discussion were professionals with history and management going over decades. I took my first final FRCS examination in London and failed. I took the next examination in Edinburgh where the patients were picked out of ward cases undergoing treatment, waiting for operations, etc. The examiners were younger and pleasanter, though no less accomplished than the London ones. This time I was successful.

It is a quaint but charming custom that the Royal College entertains successful candidates and examiners to a sherry party the same evening. During the reception, the examiners treat you as colleagues.

I took a job as a registrar in a town called Slough, forty miles from London. She moved to a small town on the England–Wales border. We broke up. We managed to get together again and during a period of reconciliation we got our respective families involved. It was a triumph of optimism over reason, but we did not know that and planned to go to Pakistan for the formal ceremonies.

In Pakistan she was in Lahore and I was in Quetta, a distance of seven hundred miles as the crow flies. We could not meet each other and indulge in our favorite pastime of hurting each other. Difficult though I find it to believe, both us thought that things would settle down after the wedding. We got married in November 1968. I left for England soon afterwards. She joined me a few weeks later.

My wife was expecting. We had rhesus incompatibility.[1] I had to take a job as a trainee assistant to a General Practitioner (GP) near the hospital in London where my wife's favorite obstetrician worked. The patients were demanding and the workload was heavy. Except for one afternoon a week, we had surgery (office) hours twice a day every weekday and on Saturday morning as well. After morning office hours I spent a good hour and a half in making house calls. I was on duty every night but one, and on alternate weekends as well. Calls at night were frequent.

My senior had given us an apartment on top of the office. It was dingy, poorly maintained and dirty. We had to scrub the floors and walls for three days before it could be made to look halfway habitable. My wife and I happened to look in a full-length mirror once at the end of the day. We looked like a particularly hard-working peasant couple returning from the fields and broke into hysterical laughter. It is one of the fondest memories I retain from the time.

As a trainee, the government paid my salary and allowed an allowance for the rent of the apartment. If I had known that I would have got a decent place. My boss was also paid an allowance to train me; all the advice he ever gave me was not to let anyone go without payment of the fee for certificates for sick and school notes.[2] I felt bad about charging the poor people and refused to do so after awhile. Once the patients learnt that I would not insist on charging money, they

---

1 When parents have different blood groups, especially of the Rhesus type, the baby has blood problems at birth.

2 It was a small charge and quite legal. I discovered later that Doctors did not usually charge patients for the notes, even in affluent areas.

repaid me for the kindness by bringing small gifts in the oriental fashion. In time they also avoided calling me at odd hours unless it was a real emergency.

It was irresponsible of my senior not to break me in. General practice involves mostly internal medicine and pediatrics. All my training was in different fields of surgery. Patients come to you for minor ailments. Treatment is symptomatic. If the patient does not respond favorably, you refer them to a specialist in the hospital. If a person were very sick he/she would be dispatched to the Casualty Department (ER). But once in awhile one came across a difficult decision.[1]

My eldest child Eram — I call her Rami — was born on January 6, 1970, in London, England. Her arrival made it all worthwhile. We lived in that apartment for a year, the term of my trainee period. We used to take Eram to the shops in the local area. She was too young to articulate well, but had only to point her finger at a toy for me to buy it. It did not matter that we did not have much money. My friends lavished gifts on her too. My wife and I continued to have uneasy relations. As compensation, I became very closely attached to Eram. Sensing my need, she reciprocated.

I briefly flirted with the idea of joining a family practice. It could be a comfortable life. My friends who opted for GP work in immigrant areas had a good time. They were lavished with gifts and invited to innumerable weddings, birthdays and other parties. GPs were also allowed private practice after office hours. Indo-Pak expatriates felt that they would get better care if they paid the doctor. But I had passed the FRCS examination, worked in surgery for six years, and did not want to give that up; I started looking for jobs in orthopedic surgery. I accepted a job in a small town called Kings Lynn in the North East of the country. Life was less hectic. Eram had more space to play in. When Eram's mother worked as a locum in neighboring hospitals, we had to leave her in the care of babysitters.

Eram contracted a chest infection and developed a high fever. The consultant we saw advised admission in a hospital. Working under a misapprehension that she would be better off nearer her mother, he sent her to the hospital where her mother was working at the time. That hospital was about twenty miles from my hospital. I got a frantic call from the nurses in the middle of the first night. Eram was screaming, and I should go there immediately. I told the nurse to get her mother. The nurse told me that she screamed louder when picked up by her mother!

Eram's mother got a job in Pakistan. Eram went with her when she was just over a year old and got sick almost immediately. She would not eat Pakistani, non-canned food. We used all our contacts to send Gerber bottles/cans, and managed to keep her in the style she was used to. At one point, however, we were so concerned that we decided to get her back to England. I had arranged a

---

1 Once I had a patient who heard voices. I gave him wrong and potentially dangerous advice. Fortunately I called a psychiatrist friend to boast of my skills. He was aghast and asked me to get him an urgent appointment with a psychiatrist.

babysitter who would keep her during the week, and at night too when I was on call. But she got better and got used to the local food as well. I visited her a few months later. She would not leave me alone for a minute while awake and cried a lot when I had to leave.

My marriage with her mother, never a happy one, got into greater trouble because of the enforced separation when the latter took a job in Pakistan. It ended in the inevitable divorce. Eram stayed with her mother. Legally I could not have asked for custody under Islamic law.[1]

After twelfth grade, Eram had to face a fundamentalist student protest against admission of non-*hijabi* girls in the institute she had got into. She decided to pursue further studies in the US and in 1988 got admitted to the University of Pennsylvania.

She had many offers for her hand. She finally accepted Adnan, one of her college mates. They had a civil marriage ceremony at our home in Bath. She later had a traditional wedding in Lahore at her mother's home.

---

1 Under Islamic law father gets custody of a male child at the age of seven but that of a girl only when she is 12.

# CHAPTER 8. STUDENT MOVEMENT IN PAKISTAN

"Hum jo Tareek rahoan mein marai gai," (We, who were ambushed in dark alleys...) — Faiz Ahmad Faiz.[1]

During their 200-year rule over India, the British colonizers had, among other self-serving measures, introduced an education system which would inhibit innovation and produce clerks for their administration. In spite of that, the movement for liberty and social justice grew among Indians.

In the last five decades of foreign rule, students emerged as a credible force for change. In August 1936 an all India Students Conference was held in Lucknow (UP). Pundit Nehru inaugurated the conference, and M.A. Jinnah presided over it. Delegates chosen by district and provincial student bodies formed the All India Students Federation (ASIF). Three months after the initial conference, another meeting was held in Lahore, (Punjab). Sarat Bose, in his presidential address, dwelt at length on analysis of the political upheaval in the country, and what he thought the role of students was.

AISF held its sixth session in Nagpur, capital of the Indian province named central province CP, (now renamed Madhya Pradesh, MP) on December 25, 1940. The agenda of this conference was to chart a line of action and policy against the colonial rule. A majority of delegates advocated a more militant stance against the British rule than the one favored by the Indian National Congress (INC) under Gandhi. Dr. Ashraf, a revolutionary leader branded *Satya Graha*, the passive resistance offered by Gandhi, a weak response to the aggressive control of the colonial power. Disagreeing with the prevalent opinion and after failure to evolve a

---

[1] The leading progressive Urdu poet mentioned in an earlier chapter, he was nominated for the Nobel Prize in literature and was awarded Lenin peace prize.

common platform, the section that favored INC seceded from the main body. Led by Dr. Ashraf and M. Mukerjee, AISF emerged as a credible player in the struggle for independence and remained active in the post independence days. In 1947 its membership was 74,000.

At the 1937 Muslim League (ML) session in Lucknow, an All India Muslim Students Federation was launched. It held its first conference in December 1938 at Calcutta (Bengal). M.A. Jinnah presided over the session, and Raja Amir Muhammad of Mahmoodabad was elected the President. Students were, as noted in a previous chapter, destined to play a vital and historic role in the Pakistan movement.

In October 1947 Jinnah, inaugurating an educational conference convened in Karachi by the government of Pakistan (GOP), declared that during the century long foreign rule adequate attention was not paid to public education. "If we are to really develop at a fast pace, we will have to give prime importance to education in our national agenda. Our education should not only reflect our history and culture, but also pay due heed to progressive thought and economic and scientific progress. We must not forget that the world is moving ahead very fast." An educational research center with a mandate to advise and guide the government was established after the conference.

Very soon after Jinnah died, the Muslim League degenerated into internecine conflict over distribution of government ministries. Muslim Students Federation (MSF) also split into factions. All the groups became an appendage of league leaders who used the students unscrupulously.

At the end of 1948, responding to the indifference of powers that be, a few progressive students founded a small group in Lahore called Democratic Students Federation (DSF). DSF participated in Union elections in different colleges. Prominent among its leaders were Abid Manto[1] in Rawalpindi and Akhtar Naqvi in Lahore. In Karachi, DSF was formed first in Dow Medical College in 1950. Islami Jamiat e Talaba, the student wing of Jamaat e Islami formed in 1948, confined itself to proselytization and convened small gatherings in mosques.

Post establishment of Pakistan, feudal lords obtained control of the government, which became total after Liaquat, Jinnah's designated heir apparent, was assassinated in October 1951.

THE STRUGGLE OF BENGALI STUDENTS

Students in undivided Bengal were, if anything, even more militant in the struggle for freedom than their counterparts in the rest of the country. Poets, Nobel Laureate Rabindra Nath Tagore and Nazrul Islam, and other progressive writers intellectually influenced them. In contrast to West Pakistan, where non-Muslims formed the bulk of students, a sizable number of Muslim students also

---

1 Now a leading attorney and a prominent progressive leader based in Lahore, Pakistan.

participated in the campaigns and were to play a large role in the 1971 war of secession. And again in contrast to the Western side, Hindus did not leave en-masse at the time of partition.

East Pakistan had two popular student organizations-East Pakistan Students Federation and East Pakistan Students League. Educationists were mostly from the Western wing and wanted to impose Urdu as the sole medium of instruction.

After partition Pakistani Bengalis, in a spirit of nascent nationalism, had accepted the over lordship of non-Bengalis in the government at the center and domination of their business, commerce and administration in the province. But they were not prepared to accept a subsidiary status for their language. Jinnah, no doubt, from motives of using one language to cement national solidarity, had declared Urdu the only official language of Pakistan. But Urdu was spoken at home by less than five percent of the total population while Bengali was spoken by 55%

Dhaka University students led the language campaign. The movement had the support of middle and lower economic class activists. On February 22, 1952 the police opened fire on a group of Dhaka Medical College students. Twenty-five students were killed and many more injured. Such a storm of protest, indignation and condemnation followed that the government surrendered and accepted the demand that Bengali be established as the state language. It also marked the first time that a struggle against a repressive regime was spearheaded by a joint front of students and the public.

## OVERVIEW OF THE STUDENT MOVEMENT

In order to get a clear idea of the student movement in Pakistan, we have to look at the religious makeup of the educational institutions in the regions which became East and West Pakistan. Before partition Hindu and Sikh students dominated the educational institutions in what became West Pakistan. In 1945, Dow Medical College in Karachi had only two Muslims out of a class of fifty. Following partition they left behind a vacuum in the Punjab which was filled by immigrants from India. Sindh, on the other hand, did not experience a whole scale exodus of non-Muslims. Refugees, though, inundated Karachi; its population quickly swelled from about hundred and fifty thousand to twelve hundred thousand.

The Muslim Students Federation was formed at the N.E.D Engineering College Karachi in 1947. Ahmad Khan Barakzai was the first President. I interviewed an activist of the time, the late Mr. Nooruddin Sarki, then a leading attorney of Karachi. After a brief mention of the federation, he went on to enumerate the names of Karachi medical students of the time — M. Haroon, M Sarwar, and Rahman Hashmi — all immigrants, as the pioneers of the student's movement.

Punjabis on both sides of the divide had borne the brunt of the worst excesses of partition. The traumatic experience they had passed through was unprecedented in the annals of human history. All they wanted was to be left alone, to pick up the pieces and live as normal a life as they could. It, therefore, took a long time for the young immigrants in the Punjab and the few among the locals to get together and plan for the future

Initially the youth wing of Maulana Maududi's Jamaat e-Islam provided the only semblance of organized student life in the Punjab. The Student wing eschewed electoral politics. In NWFP, the student wing of Khudai Khitmatgars (Servants of God) of Ghaffar Khan had been discredited as they had sided with the Indian National Congress. Baluchistan was the most feudal–tribal ridden and the least developed of the provinces in West Pakistan. Its only city Quetta was totally dominated by non-Muslims in pre-independence days.

Sindh already had a vibrant body of student activists; its traditions went back to early twentieth century. The province was known for the cordial relations between its religious groups. It did not have any communal riots till 1948 and those conflicts were between the immigrants and non-Muslims. A substantial percentage of Hindus actually stayed back in the interior of the province.

Muslim refugees from India heading towards Sindh had arrived relatively unscathed. Given the comparatively intact, though depleted cadre of activists into whom the new arrivals easily merged, the student movement in the Western wing in early years was for all practical purposes, confined to Karachi. Mostly left wing in their leanings-because of family connections, indoctrination or chaotic conditions — they launched a movement for better educational facilities such as decent classrooms, libraries, laboratories and a reduction in fees and a provision for textbooks to be free or at subsidized rates and above all the right to organize.

DSF leaders in Karachi gave the overall lead to the national students movement. Curiously enough, the core of the leadership came from Dow Medical College, Karachi that produced such leaders as Sarwar, Haroon and Hashmi. The college was also to produce arguably the most prominent of student leaders — Sher Afzal who figured prominently in student politics in the late 1950s to mid-1960s. Sarwar was the first president of DSF. Its headquarters were in room 29, Mitha Ram Hostel, in the middle of a commercial area.

By late 1952 the movement had gathered sufficient strength to take on the government. Students took out processions, and led marches in Karachi on January 6, 7, and 8 in 1953. National and International press gave them sympathetic coverage. Prime Minister Nazimuddin called the leaders to his official residence for a meeting on January 7, 1953 to discuss their demands. The education Minister Fazlur Rahman and senior officials of the ministry attended the conference. Students left the meeting with the impression that their demands had been accepted. In the official press release, however, agreement was denied.

Enraged, students went on a rampage and finding a car with an official flag on it parked in Saddar, the most fashionable commercial area at the time, surrounded it. Its occupant turned out to be none other than the police minister, Mushtaq Gurmani. The police panicked and attacked the students with tear gas. The minister succumbed to gas fumes and had to be carried away. By this time a mob had gathered. It put the car to torch and also looted some liquor shops and ammunition stores, brandishing captured guns to frighten the police.

The police retaliated by opening fire on a group of students in front of Paradise Cinema in Saddar. Twenty-six students were killed. Nainsuk Lal, a boy scout helping an injured striker, was the first fatal casualty. Several flags got soaked in blood. The public joined in the protest. The city was paralyzed and life came to a halt. All leaders of the opposition, trade unions and student groups condemned the police brutality.

The government appealed to the students to help regain peace and calm. Kazim, the overall leader of the movement, generously and in a national spirit announced that the government had accepted their demands. The GOP, instead of responding gratefully to Kazim's gesture of goodwill and considering the students' demand sympathetically, banned DSF and put student leaders in jail.

The repressive measures of the GOP could not quite suppress the movement. Student leaders from East and West Pakistan got together and gave a call for All Pakistan Students convention in December 1953. Sarwar was elected the Chairman of the convening committee. Delegates from colleges all over the country participated. M. Mateen and Khaliquzzaman came from East Pakistan. The Punjab delegation was led by Abid Manto, then of Rawalpindi. Alia Imam represented the Indian students as an observer. She ended up being deported from the country. Sindh had the largest representation, reflective not just of contiguity, but also of its politically conscious cadres. It was led by Syed Mazhar Jameel, now a leading literary critic, art historian and attorney of Karachi. There was a even a delegation from Government College, Quetta, a veritable back waters, led by Kamil Qadri, a leftist student leader who had ended up in the College and had been able to concoct a delegation.

To coincide with the Martyr's day, convention dates were fixed in January 1954. The venue was Katrak Hall in Saddar. Messages of solidarity came from student bodies all over the world. Law minister A.K. Brohi agreed to be the Chief Guest. He was an intellectual, and a bright star of the cabinet. Sarwar, at the minister's request, escorted him from his official residence to the meeting. The pair arrived at the hall only to find the place in pandemonium. Gurmani, the police minister, was still smarting at the public humiliation of his car being burnt to cinders and himself being carried away, unconscious. His cabinet colleague Brohi, notwithstanding, he had orchestrated disruption of the convention. The City administration had sent gangsters to subvert the proceedings. Police followed to quell the disorder. Both beat up the students, the latter in a more brutal fashion.

School students were special targets, probably because they were smaller in size and could be punched and kicked with impurity.

Student leaders, wise in the ways of the police, had taken the precaution of organizing a defense squad led by none other than Adeeb Rizvi, later to distinguish himself for his work in Kidney diseases and founder of the Sindh Institute of Urology and Transplant (SIUT). Sher Afzal Malik was a sort of Red Guard Lieutenant Commander of the security detail. He blocked a gangster, who was later to become a respectable small trader's union leader, from throwing a girl from an upper floor balcony, in the nick of time. Volunteers somehow managed to control the situation for long enough to enable Brohi to conclude his address, but the rest of the proceedings had to be moved to Model school premises in Pakistan Chowk, another commercial area in the town. The convention passed a resolution to form All Pakistan Students Organization (APSO), elected Sarwar as the General Secretary General and Iqbal, a right-winger, as the President. Numerous student organizations in small and large towns of all the provinces of West Pakistan decided to merge with it. Bengali delegates pledged that they would seek the approval of their groups to do the same.

Reacting to police and gangster brutality, enraged students spread all over the city. The press and public again supported them. Police dared not take overt action, so bloodshed was avoided. But many students were arrested and spent months in jail. Pakistan joined the Western Security organizations in 1954 and by a queer coincidence (or design), APSO was also banned about the same time.

National student's federation (NSF) had been a parallel moderate-right wing student body. It had been totally eclipsed by DSF. Second-generation student leaders Wadood, Sibghat and others negotiated with NSF and a merger meeting was convened in early 1955 in an apartment in a building in Moulvi Musafar Khana off Bunder Road, Karachi. Some 50-60 students, almost equally divided between left-wingers and moderates, attended. A coalition was worked out.

Life as a day scholar in those long-gone days was very chaotic. Some of us attended classes. Others spent time in the cafeteria or in jobs. Teachers fully cognizant of the parlous state of our finances, and worse living conditions at home, gave us wide latitude. But we had a vibrant social, intellectual and political life. Karachi debaters were known for their oratorical prowess and won trophies from Lahore, the only other city of note in West Pakistan, as a matter of course. The one activity of particular note I recall from those days was the procession we took out to protest the attack of Britain, France and Israel on Suez Canal. We went around to various colleges and schools and appealed to the students to come with us.

One of the notable student leaders during this period was Fatehyab Ali Khan. He later joined Mazdoor Kisan Party and rose to be its president. Another student leader to make his mark at the time was Mairaj Muhammad Khan, an emotional orator, and younger brother of a leftist luminary who was a well-known journalist. Mairaj was befriended by Z.A Bhutto, and was once introduced by him to the public as one of his successors. Bhutto appointed Mairaj to his cabinet. Mairaj maintained his links with trade unions and once Bhutto had crushed the unions, sacked Mairaj and put him in jail.

Among other pioneers M. Shafi, a brilliant debater was a spent force by the time I met him in 1955-56. Barkaat Alam, a party ideologue par excellence, had also been sidelined. He migrated to Britain and settled in Glasgow. Another prominent activist, Saghir Ahmad, joined Pakistan International Airlines and was the main force behind the airline officers' union. All these undoubtedly talented young men had to play second fiddle to and resented Sher Afzal, who was molded by Hasan Nasir, the Secretary General of the Communist Party of Pakistan (CPP). Hasan Nasir indoctrinated him in communist theology and imposed him on leaders senior to him in hierarchy. A man of great innate qualities, Sher Afzal could converse at all levels with intellectuals, students and industrial workers. Punjabi was his mother tongue, but he had gone to a school in Peshawar, and spoke Pushto like a native. In Karachi he had learnt Gujerati and Sindhi as well. He was fluent in Urdu though it was hardly chaste and managed English well enough. He had great organizational skills and had a devoted circle of admirers from all linguistic groups. He was elected president of Dow Medical students union in 1956. The union made some radical demands. The administration would not agree. A dozen or so activists, Sher Afzal among them and including a few girls, went on a hunger strike. It lasted many days and gathered sufficient public support to make no less a person than H.S. Suharwardy, the Prime Minister at the time, to visit the college and give Sher Afzal a drink to break his fast. A natural populist, Suharwardy accepted all students' demands. BBC, Tass and other international agencies flashed the news.

Sher Afzal grew from strength to strength. He had a say in the upper counsels of left wing political parties led by Bhashani and Wali Khan and was welcomed by the likes of Suharwardy in their private homes. He had a devoted band of admirers. He also earned the barely concealed hostility of the entrenched leaders of the left in Karachi. This was to have a far-reaching impact on his political fortunes. After completing his tenure of office in the students union, he became the president of NSF.

Sher Afzal chose a close friend and political understudy Mahboob Ali, as the party nominee to contest the office of the president of Dow Medical College Students' Union. Cultured, intelligent, honest and sincere, Mahboob was very knowledgeable in political theory as well, but was not an effective speaker. He spoke very fast; words ran over each other, which at times made him unintelligible. Another student in Mahboob's class, an Urdu speaker, but brought up in NWFP and therefore fluent in Pushto, wanted the nomination. He was vain, shallow and pompous and did not deserve the honor. Mahboob's opponent in the election, nominated by a right wing group, was a political nobody.

We all thought that Mahboob would certainly be elected. Out of overconfidence, he made the tactical error of designating the self same rival as his representative at the polling station. This was to cost him and us dearly. As the polling agent, the man's primary job was to object to any dubious ballots of his principal's opponent. The man never questioned a single ballot of the other candidate. Mahboob lost by one vote.

Abdullah Siddiqi, Mahboob's running mate as General Secretary, however, won the office. Abdullah had been a top ranked student and had a brilliant and incisive political mind. His dedication was total and integrity unquestioned. He became a doctor in 1958. The political bug had bitten him and he wanted to pursue a career in politics. This was the time of high ferment in public affairs in Pakistan. General elections were due in a few months time. Time was ripe to introduce new talent to the ranks. But the party bosses ignored him. Disillusioned, he left for the USA and later settled in Canada.

Martial law of 1958 intervened and changed the ground rules. Sher Afzal was soon to lose his patron Hasan Nasir to extra-judicial murder in Lahore fort. Knives were soon out against him. The bosses persuaded him to transfer to the trade union front. But they panicked when he managed to revitalize the industrial workers organizations and continued to influence students through his successor. They had inadvertently handed over two fronts to him and asked him to resume control of the student affairs. His acquiescence turned out to be a serious mistake.

Martial law had proscribed student unions and college elections. After a hiatus of two years, our military administrator, a doctor Naqi, Lt. Col. in rank, enlightened as army men go, allowed elections in 1959. Ali Ahmad, an amiable gentleman, ideologically well grounded though a bit of a practical joker, won the President's office. His term was comparatively uneventful. We were lying low. About the only agitation we indulged in was the comparatively tame affair of getting the examination date postponed.

As the next election time approached, caucuses were held to choose candidates. Hasan Rizvi was selected to contest for the presidency and I was nominated to be his running mate as General Secretary. Rizvi won; I lost to a friend who was a good debater and a likeable person too. Our nominees for other union offices lost too. Rizvi was isolated but he was an astute political worker and kept union affairs in control. We were depressed and found ourselves at a loose end. The electoral loss was a serious setback for Sher Afzal. Indians and Pakistanis are only a little less conscious of "face" than the Chinese are.

A fierce struggle was simultaneously going on between Sher Afzal and the higher party bosses in Karachi. The bosses had been firmly entrenched in their power bases, especially in the airline and journalist unions. Enjoying their perks and privileges, hands in glove with the management, they were given to selling out their followers. Rising fortunes of Sher Afzal were a mortal threat to them. Sher Afzal too was looking for an opportunity to retrieve lost ground. Patrice Lumumba, a firebrand left leaning nationalist Prime Minister of Belgian Congo had been assassinated by imperialist agents. Sher Afzal decided to pin his hopes on a successful show of strength in a student led protest march.

NSF gave a call for a day of protest marches and meetings. The call was heeded in Dhaka, Lahore, Peshawar and many other cities in the country. We went out on the streets in Karachi. But we were a forlorn group of about a hundred, carrying such banners as "Long live Lumumba," "Death to UN secretary General Dag Hammarskjöld" and "Down with imperialism," and shouting similar slogans. A few curious onlookers would stare at us, sometimes ask us a few questions, and even go along for a few minutes. Some policemen accompanied us for ten to fifteen minutes, but even they didn't find us worth the bother and most slipped away. It was a terrible let down.

About the same time communal riots had broken out in Jabalpur, India. There were persistent demands that we organize a protest march on the issue. Sher Afzal was under tremendous pressure. On the one hand, we were strictly secular and should not have anything to do with communal frenzy. On the other hand, this was the glittering prize of a really successful show of strength. The bosses had agents in place and were fully aware of our most secret discussions. They sent agents provocateurs who accosted Sher Afzal in his hostel room. They taunted him, ridiculed him and called him a lackey of the Soviet Union. As never before, his public credibility was at stake.

The next day, the premier English language daily paper, the *Dawn*, editorialized that our progressives felt more for the cannibals of Africa than for their brethren in faith in India. Our goose was now properly cooked. We were damned if we did, and damned if we did not. Left with no choice, Sher Afzal characteristically threw himself into planning a big gathering and a march to follow.

On the appointed day and time students in the thousands gathered near Pakistan Chowk, which had several college campuses within walking distance. Speeches were made pledging support to Indian Muslims. Police had taken up positions in the broad avenue flanking the meeting. The district magistrate (DM) announced that the government sympathized with Indian Muslims. We had made an impressive protest, authorities will take note and do all they could to protect our co-religionist in India. We should now dispense peacefully.

Sher Afzal agreed and gave a call to disperse. But he and the rest of us had reckoned without an agent provocateur. He snatched the microphone and screamed that our mothers and sisters were being raped in India and we were being asked to disperse peacefully and demanded that we take out the procession as planned.

It was obviously a signal. Flags and banners hoisted on long bamboo poles were grabbed and scores rushed at the police. They responded with tear gas and Lathi (Baton) charge.

I walked back to the medical college and attended a lecture. Later on, I made rounds of Hospital wards where the injured student leaders had been brought. I returned to my hostel room about midnight and had just gotten into bed when there was a loud knock at the door. Annoyed at the late callers, I opened the door and found a Criminal Investigation Department (CID) Sub Inspector Shah with another two policemen wearing plain clothes. I had been sure that I was not high enough in student leadership to be apprehended; otherwise I would have found a safe house. Shahji told me that DM had invited students to a meeting. I told him not to be ridiculous, and to tell me plainly that I was being arrested. Shahji told me not to be difficult and come along. I didn't have a choice.

They took me to a van where I found Anwar Saleem, former General Secretary of Dow Medical College Students' Union during Ali Ahmed's tenure. Anwar, who was physically quite impressive, was nattily dressed in a dark blue suit with a maroon tie. I quizzed him on the fancy dress. He told me of the meeting with the DM. I told him not to be a fool; we were being arrested. He shot back that I was the fool. We arrived at a police station about 2:00 a.m. Anwar Saleem, expecting to be greeted by a magistrate, got out first. A policeman, sighting a handsome well-dressed man, mistook him for a high official and saluted him. Anwar grinning nudged me. A moment later, a police inspector asked the same policeman to lock us up. I couldn't tell you who was shocked more, the policeman or Anwar.

We were about fifteen detainees in a 10 x 10 cell. Together, our spirits were high. We sang, joked and were quite noisy. Soon after a police superintendent (SP) visited our cell and started hurling abuse at us. He told Sher Afzal that being a Punjabi himself and a former student of his father who was a reputed head master, he felt like a brother to him. He did not expect his brother in spirit to associate with riff raff. Mairaj and Fatehyab protested. They were taken out and slapped right in front of us. They were again taken out of the cell early in the morning and mercilessly beaten.

Our sojourn in the lock up was not without its lighter side. We had settled down to fitful sleep when we were woken up by a commotion some distance away from our cell door. Hasan Rizvi asked a policeman about it and was told that a man in a suit had been brought in. Surmising correctly that it must be Mahboob, Anwar, the only other suited person, was already with us. Rizvi asked his cellmates to adopt a *murgha* pose. Entering the cell, Mahboob was stunned. Rizvi told him that they had been ordered to adopt the pose. He was clearly nonplussed. Everybody burst out laughing. The policeman panicked at the sight of what he thought was collective obeisance, rushed to his inspector that the new one must be the big boss as everyone was prostrating before him. The inspector, annoyed at the sound of loud laughter, ordered that Mahboob be transferred to another cell with hardened criminals. It took an hour's pleading to get him back with us.

About one hundred and sixty students were eventually transferred to Karachi central jail, and arrived around noon. The jail superintendent told us that he didn't care about what we had done outside, but if we didn't behave inside the jail boundary, retribution would be swift; he was the judge, jury and prosecuting attorney all in one. He further informed us that per jail regulations, a prisoner arriving about midday doesn't get lunch or the evening meal, so we would get breakfast the next day. We groaned audibly. The superintendent glared at us. An elderly man who had joined us told the superintendent not to be a damned fool. We were students, not ordinary criminals. The superintendent appeared to shrink in his uniform at the rude reprimand, especially after he had made such a pompous speech. The white-haired "angel"[1] ordered a guard to go out and get lunch for us. As an afterthought he also ordered cold drinks and cigarettes of the best brand.

From the next day food drinks and cigarettes started arriving for us.[2] It seemed the whole city was bent on bringing succor and comfort to us. About thirty of us were herded in a separate barracks, the other one hundred thirty having been released after a few days of incarceration. We spent time singing, telling stories, teasing each other and in political indoctrination. Many poems were written, some too rich and off color to narrate.

Eid (a major Muslim festival, celebrating the end of the month of fasting) fell during our incarceration. Rules were relaxed for the day. The day started with prayers. The jail Imam (prayer leader) had been commanded to lead the official congregation in the City as Maulana Ehtisham Thanvi, the official Moulvi, had had a dispute with the government and boycotted the main congregation. We were left with the deputy Jail Imam. He was a "lifer"[3] convicted for murder and given a twenty-one year jail sentence. The man could not pronounce Urdu words properly, much less Arabic. We could not help giggling during the prayers. During the *Dua* (special requests to God) after the prayers, we lost all sense of sanctity of the occasion and implored God to mete out severe punishment to our fellow prisoners.

After the prayers we proceeded to other barracks and were entertained with sweets and drinks, some spiked with Bhang (Marijuana) and raw and refined opium. The prisoners put up a stage show in our honor, with songs, dance and drama. It was pretty high standard; the performers had been actors and enter-

---

1 He was Abdullah, the head of the then notorious Bhatti clan of big time smugglers.
2 We were under trial, not convicted yet, and friends and relatives were allowed to send us food and
   drinks.
3 Murderers, if not sentenced to death, were given 21 years jail sentence and were called 'lifers'. After
   spending 7 years they were made "supervisors" to spy on other prisoners.

tainers in their pre prison life. One person, in for murdering his paramour in a fit of jealous rage, sticks to memory. He had a haunting voice and accompanied himself with music produced by tapping an empty earthenware pot (*ghara*). We also met a group of ex-air force officers convicted of some sort of smuggling. They, instead of idling away the hours, had started a crime school teaching tricks of the trade to fellow inmates. We also met an accountant, formerly a senior official in the State Bank (equivalent to the Federal Reserve Bank of the US). He had been convicted of currency fraud and had, according to his own account, stashed away millions in foreign bank accounts.

There was a young man who, after imposition of martial law in 1958, had impersonated an army colonel and held up a bank. He had been arrested a few days later in a hotel room, lying on a bed covered with currency notes. He normally would grant an interview only by appointment but relented in our case. In the world of crime, like the world of all other professions, respect is strictly related to performance.

We were eventually hauled up before an army brigadier. He reprimanded me severely; I was a grief to my father who had served honorably in World War II. It was very embarrassing. It was very humiliating as well. The man was obnoxiously patronizing. My father was greatly relieved at getting me out. There was even a hint of pride, evoked no doubt by the regard and admiration rendered us by the public.

On my first day back in college I was expecting an expression of goodwill and solitude, but the hero's welcome took me by a pleasant surprise. They wanted to shake my hands, ask how had I been treated and even my political opponents gave me admiring looks. My friends soon formed a procession, with me at its head, and protested that I should have forewarned them.

Karachi party bosses had, in the meanwhile, made inroads into the NSF. They sent messages to Sher Afzal that he should retire from student politics.

On May 14, 1965, the day before I was to fly to England, a student leader, a distant connection and an erstwhile member of my personal following, visited me. He asked me to appeal to Sher Afzal not to attend the NSF meeting scheduled for the next day, as he would be expelled. I admonished him rather severely, told him to be decent and honorable in dealing with a man whom he and all of us had put on a pedestal not too long ago. Sher Afzal, sensing the predicament he would be in, had told me to warn off my connection that he would fix the person who would move the resolution to expel him. My admonition did have some effect. Extravagant praise was heaped on Sher Afzal in the meeting. He was humbly requested to retire rather than be expelled.

The inner party struggle continued for quite long. The minions of party bosses stooped to mud-slinging.[1] Sher Afzal finally decided to cut loose his ties to

---

1 I have collected and saved the NSF magazines printed at the time.

Karachi and returned to Peshawar. By temperament and inclination unsuited to private practice or a government employment, he rightly felt that obtaining the degree was meaningless to him. He was later persuaded to come back and take the examination. He passed the examination, retuned to Peshawar again, and opened a drug store in partnership with his brother-in-law. The latter did all the work. Sher Afzal entertained his political cronies and participated in left wing politics.

With his Punjabi/Pathan credentials, work among Karachi students, abounding enthusiasm, good mind, inexhaustible energy and patent ideological integrity, he should have gone far. He should have been catapulted into national politics, but martial law allowed only sycophants to rise. It was a great national loss.

The above has been written in collaboration with Asim Ali Shah, Secretary General of National Students Federation from mid-1980s to mid-1990s. Asim has maintained his activism and lives in London, UK. Asim would like to acknowledge the assistance of advocate Zainuddin Khan Lodhi, one time Secretary General of NSF.

My contribution is based, in addition to my own experiences, on interviews with Messers Nooruddin Sarki, S. Mazhar Jameel and Fatehyab Ali Khan advocates and Drs Muhammad Sarwar, Syed Haroon Ahmad, Muhammad Khurshid and Rasheed Hasan Khan of Karachi and Dr. Hasan Raza Rizvi and Barrister Abid Hasan Manto of Lahore. Barkaat Alam of Glasgow, UK and S.U. Kadri QC of London, both pioneers of the movement, have been of invaluable help.

All the above named are stalwarts of the students' movement of Pakistan. The list is by no means complete.

I would like to dedicate this document to the January 8, 1953 martyrs and to all who believe on power of working class.

## Chapter 9. Decline and Fall of Ayub

### BD Civil War

In his weakened post-1965 war state, Ayub could never hope to withstand the combined onslaught of East and West Pakistan. The campaign against him, led initially by students and industrial workers, had caught the imagination of the people. This was the last time people of the two wings were to unite on one platform. In a desperate attempt to save his legacy, Ayub called a joint conference of government and opposition leaders. The talks broke down.

Ayub was failing so it was time for a resumption of political activities. National Awami Party (NAP) in alliance with leftist elements was expected to gain plurality in the NWFP. Baluchistan continued to remain firmly in the grip of tribal Sirdars, who aligned themselves with the highest bidder. At the time NAP had considerable support of the power brokers there. It was expected to do well in East Pakistan as well.

Agitation was resumed with renewed and ever greater vigor. Mujib drew ever-larger crowds. Bhutto drew large crowds in the Punjab. Sindhis sensing the prevailing wind, or perhaps yielding to chauvinistic sentiments, also started supporting him. He did develop some opportunistic following in the Frontier and Baluchistan provinces as well.

Ayub threw in the towel and flouting his own tailor made constitution which mandated that the speaker of the national assembly succeed him, or as some observers would have it, was forced by the top brass to hand over the Presidency to the army chief Yahya Khan, who re-imposed martial law and assumed the combined offices of the President and Chief Martial Law administrator (CMLA). Yahya made the usual noises that he had agreed to take over the government to save the country from impending disaster, as was his bounden duty as a patriot and an officer, abrogated the constitution, and dissolved one unit.[1] He further promised to hold free and fair elections based on adult franchise, one-person one vote. People listened to him with scarcely disguised disbelief. It was *déjà* vu from Ayub's first broadcast.

Calm was restored pretty soon. Politicians went about organizing their parties and gear them for an election campaign. People were cautiously hopeful. There was certainly no presentiment of impending doom.

Credit must be given where due. For all his faults, Yahya was, till then, the only ruler of Pakistan who kept his word to hold free and fair elections. He promulgated-necessary ordinances empowering the Census Board to prepare a voter list, the Election Commission to get ready for elections and lifted the freeze on political activities. He consulted leaders of political parties, exhorting them to assist and cooperate with the electoral machinery. In brief, he took all the correct and pertinent steps, including admonition to the police and bureaucrats to be impartial and to show no favor.

Political parties went into a frenzy of campaigning. Mujib offered his now famous or infamous, depending upon one's point of view, six points which were a thinly disguised plan of con-federal government. Bhutto gave a catchy slogan of Roti, Kapra aur Makan, roughly translated bread, clothes and home. He also pledged nationalization of industries and radical land reforms.

After school and college education in Bombay, Bhutto had gone to Oxford in England for a law degree. He subsequently studied at the Berkeley Campus of the University of California and returned to Pakistan in the mid-1950s. He obtained an appointment as a lecturer at the law school in Karachi. Family money and connections helped him with a private office and a lucrative retainer ship with the family shipping business of Ardeshir Cowasjee, a well known columnist and activist, who belongs to a tiny but well-knit Parsi community in India and Pakistan.[2]

The job of legal counsel to the shipping concern of Cowasjee family persuaded Iskander Mirza, the then President of Pakistan, to name him the leader of the country's delegation to a maritime conference in Geneva. Bhutto sent Mirza an absolutely slavish letter, difficult to emulate even in a country awash with toadies and sycophants, predicting that when history of Pakistan was written, the latter's name will figure perhaps even more prominently than Jinnah's!

In the NWFP, successors of the Khan Brothers had regained legitimacy. Before the advent of Martial law, the older brother popularly known as Dr. Khan

---

1 All the provinces of West Pakistan were merged into one unit to justify equal number of seats of the West and the East in the central assembly.

2 Iranians, who did not convert to Islam fled to India and are called Parsis, a distortion of the noun Farsi for Faras, another name for Iran. Koran, along with Christians, Jews and Sabians, calls them people of the book. Muslim men but not women may marry a person of the book without first converting them.

Sahib had served as a Chief Minister of the unified province of West Pakistan, called one unit. They had joined National Awami party (NAP) led by Maulana Bhashani, also known as the Red Mullah because of his egalitarian-leftist views.

The Mullahs, frightened of secular Awami League and National Awami Party, had joined hands with the feudal elements, the army and bureaucrats, thus completing the evil Quad.[1] The establishment was confident that elections will result in a divided house, and Yahya acting as a referee, would be able to get Mujib or someone else to indulge in the usual horse-trading and cobble a coalition. Hankering after office, the members of the assembly will fall out with each other once again.

But it was not to be. East Pakistan, now Bangladesh, is a hurricane prone country. With the population explosion in the twentieth century, and non-development of energy resources, large swathes of the country had been deforested for fuel. Trees and vegetation underneath hold water and soil. It thus resulted in enormous erosion of soil, which ended up in rivers, severely restricting their capacity to hold water.

A particularly devastating storm hit the region just prior to the scheduled elections. Hurricanes[2] have a vastly different impact on a poor and densely populated region like Bengal than they do in an advanced country like the United States. They wreak havoc. A large majority of the people live in makeshift mud and clay huts. Weather forecasts are at best capricious. Even if they were reliable, people won't have anywhere to escape to. The most common mode of transport is by boats, which along with whole villages, are swept away by a combination of wind and high tide. During the monsoons, people are reduced to plying boats on the roads in the capital city Dhaka and all the other major cities. The sea is dotted with hundreds of islands off shore, ranging in size from a few hundred square yards to several square miles on which millions live. They are, if anything, worse off than the mainlanders.

Maulana Bhashani demanded, and with good reason, that elections be postponed and the emergency be dealt with first. But Yahya was fantasizing about his place in history. Mujib had smelled the heady perfume of victory. Bhutto was confident that he would manage, with the connivance of the Army brass and a sizable victory in West Pakistan, to come out on top. Elections were not postponed. Bhashani boycotted them. The Awami league, without an effective competition from Bhashani's NAP, found the arena uncontested. Under the system of the front runner taking all, Awami League won 160 seats out of 162 assigned to East Pakistan, and commanded absolute majority in a house of 310 members. He could, with the support of smaller parties in West Pakistan, even garner a two

---

1 I have borrowed this from Mao's gang of four
2 I had written this before Katrina hit New Orleans.

third majority in the house. That would enable them to pass any constitution they wanted.

Yahya and the Army high command were stunned. Bhutto was too. They put a brave face on it. Yahya, during a post election visit to Dhaka, introduced Mujib to the international press as the future Prime Minister of Pakistan. He even announced the date the new parliament would meet. He and Bhutto negotiated with Mujib and tried to get him to give a little on the six points and concede a face saving formula. Talks broke down.

Yahya postponed the parliamentary session for an indefinite period of time. Mujib demanded that another date for the parliamentary session be announced at once. He permitted his minions to take over the administration, security services, transport, schools, colleges and universities, health services and courts in East Pakistan. The writ of the central government ran only in the cantonments and the Government House. Mujib, in effect, ruled East Pakistan, venturing even to welcome Yahya on subsequent visits as a guest of East Pakistan.

Yahya did announce another date for the opening session of the parliament, but things were beyond repair now. Bhutto threatened to personally break the legs of any members of his party who would go to Dhaka for the opening session of the parliament. He also warned members of the parliament from other West Pakistani parties that if they attended the meeting, they would eventually be tried as traitors.

Yahya made pious noises of national reconciliation in order to buy time to deploy enough troops in East Pakistan to crush and control the natives. Awami league leaders were aware of the plans. They tried to beef up the East Bengal rifles, a thinly armed militia manned by Bengali soldiers, all of whose senior officers were from West Pakistan. Contingency plans were drawn up for most of the senior cadre of the party to escape to India when the army made their move.

Mujib and other Awami league leaders looked the other way, while houses and businesses of Urdu-speaking immigrants were looted, scores were killed; women kidnapped and raped with impunity. They had mistreated Bengalis while they ruled the roost. They had, in common with Punjabis, looked down upon Bengalis[12] as somewhat inferior beings and kept aloof from them. They had consistently supported West Pakistani interests, politically, in business and industry. They had behaved as virtual colonizers. Let them suffer. So the argument went. Among Bengalis, members of religious parties notably Jamaat-e-Islami, timeservers and collaborators, also suffered horribly.

The massive air and sea transfer of troops to East Pakistan was a logistic challenge in itself. They were further hampered by the fact that India had banned over flight of its territory, on the pretext that two Pakistani agents had hijacked an Indian civilian plane to Lahore.[1] When Army high command felt that they had adequate forces to cow down the populace, they swooped down like birds of prey. As the first measure they disarmed, and confined the East Pakistan rifles to, what were for all practical purposes, concentration camps. The army then moved to take care of the leaders of the rebellion. A frontal assault would mean wholesale massacre. The army was not averse to it but the Governor of East Pakistan and Chief of the Navy, Admiral Ahsan[2], intervened. He insisted that the arresting squad go in quietly under the cover of darkness and behave respectfully especially with women.

In the event the assault force did beat up Mujib, push around women and break the bones of a few servants. Mujib was arrested and flown to a jail in West Pakistan, where he was tried in camera for treason and sentenced to death. Other members of Awami League high command had quietly slipped across the border to India.

Security officials, their ranks beefed up by armed soldiers, went around securing the capital city Dhaka, and the environs and spread out arresting and torturing people en route to cities nearby and did it at the slightest pretext, even without one. Other units tried to emulate the performance of the central command. After "pacifying" the cities, army personnel spread through the countryside. Out of the spotlight of the international media, they unleashed an even more brutal reign of terror of unprecedented ferocity. They did not spare even the Bengalis whom they suspected of harboring pro-Pakistan sympathies.[3]

As soon as he heard of the army action in Dhaka, Army Col Zia Ur Rahman[4] one of the few senior Bengali officers in the Pakistan army, then stationed in Chittagong, declared independence of Bangladesh (BD) from the local radio station.

Awami league High command, with blessings, diplomatic and material support of the Indian Government, set up the Government of Bangladesh (B.D) in exile in Delhi, with Mujib as the president and a cabinet acting in his name. They set about obtaining political, diplomatic, financial and armed assistance from Governments and the public all over the world. The response was tepid. Most countries, except for the Soviet Union, adopted a wait and watch policy. Nixon leaned towards Pakistan. He, along with Kissinger, was mindful of the faithful satellite status of the country. Human Rights were not a relevant concern for them.

---

1 While Pakistan was transporting troops to East Pakistan, an Indian passenger plane was hijacked to Lahore. India claimed that it was the work of Pakistani agents. It later turned out that the whole thing was planned by Indian security agencies.
2 Admiral Ahsan, an enlightened immigrant was the chief of Naval forces, and had been the first Naval attaché to Jinnah. He prevented a lot of bloodshed in the region.
3 My daughter's father-in-law, Dr. Mumtaz Chaudhury was serving as a Director of Education in a major city. The army wanted him to keep an eye on the staff under him. He told them that he would not act as a spy. A Major and a Colonel visited him soon after. In the ensuing argument, the Major called him all kinds of names and pulled a gun on him.
4 Not to be confused with General Zia ul Haq of Pakistan.

The army, not familiar with lanes and byways of towns and villages, were frequently ambushed. Reprisals were brutal. With only a few minutes' notice, shantytowns were run over by heavy armored vehicles. Escaping victims were cut down with machine gun fire. Women and little girls were abducted, some raped on the spot, in full view of the parents. Survivors of the massacre were driven like cattle to designated concentration camps.

Soldiers were also ordered to assault the places of worship and kill all who had sought shelter in the House of God. When they, Muslims themselves, de-murred, they were told that non-Muslims had occupied mosques. Some older soldiers took off the garments of the dead and discovered that they were cir-cumcised. The officers told them that the Hindus, in order to hoodwink Muslim police, had surgery performed on them.

There was a veritable avalanche of refugees across the border. Pakistan claimed that the fleeing mass of humanity were Hindus, who had never reconciled to par-tition. Few paid any heed to the blatantly dishonest attempt to whitewash the rampant repression in Muslim Bengal.

Yahya, with full support of the brass, replaced the comparatively mild, mul-tilingual and academically-inclined martial law administrator of East Pakistan, Lt. General Yakub Khan, with a barbaric general in the mold of Helegu.[1] The man, Tikka Khan, on arrival at Dhaka Airport, declared that he was interested in the land, not the people. Another of his infamous proclamations was that "We will change their race." Both events were shown on British TV. It was a blatant espousal of gang rape as an instrument of state policy. The butcher of Dhaka, as he came to be known, gave the soldiers a free hand. They specially targeted Dhaka university students. After surrounding the hostels they announced on loudspeakers that those who left peaceably would not be harmed — and fired on fleeing boys and girls. The sizable Hindu minority (they made up about 15% of East Pakistan's population) were also prime targets. All the urban areas were subjected to similar measures.

Urdu-speaking immigrants and members of Islamist parties served as a will-ing fifth column for the army. Bengali Islamists were more effective as they could easily infiltrate the ranks of the freedom fighters. They were to suffer horribly for this treachery.

Several million refugees had sought shelter in Indian Bengal and had been accommodated in hastily created tent cities. It was, indubitably, an intolerable burden on a poor country like India. Even with international aid it could not sup-port the burden of feeding and housing millions of destitute humanity.

The Indian Prime Minister Indra Gandhi was the daughter of Pundit Nehru, the first Prime Minister of India. Undivided India was an article of faith for him

---

1 Yakub was the military administrator while Ahsan was the governor. Both tried to curb atrocities of the army.

and other leaders. They would have loved to undo it, but never got the chance. His redoubtable daughter no doubt felt that destiny had offered her the opportunity to fulfill her father's dream. She was a pragmatist and was not particularly hampered by scruples. In actual fact, she was more like another leader of Independence movement Sirdar Patel.[1]

She gave an ultimatum to Pakistan. Refugees were an intolerable burden on India. Take them back immediately; settle the affairs without delay or India would take appropriate measures. Pakistan would be responsible for the consequences. She permitted Indian security personnel to clandestinely train and arm Mukti Bahini (Freedom Fighters) organized by the BD government in exile and send them on to East Bengal to harass the Pakistan forces. The assistance was not a secret to anyone. But Mukti Bahini was able to put up only feeble resistance. India massed its forces on East Pakistan border, ostensibly to prevent the flood of refugees into its territory

Indra Gandhi undertook a tour of all the major world capitals. She skillfully presented India's case, dwelling rather more on human misery of unprecedented scale, than on the crushing economic burden of having to look after millions of refugees. She was, of course, the legitimate and popular leader of the largest democracy in the world. The country had a fast expanding industrial base, and was potentially a vast consumer market. Even Nixon, though partial to Pakistan, gave her a respectful hearing.

Pakistan, ruled by an unelected, brutal and dissolute general, sent a foreign office bureaucrat who had difficulty getting an appointment with mid-level officials.

On return from a highly successful tour, Indra renewed her ultimatum to Pakistan.

Admiral Ahsan, the Governor of East Pakistan, renewed his offer to work out an arrangement under which the Pakistani Army could get out intact, without being humiliated. Pakistan would become a con-federation.[2] Yahya could continue as head of state. West Pakistani government servants would be repatriated to West Pakistan. East Pakistanis stranded in the West would be moved to the East. National assets would be divided in proportion to the populations of the two wings. It was the best possible solution under the circumstances. It would keep the country in one piece. The international community supported it. India fell in line, though reluctantly.

The civilian leadership of the West, barring Bhutto, was prepared to assist in any way and supported the Ahsan formula. The military cabal vetoed the pro-

---

1 Justifiably called the Iron man of India, Patel absorbed the feudal and semi-independent states in India with admirable speed.

2 The so called Ahsan formula under which center would control defense, foreign affairs and currency, but the provinces would have the authority to raise revenue and would fund the federation for central subjects.

posal. Bhutto endorsed the veto. Admiral Ahsan resigned and was replaced with a Bengali Quisling. The public was kept in the dark and was fed the official propaganda line that the Hindus, aided and abetted by India, were rebelling against Pakistan.

They couldn't possibly have hoped to win an armed conflict in East Pakistan. They had no means of keeping a supply line to their forces intact. India had already banned over flights over its territory. Soldiers, unless escorted by an armored convoy, could not move around. The butcher got himself replaced with the hapless General Niazi and fled to West Pakistan. The top brass had started looking for face saving excuses for transfer back to the Western wing

Expatriates could get uncensored news in the UK but were still divided along the same lines as they were in Pakistan. My acquaintances were mostly Punjabi- and Urdu-speaking people. Nearly to a man, except for the true-blue progressives, they supported the army. But the most pitiable condition was that of Pakistani Bengalis in the UK. Nearly all had a relative who had been jailed, maimed or killed by the army. The bearded Bengali owner of a shop near Warren Street in London had his store trashed twice, once by Punjabis because he was a Bengali and the second time by Bengalis because in his Islamic zeal he supported Pakistan. In the end he wished a pox on both houses.

Pakistani generals, in total denial of reality[1], deluded themselves into thinking that by initiating a conflict on the western border they would get an international intervention, cease fire, etc. Bhutto had lavished compliments on them for coming up with this brilliant idea. Pakistan would be saved. West Pakistan was the buffer between the Soviet Union and the Indian Ocean. Once the Russians controlled the ocean, they would threaten the access of the Euro-American alliance to the Far East and on and on. The US would not tolerate that. It was a rehash of Dulles's domino theory.[2]

International power brokers would have intervened, perhaps, if Pakistan had had a sustainable military position. In addition, Pakistan had earned such a bad name that even her supporters could not back her openly. Bhutto knew the opprobrium his country had already earned. He was also aware of the parlous state of the army. He still egged the army on.

The Indian Government gave a final ultimatum to Pakistan to withdraw her forces from East Bengal voluntarily and immediately. The ultimatum was rejected by Pakistan. The Indian army went into action on its border with East Pakistan. The Pakistani army withdrew after a token resistance to "defensible" strong points. The Mukti Bahini took control of the vacated areas and declared

---

1 I am quoting Akbar S Ahmad, then a civil servant, now an academic, from his book *Jinnah, Pakistan and Islamic Identity*. During a visit to the military headquarters, general Niazi told him a few days before surrender that he was going to fight through India to create a land link between the two wings.

2 US secretary of state under Eisenhower wanted to fight in Vietnam, because if that country fell to communists, all other countries would fall like dominoes.

Bangladesh sovereignty over them. Indians could afford to wait for the inevitable and pushed ahead slowly.

Pakistanis, however, adopted a scorched earth policy in East Pakistan, which would make the French action in Algeria look like a mild police raid. They destroyed all infrastructure, crops, boats, cars, buses, bridges, public buildings, industrial plants, schools and hospitals. They wanted to wreck the region, as one Neanderthal among the general staff put it, back to the Stone Age.

At this point Yahya decided to open hostilities on the Western border. Pakistani air force planes bombed some Indian airports as far as Agra, right in the belly of India. They hoped and prayed for international intervention, but it did not materialize. India counter-attacked and easily overcame the demoralized Pakistan forces. They had complete command of the skies and bombed Karachi by air, and their ships shelled the port. Lahore was hit, without a respite, by long-range artillery and from the air.[1]

Lahore was within easy grasp of India. All their army had to do was to walk in. Nixon-Kissinger warned India off West Pakistan. Nixon announced that he had ordered the US pacific fleet to move towards East Pakistan. It was a shot across Indra's bow. It worked, or as some would have it, she had other ideas.[2]

The Chinese government, in an eerie replay of a similar claim during 1965 India Pakistan war, accused the Indian border forces of abducting a few cows and goats. India, as on the previous occasion, hastily offered immediate restitution.

The Army had appointed Bhutto as the foreign minister and sent him to New York to defend Pakistan's case in the UN Security council. He made grandiloquent, dramatic, and patently futile gestures. He was playing to the domestic audience; he tore up the draft resolution demanding immediate cease-fire. He was hailed in West Pakistan as a hero for magnificently taking on the whole world to save the country. On return to Pakistan he was handed over total control of the Government. He had driven to the President's house in a plain car and driven out in a vehicle bedecked with national, presidential and CMLA flags.[3]

The Pakistani army's resistance crumbled in the east and in the west. On the eastern side, they would soon abandon even the pretence of putting up a fight. Many senior officers fled in helicopters, pushing aside women and children. But the day before surrender, they rounded up and shot in cold blood all the educated people they could lay their hands on in Dhaka.[4]

The inevitable happened. The Pakistani army surrendered to arch foe India. The ceremony was broadcast on TV all over the world. I watched it in London. It

---

1 My former wife and daughter were in Lahore. I could not get in touch with them for weeks.
2 Some Indra detractors claim that she did not want to add a huge number of Muslims to the population which takeover of East and West Pakistan would have involved.
3 Ostensibly to maintain continuity, he had taken over both the offices of Yahya-President and Chief martial law Administrator.
4 *Bangla Desh: A legacy of blood* by Anthony Marcarenhas.

was pathetic. In full view of an audience, which must have counted in hundreds of millions, the victorious Indian General Aurora tore the medals and epaulets from the Pakistani General Niazi's uniform and accepted a reversed gun from the latter as a token of surrender. Without a trace of self-consciousness, Niazi told the international press that after the surrender ceremony, Aurora invited him to cocktails.

Mukti Bahini guerillas would have torn all 90,000 Pakistani military and civilian personnel and family members to shreds. But the Indian army expeditiously threw a protective cordon round them and soon after moved them to India.

## BHUTTO TAKES OVER — POST BD

Bhutto had taken over a country universally despised for the genocide in East Pakistan. He faced immense problems. India had captured large swathes of territory in the West too. There were 90,000 of his countrymen, soldiers, their kin and civil servants with their families in India. The government of BD was demanding the surrender of the butcher of Bengal, now the army chief of Pakistan, plus scores of army men from among the POWs. Indra had not shown her hand. If push came to shove Pakistan would have had to give up the butcher. For many, it would be just retribution

All Bhutto had in hand was Mujib in a Pakistani jail. He was certainly not in a position to touch the President of BD. Had he done so; Indra's hand would have been forced. She would have had to attack West Pakistan, free Mujib and try Bhutto as a war criminal. Why Indra did not let the BD government conduct war crimes trials is a mystery. Hitler's entourage were hanged and awarded long jail terms for lesser crimes.

I visited Karachi, Lahore and Rawalpindi a few months after the Pakistani army had surrendered in Dhaka. A state of total gloom pervaded the atmosphere. Even the elite were on the edge. But they were still in complete denial. Bhutto in their eyes was the savior. They were not prepared to countenance the fact, obvious to the meanest intelligence, that the evil Quad had confronted Bengali subnationalism and with their stupid moves had promoted it into national rebellion. Bengalis never wanted to destroy Pakistan.

I embarked on a twenty-four hour long journey from Karachi to Lahore on a railway train. People tended to talk in undertones. I have seen more cheerful funeral processions. At railway stations radios blared patriotic songs by melody queen Noor Jehan, the leading singer of the country. Nobody paid any heed to the still enchanting voice. I tried to engage people into a discussion of the calamity. I told them that it was not the end of the world. The POWs will come back. BD was a Muslim country. Residual Pakistan was rich in resources. They took refuge in the refrain "Allah knows best."

I was in Lahore on the day Bhutto addressed a public meeting as the president and chief martial law administrator of Pakistan. He had carted the whole diplomatic corps from Islamabad for the occasion and had ridden a carriage pulled by eight white horses, a relic of the Raj, slowly through the streets of Lahore to the meeting ground. People did line the streets of the route. But they were not up to the effort to greet him with a full-throated "Zindabad," "long live…" slogan. His henchmen tried. All they could extract from the normally cheerful, boisterous, even loud masses of Lahoris were tepid, half-hearted clapping and subdued cheers. Bhutto made a vehement speech interspersed with his antics. The only time the crowd responded lustily was when he used an obscenity.[1]

I next visited Rawalpindi, the seat of army GHQ. This city was teeming with relatives and friends of POWs held in India. They were all desperate for news of their loved ones. Only a few had received any news through the Red Cross and other such agencies. Rumors were rife that civilians were not covered by the Geneva Conventions and were being maltreated. They openly castigated the senior army officers who had run away leaving their juniors to face the vengeful Bengali freedom fighters.

The news that I was visiting from the UK spread soon, and my host was swamped by requests to see me. They wanted my help in communicating with sons, husbands and brothers. They gave me letters to mail from London and requested me to call the Red Cross, UNO and embassies in London. They were clutching at straws. All I could offer them was that I would pass on the names, last known address, rank and relevant numbers if they were servicemen, to the Red Cross and send copies to the consulates.

On my return to England, I found Pakistanis in the depth of despair there too. Some religious older East Pakistanis joined in grieving over a lost dream. Even the jingoist immigrants from the martial race (the Punjabis were so dubbed by the British) were subdued, though the more extreme among them put the entire blame on the Bengali "traitors," their subversive activities, and intervention of India. They were on the same wavelength as the generals.

Once he had all the levers of power securely in his hands, Bhutto went to India with a beggar's bowl, to plead for release of the POWs, and return of the Pakistan territory, India had captured. Indra received him graciously, as befitted a magnanimous victor. He had to make the concession that Kashmir dispute was a bilateral issue between India and Pakistan, and not an international issue, as had been hitherto accepted by the world bodies.

It was, under the circumstances, not a bad bargain. Indra could have forced him to drop the issue altogether, and made him sign the kind of treaty the allies made Germany do post World War I. She did not humiliate him to the extent that he would lose all credibility in residual Pakistan. She wanted a stable though weak state at her border. India had to feed 90,000 POWs and keep them secure.

---

1 He called his predecessors sister F…

It was not an inconsiderable burden. But when all is said and done, Indra behaved like a statesman, stateswoman if you will.

Mujib was still in a prison in West Pakistan. Bhutto grandiloquently declared that if Mujib agreed to a reunified Pakistan, he would order the latter's release from the jail and hand over reins of power to him as the Prime Minister of All Pakistan. Wali Khan, a veteran politician, offered to visit Mujib in jail and convince him to take over for Bhutto. I am paraphrasing an article by Wali Khan that I read in a Pakistani magazine that Bhutto thanked the Khan for the offer, but the next thing the Khan heard was that Mujib was put on a special and secret PIA flight early one morning to London. Mujib had been held incommunicado and did not learn of the establishment of BD as a sovereign state till he landed in London.[1] Wali Khan later ridiculed Bhutto in the parliament for his insecurity. The latter did not deny the charge. Wali stood vindicated.

The British Government received Mujib as a state guest and lodged him in a suite of rooms at the Claridge Hotel, usually assigned to heads of state. The suite was immediately swamped by his followers, inundated by phone calls from BD, Indra Gandhi and the British Prime Minister Edward Heath, among scores of other callers. He was unaware of the genocide perpetrated by the Pakistan army. The truth would not sink in till he reached Dhaka. Mujib stopped in Delhi en route to Dhaka and was given a historic reception. He, of course, had a much bigger welcome when he landed in Dhaka and quickly established absolute control over the government.

After the surrender of the Pakistani army to the Indian forces, Mujib's assistants had returned in triumph to the Independent state of Bangladesh, and installed themselves as the provisional government of the republic. They behaved as all revolutionary governments do; sought revenge, put opponents in jail, conducted kangaroo court trials, appropriated property, businesses, and even houses of their opponents. Urdu-speaking people became special targets.

The Indian Army restrained them from blatant excesses. The leaders should have put their heads together to initiate the process of rebuilding. The country had been devastated. There was little food, clean water, electricity, fuel or adequate shelter for the bulk of the people. With no accepted leader, they fell to infighting instead. The situation was saved from degenerating into mass starvation, rampant epidemics, and enormous loss of life by the unprecedented scale of international help, and by the logistic support provided by the Indian army.

About half a million Urdu-speaking persons had been left stranded. They were herded, for security, into hastily erected refugee camps. They were legally Pakistani citizens, and did not want to relinquish the citizenship. BD did not want them. There were lengthy negotiations between the respective Govern-

---

1 Anthony Mascarenhas in his book referred to above claims that Mujib had made a deal with Bhutto to maintain some kind of link with Pakistan.

ments and international agencies on what to do with them. Pakistan had to accept their claim of citizenship, but pleaded lack of resources for their repatriation and resettlement. Saudi and other gulf governments set up a trust fund for the purpose. Pakistan hedged. The province of Punjab offered to take them all if housing, jobs and means of sustenance could be provided for them. But Sindhis were apprehensive that regardless of where these Urdu speakers were initially resettled, they would eventually gravitate to its cities. They started talking of being "Red Indianized."

A few thousand houses were, nevertheless, built in the Punjab, and those with close relations in Pakistan were repatriated. Some made their way to Pakistan by bribing the border guards. The rest, over one hundred and fifty thousand in number are still (2008), languishing in UNO refugee camps.[1] Trust funds for their rehabilitation have, in the meanwhile, grown enormously.

The repatriates from the then East Pakistan did gravitate to Karachi, and live in a vast sprawling makeshift colony on the out skirts of the city. They are, however, an enterprising community and have established a large number of cottage industries making garments, weaving cloth, metal works, you name it. They were trained in sabotage by the Pakistan armed forces to fight the BD insurgents. They put the training to good use in periodic confrontations with the police, army and other security agencies. They played a large role in ethnic riots promoted by Zia, which were to break out in Karachi during his dictatorship. They also proved a great source of strength to the ethnic Mohajir Qaumi Movement (MQM), that Zia was believed to have sponsored.

BD was so poor that a large number of ethnic Bengalis were to migrate illegally to Pakistan. They lived in Karachi and other urban centers in Sindh and did menial work. They were exploited by employers, victimized by security agencies and looked down upon by other ethnic elements. Many, when compared to the average Bengali, are tall and fair. They are believed to be the products of the genetic engineering practiced under the aegis of the butcher of Bengal. The country remains much less developed than Pakistan. The population of the country is, though, now less than that of Pakistan. BD government was remarkably successful in promoting family planning.

Causes of poor economic progress of BD are many. Detailed analysis of the subject is beyond the scope of this narrative. Briefly they include early neglect, unstable governments and lack of resources superimposed on two hundred years of colonization.[2] Flood control measures have remained elusive. One private ven-

---

1 Those born since 1971 have been offered citizenship. They had turned down the earlier offer of full citizenship made a while after independence from Pakistan . In July 2008, the BD Supreme Court handed down a decision to allow them to vote in elections.
2 Bengal was fully colonized by 1757, while it took another hundred years for the rest of India.

ture the Grameen Bank[1] lends small amounts of money to finance small home based industries like garment making etc. But that is a drop in the ocean.

In Pakistan, Bhutto took full advantage of the humiliation of the armed forces. He retired many in the top brass, exiled others to comfortable sinecures as ambassadors and changed the designation of service Chiefs from that of Commander in Chief (C-in-C) to that of Chief of the staff (COS). A new post, Chief of Joint Staff was created, but its occupant had only an advisory capacity. The President of the republic became the C-in-C of all the services. Bhutto sacked the first army chief he had appointed and replaced him with the butcher of Bengal, Tikka Khan. Tikka was quite subservient to Bhutto and kept the army under control for the boss.

On the civilian front Bhutto had lists of undesirable functionaries prepared and dismissed them without recourse to legal proceedings, as Ayub and Yahya had done. The criteria for inclusion in the list varied from the highest offence of ever disobeying the man himself to crossing the path of the lowliest PPP partisan. Ethnic prejudice once again played a large role.

But Bhutto did introduce far-reaching reforms in the administration. Special cadres, like administration, police and customs, were organized. Previously a Superior Services officer could be a magistrate, judge, a district collector, and secretary of a department or serve in the Foreign Service. Now the successful entrants had to stay in their field. He also let professionals be promoted to senior most ranks. A doctor could, for example become Secretary of the Health Ministry, an engineer Secretary of Communications and so on. These positions had hitherto been an exclusive preserve of superior services. Under the pretext of attracting talent, he, however, appointed favorites directly, without the benefit of any experience or training, to senior bureaucratic positions. This procedure was called lateral entry.

On the political front, Bhutto offered a liberal democratic constitution. He even conceded the demands of the opposition that if he wanted executive power he should step down from the office of the President. The constitution provided for a head of the state with reserve powers, a powerful Prime minister, whose dismissal was automatically followed by dissolution of the parliament and any member of his party voting against him in a vote of no confidence would lose his/her seat if the measure failed. A constitutional draft was presented to the parliament. After careful deliberations, the ruling group accepted most of the amendments presented by the opposition. The document was passed by a unanimous vote in 1973. After the President had signed the document, martial law was lifted.

It lasted all of five hours. In a malicious and Machiavellian display of bad faith, Bhutto declared a state of emergency, suspended civil rights and curtailed the

---

1 The head of the enterprise won a Nobel Peace prize in 2006

authority of courts to entertain cases against the Government. The opposition cried foul, but they were helpless.[1]

Bhutto ran the country as a fiefdom, jailing opponents at will, and having them tortured as a matter of routine. It is widely believed that the head of a leading religious party, a venerable old man, was sexually assaulted while in jail.[2] Bhutto personally threatened a high court judge with dire consequences, and pointedly referred to his daughter who went to college every day. The befuddled judge took a long leave of absence. Bhutto did not spare even benefactors and friends. A senior civil servant and a member of his cabinet J.A. Rahim,[3] who had been his mentor, was not immune to his wrath. His first law minister Mahmood Qusuri, author of the 1973 constitution, appeared to grow too big for his britches. He was sacked with the usual admonition to take care lest things were to happen to the females of the family

Before elections Bhutto had given catchy slogans of "Roti, Kapra aur Makan" roughly bread, clothes and housing for all. He had also declared that factories and mills belonged to the workers. On his ascension to power the workers in many factories had taken him at his word. In a few cases the bosses were kept without food or water for extended periods of time. This was termed *gherao*, encirclement. When Bhutto used the iron fist on trade union workers, they looked up to one of his close associates, Mairaj Khan. To assert his independent status, he joined a trade union procession and was publicly beaten up. I have not been able to find a precedent, in non-communist countries, when the police had manhandled a sitting minister.

Bhutto maintained a lavish court in the style of potentates of yore. He just stopped short of declaring, like Louis XIV: "I am the state." Drunken orgies, wife swapping, and seduction of the wives of associates were reported to be common. I am sure his detractors told some malicious lies too, but the known fate of close associates lent credibility to the stories. If he looked cross eyed at them, ministers, generals, bureaucrats and governors were reduced to a quivering jelly. He specially favored yes-men in high office and appointed Zia chief of the army after the Butcher of Bengal retired. Zia was widely regarded as a mediocrity and used to follow Bhutto like a loyal henchman, usually with a tray of whisky in his hands.[4] The print media, dependent on government advertisements for their

---

1 Indra in India also got power drunk. When a court invalidated her election to the parliament on the grounds that she had used government transport for the campaign, she declared a state of emergency, jailed all her opponents, but could not overcome the innate strength of bourgeoisie democratic institutions. She had to call new pre-term elections, lost her own seat and was harassed by the new government.

2 These incidents were reported in Pakistani press, but have not been fully authenticated.

3 I read a report in a newspaper that Rahim left a party saying that he could not wait for Bhutto forever. Bhutto sent security personnel to the minister's house and had him beaten up. Rahim was "discovered" in solitary confinement in a house in Karachi, after Zia had overthrown Bhutto.

4 I have this on the authority of a retired Brigadier. Zia had blocked the man's promotion, so he may have embroidered it a bit.

daily bread, never virile in Pakistan, was reduced to abject servility. Radio and TV were under government control already. One could easily dub the media, Bhutto voice.

Perhaps the greatest disservice he did to the country was to bring to surface the latent animosity between the older inhabitants of Sindh and the newer ones who had migrated from India. He used state machinery to lavish favors on people who had done him a good turn in the days of his adversity.[1]

Bhutto was bright and educated enough to understand that the feudal system and capitalism were a contradiction in terms. His erstwhile patron Ayub had promoted industry and even managed to initiate pharmaceutical industry in East Pakistan. Bhutto decided to revive the fortunes of his class. He had given populist socialist slogans before assuming power. Workers had shown him the way by taking over industries. He would go the whole hog. He nationalized — read expropriated — industries, banks, schools, commercial concerns, even cottage industries like flour mills. Capitalists fled the country, taking their money and skills with them.

Banking was one of the more efficient and robust sections of commerce in Pakistan. After nationalization, hundreds of millions in loans, without any collateral, were given to sycophants, relatives and hangers on of the ruling clique. One favorite technique was to mortgage barren and worthless land, take a huge loan and then default on the loan. Qualified and experienced officers were summarily sacked to make way for cousins, supporters, and contacts of Bhutto's political party. The institutions were soon on the verge of bankruptcy and had to be bailed out by the government, further burdening the national exchequer. Many years later, when the Government offered the Banks to past owners, they declined to accept.

Private schools, a relic of the colonial past, run by Churches, and a few other parochial groups such as Parsis (Zoroastrians) provided high standard education for the progeny of the elite. The Government took them over. They started, like the government schools, churning out semi literate unemployable degree holders. The Church and a few other high-powered schools managed to retrieve control in due course, but many other less well connected were reduced to low standards.

Bhutto was much more successful in his dealings with the international community. He convened a meeting of the heads of all Muslim countries in Lahore and used the cover of the conference to obtain a "consensus from the conference to recognize BD," publicly embraced Mujib and buried the fictional existence of a "United" Pakistan.

---

1 One of my classmates from Quetta, an absolute pedestrian as a student, was barely able to keep body and soul together with his law practice. He made speeches in the Bhutto's favor in Lahore bar association. Bhutto, on ascension to power, had appointed him to the high court. Over the course of time he ascended the departmental ladder to a seat in the Supreme Court!

Political leaders the world over are known for public posturing. The discerning public takes these grandiloquent gestures for what they in actual fact are — low comedy. Bhutto was an expert at grandstanding. India had exploded a "peaceful" nuclear device in 1974. Bhutto had pledged a thousand years war with India and vowed to eat grass if it took that to make an "Islamic" atomic bomb. He was aided and abetted in this pledge by other heads of the state, especially the likes of the wild-eyed fanatic Moammar Gadafi of Libya.

CHAPTER 10. HEALTH SERVICE AND SOCIETY IN NORTH AMERICA, 1973 –2007

## SYDNEY, NOVA SCOTIA (CANADA) 1973–1974

Sydney was a small and economically depressed town. Besides a few lobster and shrimp farms, which provided subsistence living for a substantial part of the population, there was little economic activity. It had been a busy mining town, but they had run out of coal a long time ago. A jail and the medical establishment, consisting of two general hospitals and a long-term psychiatrist facility were the main employers. Unemployment was high and alcoholism was rampant. A native Indian reservation was an hour's drive away. An airport and a seaport were shared with another, a rather smaller town thirty miles away, called Glace Bay. The airport received two flights a day, one incoming and the other outgoing. An average of ten to twelve ships per week called at the port.

Sydney was the "capital" of an offshore island called Cape Breton. Patients from outlying cottage hospitals were referred to the medical facilities in Sydney. Complicated cases went to Hospitals in Halifax, the Capital of Nova Scotia. That city of about 350,000 people was three hundred miles away. It boasted a university, a medical school, a busy port and some industries. The total population of Nova Scotia was less than a million.

Cape Breton was dotted with villages and hamlets of a few hundred to a few thousand people. The total population of the island was one hundred thousand. A causeway built across a narrow strait connected it with the rest of Nova Scotia. The area was quite scenic with forests, trails, lakes, and hills, wild animals with good hunting and fishing. A particularly scenic hundred and twenty miles long trail, named after the French explorer Cabot, was quite popular among hikers and tourists.

The office I had engaged to work in was called the Guam clinic after its founder, Abraham (Abe) Guam. Abe was a qualified surgeon who practiced every specialty except Orthopedics, Ophthalmology and Ear, Nose &Throat. He was around seventy years old, but very well maintained and worked from 7:00 a.m. to 9:00 p.m. almost non-stop six days a week. He employed several family prac-titioners. They were all foreigners. We worked from 8:00 a.m. to 6:00 p.m., with half an hour for lunch, six days a week, and were on call once every three or four nights. Call started at 7:00 p.m., an hour after a full day's work. Our cars had been fitted with radiophones. An answering service would forward a patient's address to us on the car radio. One would be lucky to snatch two or three hours of sleep.

Abe had organized the clinic on the pattern of an assembly line. There were about ten cubicles, all equipped with syringes filled with penicillin. He would move from one room to another, place the stethoscope on the patient's back with a preoccupied look on his face and start scribbling with a pad in his right hand (he was left handed). Before the patient had finished the first sentence, he would hand the note to the patient. The note may have the name of a drug or two, but more often would have an order for an x-ray of the kidney, gall bladder or some other part of the body. If x-rays showed any abnormality, he would perform a surgical procedure. If the report were normal, he would simply tell the patient not to worry, regardless of persistence of symptoms. On average, the consulta-tion took all of two minutes.

Sydney had two hospitals. One, Sydney General run by the state, had two hundred beds. The other hospital was run by a Catholic charity. It was called St. Rita's and catered to the affluent. Bone, joint and spine cases had to be sent to Halifax. Not all patients could afford to go, so they simply put up with it and suffered.

The town had lost its orthopedic surgeon several years before I arrived on the scene. I had had four years of first-rate orthopedic training, and had qualified the specialty examination of the Royal College of Surgeons at Edinburgh, the oldest such college in the West, but the local hospitals would not give me full surgical privileges[1] because the Royal College of Surgeons in Canada had not granted me eligibility[2] to appear at their specialty examination. I was British trained but my basic medical degree was from Pakistan and the Royal College of Surgeons in Canada granted eligibility to British but not to medical graduates from the sub-continent, though the two had identical training, and qualifications. Canadians, unlike their American counterparts did discriminate[3] on grounds of race.

---

1 American courts routinely decided against hospitals and universities if there was a hint of discrimi-nation on racial grounds. Canadian courts held that privileges and eligibility were entirely the prerogative of the institutions in question.

2 The Royal College of Surgeons in Canada and American specialty Boards scrutinize qualification before granting permission to appear at the respective examinations.

3 In North America a doctor applies to hospitals for permission to admit patients and treat them. The hospital grants the privilege based on the qualifications and training of the doctor.

Abe Guam, who occupied the largest number of beds in the hospital, insisted that I be allowed to perform surgery. They reluctantly permitted me to perform surgical procedures under supervision of his brother, Dave Guam, who was not a qualified surgeon but had full privileges. He had had little exposure in orthopedic surgery and was in no position to advise me, much less supervise me.

One evening I had gone to the x-ray department of the General hospital. The sight of a patient lying on a stretcher struck me. He had his head bent at an ab-normal angle. The x-ray technician saw the look on my face and asked me to look at his x-rays. To my acute horror, it showed a high fracture dislocation of the cervical spine which if moved improperly could result in paralysis from neck down. I immediately called his general practice doctor (GP). He initially objected to my looking at x-rays of his patient, even upon his request, but when I told him of the possible dire consequences it properly put the fear of the Father, the Son and the Holy Spirit in him (he was a devout Catholic). He begged me to wait for him in the hospital.

He practically ran to the hospital. He was properly flustered and asked me if I could fix it. I told him I could if I had a neurosurgeon to advise me. We called the surgeon in Halifax. He advised that the patient be put on a plane with me by his side. But the only flight for the day had left. An ambulance journey over the hills and vales in the middle of the night over a route under several feet of snow was not a practical proposition. The neurosurgeon asked me if I would be able to insert calipers[1] on the man's skull and reduce the dislocation while he gave me instructions on phone. I agreed to the highly unorthodox procedure as long as the patient understood and took the responsibility of consequences in writing. The GP thought I was being overly fussy.

Even after passage of over three decades, the following two hours are still vivid in my mind. A crowd had gathered around the patient's bed. I was liter-ally sweating. Any maneuver I performed could have damaged the spinal cord irreparably. After a while the dislocation reduced with an audible click. My heart started beating again and I resumed breathing too. There was a round of applause from my now quite impressed and admiring audience. The patient stayed in the hospital for eight weeks. Finally it was time to remove the calipers and put him in a body cast. I still have his photo in the cast.

It was in Halifax that I first heard of Halal bread. I was intrigued. How do you slaughter bread, in a halal or, for that matter, a haram way, I asked a friend.[2] He laughed; they look at the list of ingredients and make sure no lard was used. In England alcoholic drinks were freely served in all Muslim "Desi" parties. Not so in Halifax.

---

1 This is an instrument that is fixed to two sides of the skull and attached to a pulley system to hang weights on to keep the neck and head in the desired position.
2 Roughly Kosher. Jewish rabbis charge considerable fees to certify wine and bread as kosher.

I found a jewel of a man in a British-trained Indian surgeon, Dr. Chaturvedi.[1] He was secular in the Nehru mold, religious in the Gandhi style, national-linguistic chauvinist like a good Indian, a traditionalist like a good Brahmin and liberal in his overall outlook. Chat Ji, as he was affectionately called, used to arrange a flag raising ceremony on India's Independence Day, August 14. He invited me to give a short talk on the occasion. Some Indians from Gujerat and Indian Punjab objected. I was a Pakistani. Chat Ji reassured them that it was simply a gesture of good will.

In mid 1973 I appeared for the US licensing examination. I was lucky enough to pass the test and in due course got a license to practice medicine in New York State and started applying for jobs and private practices. After several interviews I accepted a job in Kingsbrook Medical Center, Brooklyn, New York.

## BROOKLYN 1974–1980

I flew to New York on a sunny afternoon in mid-March 1974. The cab driver who drove me from JFK to the hospital wanted to know what I did for a living. On being told that I was a doctor, he asked me with a mix of envy, wonder and admiration, "How come all the Indians are doctors"?

Life in American hospitals was very different from that in the UK.[2] The hospital, on my specific request, had given me a room in a building attached to the main building. On a Saturday evening I went to the hospital reception and asked in an exaggerated British accent where the doctor's mess was. Americans have a sense of humor. The man said that he knew that their doctors were a mess, but had not realized that the news had spread to Europe. I had to explain; there must be a place where doctors on duty stayed. Oh yes, and they pointed me to a building. It had a decayed look.

The common room was on the second floor and was small, rather shabby and had a desolate look. No wine or women in sight. I waited impatiently. After about half an hour a resident arrived. I asked him where the others were? "What others?" was his response. Very few residents ever visited the room; they didn't have time. Most residents were married and lived in nearby apartments

During my wanderings in the area I came across a "To Let" sign and went in to the rental office. A scruffy looking man showed me an apartment. I was to learn soon afterwards that the building was located in a high crime area, but rent was low. I signed a lease. My colleagues were aghast. I lived in the apartment for a year and often came back late at night. Nobody ever bothered me. They perhaps

---

1 He was born in Banaras and brought up in Ajmer. Ajmer is known for the shrine of the most revered Sufi-Saint of India, Khawaja Moinuddin Chisti. During the Saint's annual celebration, my new friend's father hosted both Hindus and Muslims at his home.

2 In the UK doctors in training live in quarters attached to the hospital compound. Nearly all bachelors, we had a party in the residence common room almost every Saturday. Hospital kitchen would provide the food and we had beer at a subsidized rate. Nurses would be invited and were eager to participate.

thought that a person daring to enter the area after dark must have at least a ma-chete up his sleeve. Or I was just lucky.

My colleagues advised me not to buy a foreign car. American mechanics did not know much about them. About the only foreign car one came across was Volkswagen. I asked questions about engine size, gas consumption, time taken for 0–60 miles, etc.[1] The salespersons were blissfully unaware of all these crite-ria. One finally blurted out, "in what other country can you buy this much of a car for this much money?" Americans, always partial to size, were used to mam-moth gas-guzzlers. Gas was plentiful and cheap. I bought a huge 6.0-liter Cutlass which could not outrun a 1.0-liter Japanese car.

I had arrived in the US after the 1973 Yom Kippur war. In Canada the im-pact of the war was minimal. Whatever the Jewish people there may have felt, they did not express it openly. The situation was entirely different in the United States. Media coverage was intense and the oil embargo in 1974 after the ces-sation of hostilities changed the perception abruptly. People suffered, gas lines were literally miles long. Fistfights broke out frequently, and some serious in-juries were reported (I think one death too) for cutting in the line. The country briefly started making and importing smaller and more gas efficient vehicles, and the first stirrings of sympathy with the Palestinians appeared.

Simultaneous with the war and oil embargo, the Watergate crisis was brew-ing. Nixon had been caught with his pants down-metaphorically. His attempts at evasion, excuses and diversion, did not help much. He went to China and ordered Kissinger to get a face-saving deal with Vietnam, to no avail. It was rumored in interested circles that he had procrastinated in sending emergency military sup-plies to Israel. The radical left put out that conservatives wanted to punish him for opening up to China. But his successor gave him an unconditional pardon, and he did not have to spend jail time as his co-conspirators had to do.

Situated in the middle of a residential area, the hospital medical staff was as-sociated with several nursing homes and largely catered to diseases of the older people. It was my first experience of security guards at every entrance of the parking lot. Armed officers in police cars made regular rounds around the hos-pital. We had close working relationship with Brooklyn Jewish Medical Center a few miles away. Einstein had been a patient there. Foreigners dominated the junior staff and resident ranks. American graduates tended to gravitate to the suburbs. Half a mile away was Down State Medical School and Hospital, which catered to more affluent patients. King's County Hospital, second largest in the country, after Cook County Hospital in Chicago, was next door to it.

Because of our proximity to King's County hospital we received only a few emergency cases. But I recall one patient and her husband vividly. She had been in a car accident and had sustained a lot of wounds. Though born and brought

---

1 Salespersons in the UK were well informed on performance of the cars.

up in New York, she spoke only Italian.[1] She picked up a little English during her long stay in the hospital. After discharge she came to my office and started crying. I and asked her why? She blushed and said that I didn't know what she used to call me while I changed her dressings. She was sorry and wanted to be forgiven, and insisted that I loudly say, "I forgive you." I did as I was told. After escorting her to the waiting room, her husband came back and asked me confidentially if I would like him to take care of anyone. I did not quite understand. He volunteered that he could have the legs of anyone I did not like broken. I politely declined the offer.

I had had little exposure to pediatric orthopedics before, so the adult side was assigned to me. I was, however, more skilled than my colleagues in joint replacements. They were initially developed in the UK and till shortly before 1974 the FDA[2] had allowed the procedure only in select medical centers.

Because of the high premium of mal-practice insurance I was very apprehensive of launching into private practice. I remember the premium for orthopedic surgery was $8,000 per year,[3] but the director of my department persuaded me that it would not be a problem. With a great deal of reservations I started private practice.

I had treated a patient injured in a car accident. Some two weeks later, an attorney called on her behalf and asked me to send him a bill for her treatment. I sent him a bill for $135. He called me a few days later to say that the bill was too low and if the case went to a court, he would be laughed out of the room.

Free enterprise in medicine has certain grave deficiencies. In my thirty years as a doctor in the US, I have come across hundreds of patients who had to go without essential medicines and treatment because they did not qualify for welfare and could not afford private care. Government statistics tell us that 46 million Americans out of a total of three hundred million do not have health insurance. Another ninety million are inadequately insured, so that hospital bills are the largest cause of personal bankruptcy.

A colleague referred me to St. John's Episcopal Hospital in Bedford–Stuyvesant area in Brooklyn. That was really a rough and tough neighborhood. It had seen the worst riots in the aftermath of Martin Luther King's assassination. On payday, nurses used to go to the bank with an armed escort. It was a terribly disorganized place. In outpatients, case notes and x-ray films would be missing. On paper they followed an appointment system, but that was honored more in breach than in compliance. The operating room was decrepit.

---

1 In the UK, many persons from the sub-continent could not intelligibly communicate in English. Their English does not improve because they live in racial ghettoes.

2 The Federal Drug Agency regulates many aspects of medical practice in the US. It conducts lengthy tests, though it drags its feet and does not withdraw drugs from the market expeditiously, even after credible adverse reports on harmful side effects have been published in respected medical journals.

3 I had paid $ 300.00 the year before in Canada.

---

I had my first malpractice suit there. A butcher had been in the habit of curs-
ing his assistant. One day the lad could take it no more and beat him up with a
baseball bat. The man had sustained a very bad elbow fracture. I operated on him
and to keep bone fragments together inserted a metal plate and several screws. On
discharge from the hospital, I had given him strict advice not to lift anything with
the arm. With nobody to help him, he had lifted heavy carcasses. The hardware
broke. I admonished him. He blamed me and went to an attorney. For uncannily
similar reasons, I had several other malpractice suits while at the hospital.

Manhattan has more attorneys than the whole country of Japan.[1] The system
promotes malpractice litigation. Attorneys are allowed to accept part of the settlement as their fee and expenses. It is called a contingency fee arrangement. In
Canada and Europe this would be called fee splitting, and would be grounds for
disciplinary action. Mal-practice insurance companies usually settle out of court,
as it costs less to pay up than fight an expensive court battle.

It is not only the cupidity of lawyers and patients that causes a deluge of
such cases, though they are far more numerous in high lawyer concentration and
more socially disrupted regions like New York city, the counties around it, and
in parts of California, Florida and in Washington DC. In a system in which the
income of a doctor is related to the amount and kind of work they do and being
subjects to vagaries of human nature like others of the species, they would make
every effort to enhance their income. This statement is borne out by the fact that
legal suits are filed much less often against doctors who work on fixed salary for
health maintenance organizations (HMOs) and have no incentive to perform unnecessary procedures.

On my second or third day in the hospital I came across a young lady wearing
a Muslim *hejab*.[2] She asked me my name. I told her. She inquired if I was a Muslim.
I nodded in affirmative. Her next question floored me. Had I prayed in the morning? I stared at her in disbelief. She was very annoyed. And told me, "Don't try to
browbeat me with haughty looks. I am your sister and have every right to ask
you such questions." I am glad I conceded the rights to her. She protected me and
stood by me in many awkward and potentially hazardous situations.

The year 1979 was remarkable for the takeover of Iran by Khomeini. It is difficult to understand how the US policymakers kept themselves from learning the
situation on the ground. The CIA was believed to have more agents in Teheran
than in Langley, VA and monitored all of Asia from Iran. Jimmy Carter had called
it an island of stability in the region shortly before the Shah was overthrown, and
a US general tried to persuade Iranian generals to take over. The idea of making
Khomeini the regent with the Shah's son as King in waiting was floated, but it

---

1 In New York after a car accident, unless you could not move at all, you went to your attorney first.
2 A head covering that conformist Muslim women wear in public.

was too late. All they could assure was the safe flight of the Shah with his family. His loot was already out of the country.

Iranians kept on finding evidence of listening posts and saboteur activities in the country, directed by the US embassy. They finally took things into their own hands; took over the embassy and took the personnel hostage. They painstakingly put together the shredded documents, which gave them details of all the plans for undermining the country. The hostage crisis lasted a long time and the period included a botched attempt at a rescue, which must go down in history as one of most poorly planned and worse executed endeavors. Coming on the heels of the fiasco in Vietnam, it was a body blow to the American psyche and cost Carter the presidency.

My mother had been insisting that I get married again. I was lonely too, but was not inclined to develop permanent relationship, once burnt, twice shy. I left the choice to her and she married me off on January 14, 1979 to Rafat.[1]

Rafat arrived in New York a few months later — on the same flight my summer vacationing daughter had taken. They had never met before. During the flight Eram, an extrovert, had invited her to visit our home! My new wife was very kind and affectionate to Eram. I will remain eternally grateful to her for that. If she had acted like the proverbial stepmother, she could have made my life miserable. I was strongly attached to my daughter and would not have known what to do.

We had our first baby in Brooklyn and named her Sarah.

I had for quite some time wanted to move back to Pakistan as my mother and sister were finding it difficult to live on their own, but I couldn't sell the house I had bought in Brooklyn. The housing market was in a slump. I decided that instead of waiting for the sale of the house I should find a practice in a small town and work for another 3–4 years. A colleague referred me to a hospital in Bath, New York. It was three hundred miles from Brooklyn. The hospital offered me a package deal guaranteed income, mal-practice insurance and rent-free office for a year plus moving expenses. Everyone I met assured me that the people of Bath would welcome me with open arms.

I resigned from hospitals in Brooklyn and notified my patients that I would be leaving shortly. A lot of my patients visited the office to say good-bye.

## BATH, NEW YORK 1980–83

One fine day at the end of August 1980 we packed our car, tied a camp bed on the roof and drove to Bath via Interstate Route 17. It was highly scenic but very circuitous and very slow; at the time it was a two-lane highway along most of the route. We arrived in Bath, tense and tired, at about 11:00 p.m. Compared to Brooklyn, it was chilly.

---

1 She was from a conformist family, a distant connection and a college graduate. It would appear strange to Western people, but as per custom she agreed to marry me sight unseen. I gave her a pet name Paro — roughly, lovely.

The radio alarm woke me up the next morning. I burst into uncontrollable laughter. Paro was alarmed. The news broadcast had announced that there was no traffic congestion! Bath,[1] at the time, had two regular and one blinking traffic light. For one recently arrived from Brooklyn, the roads had a deserted look. But everything is relative. For the people of Bath, four cars at a traffic light were akin to the Times Square during rush hours.

I called the hospital to inform them that I had arrived. They had a bad compound fracture case and asked me to go there right away. The surgeon on call had advised amputation. The fracture was bad, but I thought the leg could be saved. The surgeon left abruptly, muttering, in all likelihood, curses. It did not let up. The three years I spent in Bath were an uninterrupted continuum of work.

The office was soon set up. I was lucky to find an efficient secretary who was actually a college graduate.[2] She even badgered the local congressman's office to put pressure on insurance companies that had not paid bills from my Brooklyn office. The US consulate in Karachi had declined a visa to my mother-in-law. She sent them a telegram with a copy to the state department in DC, that the patients in Bath were suffering as the doctor had to spend time looking after his wife and a tiny baby. My mother-in-law got the visa.

Bath was an interregnum for me. We did not make any long-term plans, as I wanted to go back to Pakistan. We had two more additions to the family, Umar born on March 6, 1981 and Laila-Sana on February 12, 1983. I had been in touch with a lot of fellow physicians from Pakistan and had found a surprising degree of resonance. They shared the same passionate desire to return home. We formed a partnership to build a hospital in Karachi.

## BACK TO BATH 1991–2001

I had done well in Pakistan, but the near civil war situation and several incidents of abduction of children and physicians for ransom had unnerved me. During a visit to Bath my old hospital offered me my old practice. I was glad to accept. I flew back home and told my partners that it was all theirs.[3]

It was a wrench. I was making enough money for my needs, had developed a circle of friends, most from my old days in the town. The hospital was doing well;

---

1 I do not mean to denigrate Bath, but it is tiny. It has a winter population of six thousand, which with tourists in the summer swells to nearly ten thousand. But our wine has the highest concentration of the chemical, which prevents heart attacks.

Twenty miles down the road is Corning whose claim to fame is Corning Inc. It has diversified into fiber optics, but still maintains a glass museum with specimens of glass many thousands of years old, and makes the very expensive Steuben glass. President Carter gave Secretary General Brezhnev two peace doves worth $30,000 in late the 1970s.

2 It is a paradox. Countries in the West have high literacy, nearly every one finishes high school, but the percentage of high school graduates who go on to college is actually higher in the subcontinent. College graduates are therefore more highly valued in the West.

3 I had built a hospital in Karachi described more fully in the chapter Pakistan 1983-91

I was fast developing a reputation as a highly accomplished orthopedic surgeon. My mother and sister would be left alone again.

Physician colleagues told me that there was far more State and Federal regulation; health insurance companies had become emboldened and very intrusive.[1] Tiresome paperwork had become obligatory; reimbursement had been reduced uniformly, though cost of living and practice had gone up. I better buy a computer and get my staff trained to use it. I could not believe them. But they were right. Insurances paid less for the same procedure in 1992 than they did in 1983, never mind the inflation. More forms with all kinds of codes had to be filled out; insurance companies made more objections. It was an uphill struggle, with tons of paper work.

To make matters worse the hospital was passing through a bad period; it was actually in an acute financial crisis.[2] Many businesses and industries had left the region or gone bankrupt. Winemaking and farming, the two main props of local economy, were on a downward slide. Manufacturing sector had moved overseas and cheaper foreign produce was flooding the country.[3] They had to close one of the two-inpatient floors in the hospital.

During my 1974-1983 stay I had been only biding time so I could save enough to live on in Pakistan till I had developed adequate private practice to meet our needs. Now we were here to stay. I started looking for a house to buy and finally settled on a large five-bed room house on nearly three acres of land. It sat beneath a hill with a lot of trees. Paro and the children arrived in June 1992. We contacted our local school. Children were promised admission in appropriate grades. Sarah, Umar and Laila-Sana did not take too long in adjusting, but Hasan born during our stay in Pakistan had a bit of a problem and we solved it by getting him into a private school for a year. But they were all much happier and thrived on the fresh and clean air, pastoral life and security.

We tried to live as normal a life as we could. Bath and the area surrounding it are very picturesque. We have parks, lakes, farms, amusement parks, zoos and a notable glass museum. The famous Keuka[4] Lake is eight miles from Bath. Our neighboring village Hammondsport sits on one end of the lake and the town of Penn Yan at the other. The lake is circumscribed by homes some of which are quite luxurious. The actor Paul Newman has a mansion there. Boating, fishing and cruises are quite delightful and popular. We went on day trips, picnics and

---

1 They objected to the treatment physicians offered, delayed payment inordinately and paid the CEOs millions as salary and year-end bonus. Their overhead is about 35 to 40 %. Contrast that with about 8% in Veterans in Health Administration (VA System). Drug companies sell medicines to the VA at a fraction of the cost that they charge HMOs and hospitals and charge ordinary patients, who do not have insurance, an even higher rate.

2 There was spate of hospital bankruptcies in the seventies. Health Maintenance Organizations bought hospitals and made money by ordering doctors to offer low cost treatment. Please see the Michael Moore movie "Sicko"

3 I have discussed the issue in the chapter on Globalization

4 Keuka is an American-Indian name and means crooked.

traveled to Toronto, Canada and made several visits to Cape Cod. The children thoroughly enjoyed the museums and amusement parks in Toronto and Cape cod. The latter had additional attractions of whale cruises and boat trips. A month long Christmas time visit to Pakistan remained a routine till my mother passed away in 1995.

A new field of business, Independent Medical Examinations (IME), had developed in orthopedic practice. If a worker who got hurt at work and did not return soon enough to suit the employer, the latter asked for an independent medical examiner to assess the disability. The employer's Insurance carrier would engage an IME company to send the worker to a Doctor of their choice to perform an examination.

IME companies could not find enough Orthopedic Surgeons to do this kind of work.[1] In 1994 one IME company owner had approached me. I had initially disdained the offer. But my practice did not pick up to my satisfaction and in 1995, I reluctantly made a deal with several IME companies

In a clinical setting there is a lot of goodwill between the physician and the patient. During an IME encounter, apprehensive that their benefits might be adversely affected, most of the examinees would be in a defensive mode of behavior. Sometimes their attorneys would accompany them. Further, one had to go to courts to defend the findings in IME reports. Many of the IME companies were of the fly by night nature. You were never certain when one would fold up and abscond with your money. Even the large ones would sometimes go belly up. I traveled over a wide area driving several hours each way and had to stay overnight in motels twice a month to enable me to work the next morning. It was good money, but it was a hassle and driving was a great hazard in the winter. Finally I decided to give up clinical work. It would drastically reduce my mal-practice insurance premium.[2]

I did fulltime IME work between 1997 and 2001. The only part of the work I enjoyed was matching my wits with attorneys in court. Not all of them had dialectical skills needed for the profession. As one would expect, the ones practicing in the higher courts were better debaters. IME work gave me free weekends. But the extensive driving became too much and I decided to stop working.

I had the good fortune of coming across an academic from Cornell University. Dr. S. Naqi, who was a high minded, liberal, very well read and widely informed gentleman. He called a meeting of like-minded persons. After a lively discussion we decided to launch an organization. Naqi was elected the President and I accepted my favorite position of General Secretary. Our meetings were well attended and the input of participants was serious and productive. After several sessions, some heated, we decided to adopt strictly secular byelaws and settled

---

1 I have made a special mention of Orthopedics, because about 90% of IME's were in the specialty.
2 For IME work one could get by the much lower Rehabilitation medicine insurance rate.

on Concerned Citizens for Peace and Understanding (CCPU) as the name of the group.

We launched a membership drive, which evoked generous response from local expatriates academics, scientists, physicians and other peace groups. We decided to broaden our quest, and practically every weekend drove to towns as far away as Rochester, Syracuse, Binghamton and Buffalo. I addressed a large gathering at the Rochester, NY, Islamic center. The local congresswoman MS Slaughter was among those present. She was very receptive and offered help. I was surprised to learn that expatriates in larger towns did not approve of our secular stance.

Our first public meeting was a full day session held in a hall in Cornell University. People of all creeds, Muslim, Christian, Hindu, Jewish and others were in attendance. Among others, Shibli Telhami,[1] then a professor at Cornell, addressed the group. Delegates from as far away as Boston and Long Island attended. The American Muslim Alliance (AMA), a liberal Muslim organization, sent its national vice-president who pledged cooperation and asked us to form an AMA chapter as well.

I did end up founding an AMA chapter in the fond hope that Muslims in the area would participate in and be politically energized by the name. We again visited all the major cities in upstate NY — Rochester, Buffalo, Syracuse and Binghamton. The response was tepid and the reaction equivocal. Our (subcontinental) culture is not conducive to working together. I attribute it to long years of colonial rule, which stifles initiative and dampens self-confidence. Naqi retired and went to Texas. I was getting bored and went to the UK. Our organizations are person- and event-centric. Both the CCPU and AMA chapter gracefully subsided.

I worked in the UK off and on for two years and came across startling changes in the heath service and social conditions which I have described in a later chapter.

## BACK TO BATH, 2003

Fed up with living alone in the UK, I decided to return home to Bath in January 2003. Now I had time to indulge in my favorite pursuits, reading, writing and political activism, full time. Together with local expatriates I organized a community group and we invited an attractive and young Democratic hopeful for the US congress to one of the meetings. She did give a creditable performance but was pitted against an entrenched republican candidate, a politician with 25 years in the state senate and lost by a small margin. Our area is republican anyway.

A young colleague introduced me to Asian American Network against Abuse (AANA), a secular democratic advocacy group. Initially it was an offshoot of the

---

1 He has since moved on to the Sadaat Chair of Public Affairs at Johns Hopkins University.

Association of Pakistani Physicians of America (APPNA). For lack of resources, it focuses only on the social evils in Pakistan. The group sponsored a seminar on future of democracy in Pakistan, simultaneous with an APPNA annual session.

In January 2005 we heard that a lady Physician, Shazia Khalid was gang raped in her quarters in Sui, Baluchistan, allegedly by army officers on active duty. The grandfather of the husband was to convene a Jirga (tribal council) soon after, and have the lady declared "kari."[1] I was on my way to Pakistan and during a tele-conference called by APPNA offered to visit the lady in Karachi. I found her in virtual house arrest in an apartment in Baluchistan House, a hostel for the province's officials.

An earlier gang rape victim, Mukhtaran Mai had become a *cause célèbre*. What was more poignant about the case was that the village council had ordained the heinous act at the behest of the local feudal lord. The charge against her was that her brother, ten or eleven years of age, had brought dishonor to the feudal family by having illicit relations with a sister of the chief of the village. In actual fact the village chief wanted to have homosexual relations with the boy. He had declined the "honor" and Mukhtaran had had the temerity to speak up for her brother.

To give the devil his due, Musharraf, who was in his liberal phase at the time, intervened and ordered the police to take proper action. Nicolas Kristoff of the *New York Times* got into the act and wrote a column in his paper asking for funds to support the victim. The case went to the courts. The Punjab High Court, citing lack of credible evidence, dismissed the case. Potential witnesses had been scared away by the perpetrators of the crime and their patrons. The Supreme Court, however, heard the appeal and ordered the re-arrest of the perpetrators.

AANA picked up her cause and invited her to a meeting in the United States. Government of Pakistan functionaries decided that her trip would bring bad name to the country. In their usual ham handed fashion, they stopped her from leaving the country. On the point of leaving for Islamabad to get her visa to visit the US, she was abducted by the security agencies and kept incommunicado. After an interval of several days she was presented to a news conference in the capital, Islamabad, and made to read a statement that she agreed that her visit would tarnish the shining face of her country, and she had decided to withdraw her application from the US consulate of her own free will. Musharraf, during an overseas visit, declared that he would not permit anyone to wash the country's dirty linen abroad. He added fuel to fire by parroting a statement by a woman member of Benazir's party, Fauzia Taufeeq, who had opined that these women had staged a rape for publicity. In any case pressure built up on the GOP to let Mukhtaran go.

---

1 A tribal term for a woman who has brought shame on the tribe, she is liable to a death sentence regardless of whether she was guilty or not.

To highlight the issue during Musharraf's annual pilgrimage to the UN general assembly, AANA had in the meanwhile, decided to hold rallies in New York at the Pakistan consulate and near the country's embassy in Washington DC. The rallies were moderately successful. The Pakistani government had to give in. Mukhtaran duly arrived and was feted at a public reception and award ceremony funded by *Glamour* magazine.

In this phase of my life I came across the problems and expenses of sending children to undergraduate schools in the United States. Good schools are highly competitive and very expensive. Expatriate parents are very ambitious and push their children to set high goals and pursue them relentlessly. We were no exception and achieved higher than average success. Umar went to the University of Rochester and is pursuing a career in finance. Laila-Sana chose Duke University in Durham North Carolina and is trying her hand in a publishing firm in New York City. Hasan is following in the footsteps of Eram and Umar at Stony Brook University in New York.

Higher incomes (and lower taxes) of professionals and others in the US are spent in private education and health care. Given free health care and education, my colleagues in the UK and Canada did as well as I did in the US, sent their children to prestigious universities, built houses, visited Pakistan-India as frequently and had more time for relaxation as their working hours were much shorter.

CHAPTER 11. THE RISE OF FUNDAMENTALISM


IN PAKISTAN

Bhutto fell victim to a delusion, common to all tin pot dictators; he started taking his own bombast seriously and made a critical mistake. He called a conference of all the nuclear physicists of the country and demanded that they produce a workable nuclear device in the next four to five years. The nuclear scientists in Pakistan were, one and all, jaded bureaucrats living a comfortable life in cushy sinecures. Professor Salaam was among a few exceptions.[1]

The group of scientists humbly expressed their inability to deliver the goods, proffering the valid excuse of lack of equipment, infrastructure, technical staff, laboratories and supplies. Bhutto offered to get all the equipment they would need. They still demurred. He heaped obscene abuses on them and literally shouted them out of the hall. Tail between their legs, they slinked out.

A Pakistani metallurgist, A. Qadeer Khan, married to a Dutch lady, was employed as a translator in a nuclear reprocessing plant in Holland. He was trusted by his employers, and given the freedom of the plant. His work gave him unlimited access to all the records. He wrote to Bhutto that if he was given a personal audience, he could suggest a method of achieving the goal dearest to all their hearts. Bhutto was shown the letter and sent word to the man to present himself forthwith.

---

1 From a family of modest means, he was a scholarship student and obtained a master's degree in physics from Punjab University in Lahore. He had won a scholarship for a PhD program at the Imperial college of Sciences in London and obtained a PhD in physics in a remarkably short period of time. The college offered him a job on its faculty, but he told his professor that he owed it to his country and himself to return and teach there. He was treated shabbily in the country and returned to England.

Qadeer[1] brought photocopies of relevant documents and a complete list of supplies, equipment, and materiel. Bhutto ensconced him in a secure location, ordered that phony companies be set up to smuggle supplies in, and the man be given the highest priority in all he needed. He was given extraordinary protection.[2] Khan turned out to be true to his word. He produced the bomb in about five years, though due to the fear of international opprobrium the device could not be tested.

Kissinger saw red in Bhutto's plans to develop an atomic bomb and flew to Pakistan to upbraid him. Bhutto blandly denied the whole affair. Kissinger, as arrogant as they come, was incensed. He told Bhutto that the latter was insulting his intelligence and that unless he ceased and desisted, "we would make a horrible example of you".[3] Bhutto, a megalomaniac of equal caliber, handicapped though he was as the leader of an underdeveloped country, did manage to stand on his dignity. But the confrontation with Kissinger sealed his fate.

An opportunity to exact revenge, and make a horrible example of him, came soon enough. Elections were due in Pakistan. It was widely perceived that Bhutto and his PPP would win the elections hands down. There was no credible alternative to him. He announced the date of election with his usual theatrics. They thought that, bar the shouting, all was over. But he had reckoned without the good old Almighty Dollar. The opposition, hitherto rather laid back, was suddenly energized and flush with spare cash. People in urban areas were particularly disaffected. In Karachi, the opposition candidate, a politically inept and colorless former chief of the country's air force, Air Marshal Asghar Khan, drew huge crowds. The fates were finally looking kindly on Bhutto's detractors.

Elections were held in due course. As polling results started trickling in, people looked at each other in dismay and disbelief. The final straw was the defeat of the air marshal in Karachi. Bhutto's Pakistan People's Party "won" the requisite two-thirds majority which would enable it to amend the constitution or override a presidential veto. There were howls of outrage. People would have accepted a simple majority for the party. But this was beyond the norm even of "Banana Republics." The PPP had "won" even in the urban centers of Sindh dominated by Urdu-speaking immigrants, whom Bhutto had managed to alienate during his five-year rule.

The opposition took out mammoth processions in all the major cities of the country. The army, called in to assist the police, was only too willing to use force in Sindh and Baluchistan. But they hesitated in suppressing the uprising when

---

1 This was widely reported after his ring of export of nuclear technology was discovered.
2 Once, two Frenchmen were found loitering near his house. They were unceremoniously manhandled by the guards, their white skin notwithstanding.
He "saved" Pakistan on another occasion. When India massed troops on Pakistan's border in the mid-1980s, he said during an interview with Indian journalist Kuldeep Nayyar that he could assemble an atomic bomb in a matter of hours. India withdrew from the border.
3 This was widely reported in the newspapers.

it came to the Punjab, and to a lesser extent in NWFP, the heartlands of the harvesting fields of the armed forces.

The Air Marshal gave a public call to the armed forces not to obey Government orders. This was seditious. But the Government was in no position to try him on the charges. The Government and the opposition held off and on negotiations. Bhutto offered to have polling held again in the disputed seats. The opposition wanted new elections held under the auspices of an all parties Government. The agitation continued. From fawning sycophants, army officers and bureaucrats turned into neutral observers. Newspaper editors, trade union leaders, professional bodies, till lately perfect toadies, passed resolutions against the Government. Students were indifferent. Bhutto resorted to strident, shrill and undignified speeches. Gone was the statesman-like posturing.

Bhutto was reported to have finally agreed to cancel the results of the elections, and hold new ones under the auspices of an independent election commission, which would have opposition nominees too. The agreement was to be signed the following morning. Ghulam Ishaq Khan,[1] a grizzled bureaucrat in cahoots with the army was privy to all the negotiations, and had kept Zia well informed. The Army struck the same night. They took Bhutto and all the ministers in "protective custody." Zia declared martial law, suspended the constitution, dissolved the National assembly and promised new elections in ninety days.

People took a sigh of relief. The nation had stepped back from the edge of another precipice. The opposition was satisfied at the turn of events. Their demand for a whole new election had been accepted. No one was prepared to lead and organize another insurgency. But the public had not forgotten the humiliation of 1971 civil war in East Pakistan. They wanted the men in uniform back in the barracks expeditiously. The army went on a propaganda offensive. Pictures and statements of concentration camp detainees were given wide coverage in government-controlled media — radio, TV and newspapers. Other scandals were publicized. White papers were issued.

Zia, as yet unsure of his ground, called on Bhutto in his jail cell. Standing at attention before the prisoner, maintaining the façade of a humble man, he plaintively asked, "Sir, why did you have to do it?"[2] He was perhaps giving Bhutto a false sense of security. To test the waters and to see how much popularity the man retained, he released Bhutto soon afterwards.

Prisons in South Asia are wonderful places for political rejuvenation. People started recalling Bhutto's "good" deeds again. He had managed to get 90,000 prisoners of war released from India. He had given a measure of self-respect to the poor, the workers, the dispossessed, and the wretched. He had convened a grand

---

1 That he went on to serve as the Chairman of the senate and succeeded Zia as President would lend credibility to the conjectures.
2 That is rigged elections-Newsweek published a photo with Bhutto sitting in a chair and Zia standing at attention in front of him.

conference of all Islamic heads of state. He was making atomic bombs. What if he drank a little alcohol and womanized a bit?[1] In any event he was given a wild, ecstatic, tumultuous and overwhelming reception in Lahore.

Mass adulation went to his head. He shouted defiance and vowed a colorful and sexually explicit vengeance. He denounced the political legitimacy, and cast doubt on birth antecedents, of Zia. He would try him for treason. He was the savior of Pakistan. People loved him. He would smash the capitalists, make senior bureaucrats (he called them the progeny of pharaohs) — sweep the streets, and set the generals to cleaning latrines. He would force the mullahs to make an honest living. Property of all the feudal landowners, who had aided and abetted the army, would be confiscated and distributed to their peasants/tenants. It was a rollicking show. People loved it.

Zia was not too put out by the insults. He was thick skinned. But the threat to try him on charges of high treason was a real risk. Bhutto was vindictive. He was arrested again. There was surprisingly little public outcry. His supporters expected that after further deals, he would be released soon.

Zia broke his pledge and brazenly declared that elections would be held only after a "positive" result could be assured. The opposition, spear headed by obscurantist groups and the retired Air Marshal, did not mind. They would rather deal with the military than with a resurgent Bhutto. Bhutto used to ridicule the Air Marshal that he had spent too much time in low oxygen high altitude areas and that had affected the latter's brain. The statement had received wide publicity. After several postponements, elections were put off indefinitely.

The military regime started churning out propaganda again. Several more voluminous "white papers" on Bhutto's "misdeeds" were published. Courts were moved that the publicity would prejudice Bhutto's case. They agreed.

Zia piously proclaimed his intention to introduce laws according to Islamic Shariah-jurisprudence.[2] He co-opted religious and other disaffected and disenchanted anti Bhutto groups into the government. There was no shortage of turncoats from PPP either. He issued ordinances legitimizing his deeds, past, present and future through the legal framework order (LFO). The LFO was drafted by the presiding genius of such affairs, a prominent attorney, Sharifuddin Pirzada.[3]

In the ensuing months and years Zia had political opponents publicly flogged, jailed and tortured — in the name of Islam. Under the Hudood ordinance raped

---

1 Alcohol is absolutely prohibited in Islam. He had once brandished a glass in a public meeting proclaiming that yes, he drank wine, not the blood of the poor. Womanizing is frowned upon, though it does not carry the stigma of alcohol. Islam has actually made extra-marital relations redundant. A man can have four wives simultaneously and keep on replacing them as long as he does not exceed the prescribed number. In July, 2008, a newspaper reported that a man had been arrested in Saudi Arabia for having six wives instead of the permissible four.

2 The so-called Hudood-restrictions-laws are supposed to be based on the Body of Islamic codes and jurisprudence.

3 He has advised all the dictators from Ayub down to Musharraf.

women were tried for adultery, unless they had four adult male practicing Muslims as witnesses to prove that the sexual act was not consensual. The rapist, for want of such evidence, would on most occasions go Scot-free. The victim, if she conceived, could not deny that she had had a sexual act. By implication, Zia legitimized honor killing, which is a tribal custom in which an aggrieved party whose honor was besmirched can kill the offending male or female or both and pay blood money with the agreement of the victims heirs. Hudood law made honor killing an offence against the family who could forgive the killer.[1] In practice, the cover of honor killing is used to keep the girl's share of land and property from going with the girl to her husband's family. Another subterfuge is to marry women to the Koran. There is no provision for such an act in Islam, but the Koran does not ask for the girl's share.

Bhutto had threatened to try Zia for treason. He would pose an unacceptable risk in exile. He could come back. A murder case was the only recourse. Some judges had to be replaced before Bhutto was put on trial. The presiding judge was the same person whom Bhutto had threatened with abduction of his daughter.[2] The death sentence, for allegedly ordering the execution of an opposition politician, was duly handed down by the Punjab High Court. A while later the Supreme Court confirmed the sentence. Foreign observers, including a former highly regarded U.S. Attorney General Ramsey Clark, stated categorically that proper procedures of Pakistan penal code had not been followed. Judges had acted with impropriety, openly favored the prosecution, and accepted dubious evidence.

I was on a visit to Pakistan when Bhutto was hanged. To keep people at home the government had closed all offices, schools and colleges and declared a public holiday. There were a few riots; one man torched himself publicly to death. The people had been thoroughly cowed. If Bhutto had not so callously betrayed the working class, they would have stood by him. In the end his support had dwindled to a narrow group of courtiers with no constituency of their own. His ambition and arrogance was overwhelming. He had no scruples either. All his political life he had let his mentors down. Once entrenched in power, he took on all the centers of power in the country and the US simultaneously. It was a tragic though perhaps a fitting end to a life of great promise.

After postponing elections several times, enacting discriminatory laws, and violating human rights, Zia became an international pariah. Bhutto's legally contrived assassination drove his personal standing even lower. Harsh economic sanctions were imposed on the country. Once again it was on the brink of eco-

---

1 The British government, unwilling to alienate powerful interests, accepted the custom. They had, nevertheless, imposed stringent conditions. The act had to be witnessed and witnesses willing to testify. The aggrieved party must be an actual relation of the girl by blood or marriage. The act was made a crime against the state, and not just against a person or a family

2 Justice Mushtaq Ahmad. Bhutto, a feudal lord, had the habit of threatening anyone who did not do his bidding with abduction of the female relatives.

nomic collapse. The whole rice crop had to be mortgaged to the Bank of Commerce and Credit International (BCCI).[1]

The fates came to his rescue. The Soviet government decided to install their
man in Kabul.[2] "Invited" by the Afghans, Soviet forces removed the double agent
masquerading as a communist loyalist, took over the capital and handed it over
to loyal cadres headed by Babrak Karmil, who had fled the country in the wake
of the massacre of the erstwhile Prime Minister and his faction. Karmil revoked
all anti-religious orders. Things seemed to settle down, but Afghans remained
suspicious

The Americans had not forgotten their humiliation in Vietnam. The image of
senior officers scrambling to get on fleeing helicopters, stamping on the hands of
women and children while trying to hold on to the boarding ramp of the planes,
was indelibly printed on their conscious mind and thought. They had blamed
the Soviet Union for the debacle. Now they had been given a chance for sweet
vengeance on an old adversary. Led by Brezhnev, a man in his dotage, the Soviet
Union answered its prayers.

As a by-product of the superpower tussle, Zia got a reprieve. From a pariah
he metamorphosed into a saintly defender of all Godly faiths. He was offered a
few hundred million dollars by President Carter, which he contemptuously rejected as peanuts. Zia offered Afghan rebels moral, political and material help.
They needed it and gratefully accepted it. By waging a "holy" war on the infidel
Soviets, he could also rehabilitate himself in the Muslim world and could get into
the good books of the West as well. Officers in the hundreds were sent to the
US for training in military academies. The British Commonwealth, a fossilized
elephant that had removed Pakistan[3] from its membership, invited Pakistan back
as a member. Zia was welcomed with open arms in the brotherhood of Muslim

---

1 The enterprise was the brainchild of a financial wizard Agha Hasan Abdi, who used Arab money
to launch a major house of finance. It grew phenomenally, and was emerging as a robust rival
to Western banking interests. It lured such luminaries as former Cabinet secretaries in the US
and Europe, Arab Princes and Amirs on its board of directors. Agha Abdi co-chaired a charity
with Jimmy Carter. He had a severe heart attack, and eventually had to have a heart transplant.
Without Abdi at the helm, the bank was accused of money laundering, financing arm and drug
deals, and giving billions in unsecured loans. Its advisors and employees were indicted. The number included several prominent corporate attorneys of the US, and Europe, and that *eminence gris*,
advisor to several US presidents, former cabinet secretary Clark Clifford. Pakistan refused to
extradite Abidi. Western countries did not twist Pakistan's arms to get him. The likes of Carter
would have to testify.

2 A few communists backed by some army officers had overthrown the government. They fell out
amongst themselves, the deputy Prime Minister killed the Prime Minister and started ordering
people not to pray or announce call to prayers, women to shed their veils and schoolteachers to
learn and then impart the knowledge of Marxist lore. Widespread riots broke out. Soviet government correctly surmised that man was a reactionary agent provocateur. They should, nevertheless, have known that no one had been able to control Afghans for long.

3 In the wake of the Bangladesh civil war, Bhutto had withdrawn from the club. The country's membership was suspended when Musharraf arrested the Chief Justice and imposed emergency rule
in 2007. After the March 2008 election, it was allowed back in.

heads of state and was able to extract arms and financial support.[1] Having established his Mujahid (holy warrior) status, he could also impose his vision of Islamic rule on Pakistan. With money and material to spare, he was successful in making the whole country one vast detention camp. Afghan rebels supported by elements of the Pakistani army, Al-Qaida and Taliban, had pinned down hundreds of thousands of Soviet soldiers, draining their resources and grinding the Soviet economy to a near halt. Pakistan's military arsenal was overflowing.

Zia was averse to the risk of holding an election. His patrons in the West and public opinion at home forced his hands. He resorted to a time worn subterfuge. Harking back to the Islamic traditions that the rightly guided Caliphs were chosen by consensus, that candidates did not present themselves for office and that there were no political groups-parties in Islam, he hit upon the idea of referendum to choose a President. His was the only name on the ballot and the question was something like, "If you believe in the rule of Islamic Shariah, Zia ul Haq is the President." No Muslim could deny Shariah, so there were hardly any negative votes.

I made a tour of polling stations in Karachi, the most politically savvy, aware and conscious city in the country. Few went to the polling booths. I found only the agents of the election commission lounging around in most of the polling stations. There were actually more armed policemen in the tents housing the ballot boxes than there were voters. Elsewhere in the country, police and other officials bussed and coerced people to vote. That could not be done in Karachi. Denizens of the city, veterans of numerous uprisings, are not easy to cow down. It has a concentration of foreign press too. According to neutral observers, less than 15% of the people voted. Zia got 99.9% of the votes cast. Included on the ballot papers were names of candidates for membership of a Majlis e Shoora (consultative assembly). Candidates were barred from declaration of affiliation to a political party, though the restriction was honored more in breach than in compliance. Only second-rate timeservers participated in the elections. The assembly was a motley crowd of rank outsiders and nobodies. After picking up a non-entity for the office of the Prime Minister, Zia even engineered deposition of the first speaker of his handpicked assembly, Fakhre Imam, head of a Pir house, who though an erstwhile disciple of Bhutto was a man of some integrity.

Zia also created a senate. The Shoora elected some members of the senate, others were chosen by the President from different professions. Professional bodies of journalists, doctors, lawyers were asked to offer their choice, with the

---

1 He was chosen to represent the Organization of Islamic States for an address to UN General Assembly but Yasir Arafat shunned the session as Zia, as commander of the Pakistan army contingent, had been instrumental in massacring thousands of Palestinians, when King Hussein had asked for Bhutto's help.

admonition that only compliant persons be designated. The first choice of the Pakistan Medical Association was rejected.[1]

The Afghan Jihad, in addition to corrupting Pakistan with easy money, was to have serious and far-reaching deleterious consequences. The Soviet Union had lavished an enormous number of Kalashnikov assault rifles on the Afghans who, though second to none in loving combat, do not enjoy fighting for others. They, in any case, prefer a buck to a bullet. With touching impartiality, they sold the arms, Russian and American, to any who could pay. The arms ended up in Iran, Pakistan and in some Arab countries. Drug dealers, warlords, racketeers and smugglers also bought the arms. They could now outgun the police and militia and outclass the Pakistani coast guard. International arms dealers made profits beyond the dreams of avarice. The Pakistani army, the handlers of the traffic, kept a large portion for themselves.

Afghanistan's main cash crop is poppy out of which opium is extracted. They had, hitherto, sold the low-tech product. Opium addiction, innocuous compared to that of its sophisticated end products morphine and worse still heroin, was fairly common in South Asia and China.[2] The Russians, in a calculated move, imparted the know-how and wherewithal for making heroin to the Afghans. Bulk heroin ended up in West Pakistan, now the transit territory, and this also spawned a large crop of drug dealers. From a minuscule number in the 1960s, the count of addicts rose to a million by the time Zia died in 1988. In 2007 they were estimated at three million.

Army generals supervised the traffic, provided safe logistic support, and raked in millions of dollars. A feudal lord of the frontier province of Pakistan, Nawab Hoti, with land holding larger than the area of many small countries, reportedly offered to exchange all his property for a general's drug income in a month. Other entrepreneurs joined in. Many ventured abroad. Some were caught and are still languishing in European and American jails.

Benazir, released from jail on health grounds, went to England for treatment. She now had freedom to lobby foreign governments. Zia's administration was riddled with scandals, financial and salacious. After using them in early years of his rule, he had ditched Mullahs. They were getting restive too. A combined front, Movement for Restoration of Democracy (MRD), was rigged.

Past master at the game of divide and rule, Zia created an immigrant party, the Mohajir Qaumi Movement (MQM) — and two second-string native ethnic groupings, the Punjabi-Pakhtoon Front and Jeay Sindh. The Punjabis and Pakhtoons were in direct economic competition with the Mohajirs, while the Sindhis,

---

1 Pakistan Medical Association, dominated by graduates from my alma mater Dow Medical College, is one of the very few progressive organizations in the country. It had nominated one of the godfathers Rahman Hashmi, a stalwart of student movement in Pakistan.

2 Zia, as a part of his "reforms" cancelled the licenses of the native opium shops. That measure only sent them underground.

in denial of the reality that Mohajirs comprised at least forty-five percent of the population of the province and were the majority in all but a few urban centers, disdained any dialogue with the former.

The "law and order" situation, as the governments are so fond of calling it, deteriorated and would lead to the birth of armed gangs. They would make daring day light raids into businesses, banks and wedding receptions.[1] Kidnapping for ransom became a routine. The police, of course, gave backup support. In honor of the occasion they would exchange their official garb for civilian dress. The gangs recruited unemployed university graduates. They were invariably polite, respecting women, and considerate to children and elders and would shoot only when they had to, on meeting resistance. They always warned men folk, that they would not be harmed if they were sensible.

Russians, meeting more organized opposition in Afghanistan and in a desperate attempt to save vestiges of superpower status, were surreptitiously looking for a way out. They offered a deal to the Americans. The Americans knew that Zia was taking them for a ride. Their main clients were Osama bin Laden and Mullah Umar of Taliban fame. Though not able to foresee the grief the men would cause them, they wanted to disassociate with the likes of these people too. The Soviet Union had a glamorous, articulate sophisticate in Gorbachev, who played skillfully on fears of the West.[2] He offered a deal to America to get his forces out of Afghanistan. Zia sent his Prime Minister Junejo to sit in on the parleys and look out for Pakistan's interest. Going beyond his brief, he agreed to the Soviet-American agreement.

Zia wanted no part of it. He had visions of restoring glory of Islam by annihilating the Soviet army in Afghanistan. He had made his opposition to any accommodation known all over. Fully aware of the reach of powers that be, he became jittery. Far from being unfailingly polite, he became rude and short tempered. He dismissed the Prime Minister,[3] refused to call off his hounds, and vowed to ambush the retreating Soviets. But the Americans would not take lightly to their own poodle snapping at the heels of their new bosom buddy.

An incident had to be contrived to get rid of Zia. He was scheduled to observe a test run of a tank America wanted to sell to Pakistan in a place called Bahawalpur, and invited a very reluctant U.S. military attaché and the ambassador to accompany him. He also took along a dozen senior Pakistani generals on the ride. On the return trip, Zia invited the vice chief of the army, who had flown in his own aircraft, to join him on the plane to discuss the merits of the tank. The man

---

1 In the sub-continent women at all parties, but especially at wedding receptions, are laden with gold. Married for many years, they still dress up as brides.

2 In one of the summits he got Reagan to agree to total nuclear disarmament. After his advisors had told him in simple words what he had conceded to the Russian, Reagan had to retract.

3 The poor man was told of the shove when he landed at the Islamabad Airport, after what he thought, had been a notable achievement.

politely declined the honor on some pretext. Zia's plane C 147, transport work-horse of US army, with a very high safety record, exploded a few minutes into the air, taking him and fellow generals into their cherished paradise.[1] It was rumored that just before the plane took off, a crate of choice mangoes, a gift of the sacked Prime Minister, had been taken aboard and had explosives tucked inside.

The vice chief, turned his plane around, landed at the airport, made sure Zia was good and dead, and flew to military headquarters to a hastily convened meeting of Lt generals, which decided to abide by the constitution and hand the presidency over to the chairman of the senate. The latter gentlemen appointed an interim Prime Minister and a cabinet. They, in their turn, rubber-stamped the US-Soviet agreement on Afghanistan.

## TALIBAN

An undercurrent of messianic zeal is never far from the surface in Muslim societies. It goes back to the Prophet's time. The prophet, however, tempered his message with due consideration for human frailties and preferred persuasion to coercion. On the occasion of the signature ceremony on the peace treaty document (Suleh-e-Hudaibiah) between Muslims and the Quraish[2] of Mecca, the latter objected to his title "Messenger of God" under his signature. He scratched out the title when he signed the document, rather than forego the obvious advantages of the treaty.

He was to capture Mecca the following year without firing a shot, or in his case, without launching an arrow. He did not seek revenge from the leaders of Mecca, forgiving even the woman Hinda of the Umayyad clan who had, after the defeat of Muslims in the second battle against the Quraish, chewed the raw liver of his favorite uncle Hamza.

The Prophet was gradualist and tolerated affronts to his person with a smile. He forbade alcohol in stages, first asking the believers to abstain from it before the congregational prayers. At the height of his power a Jewish woman on a street in Madina verbally assaulted him. His devotees wanted to lynch the woman. He restrained them and listened to her patiently. He left the Koran as his legacy and specifically forbade documentation of his sayings, lest they be equated with the holy book. His immediate disciples honored his instructions, but later ones started documenting his sayings based on oral tradition, about a century after his demise.

---

1 See *Confessions of an Economic Hit Man* by John Perkins for how fruit baskets were used to assassinate heads of state in Latin America.

2 Muslims were not allowed to visit Kaaba. After having inflicted several defeats on his opponents, the Prophet asked that his followers be allowed to make the pilgrimage. He agreed to leave all arms outside the city of Mecca. In the second battle against the dominant section of his tribe called Uhad, Muslims had suffered a bad reverse. The Prophet was actually left for dead. Most of his followers were drunk. It was pre- alcohol prohibition time

I have gone to some length in describing the Prophet's sagacity to emphasize the fact that his followers, soon after his demise, cast aside his open minded and judicious approach to problems. After him Umar, who was to be the second caliph, imposed the first Caliph Abu Bakr on the populace. About a hundred and fifty years after the prophet, Abbasids who took over the caliphate, which was by then a full-fledged hereditary office. They got the clerics and jurists to meddle with the traditions of the prophet. In the process all the sayings which emphasized tolerance, compromise, free will in adoption of any creed, proscription of coercion in conversion, near equal status of women, fair treatment of minorities, pursuit of education, etc., were eradicated from the texts. A noted scholar Imam Bokhari[1] found only about six hundred fifty credible traditions, among the seventeen thousand then extant.

One scholar Ibn-e-Tamiyya in the early Abbasid period promoted an intolerant version of Islam, as propounded by one of early jurists of the creed Imam Ibne Hanbal.[2] Another disservice the scholars did to the religion was to proscribe Ijtehad — research, innovation and critical thought, thus closing the gates of rational analysis, leaving only blind belief instead. The name of Imam Ghazali, an eminent jurist of his time, springs to mind. His influence was overwhelming. His stated intent was to discourage dissention in the ranks.

Fortunately for the faith, the intolerant version did not take root; that is till the eighteenth century, when a mediocre Arab cleric by the name of Abdul Wahab[3] revived it. He was not very successful either, till he made a compact with an ambitious chieftain, the founder of the House of Saud. Wahabi beliefs were largely confined to what is Saudi Arabia now, though a tiny percentage of Muslims did follow the system in other countries. Mainstream Sunnis in India shunned them before independence.

The Wahabi sect was given a tremendous boost by the discovery of oil in Saudi Arabia. Erstwhile minor tribal Chiefs wanted to live it up. The Mullahs objected. The Chiefs palmed them off with funds for madressahs, seminaries outside their own country. Literally thousands were established in Pakistan and other Muslim countries. The countries suffered from grinding poverty and an abysmally low literacy rate. If anyone offered food, clothes and shelter, millions would swamp him. The seminaries offered religious education too; it was actually memorizing the Koran and indoctrination in fantasy of wine, women and dance in the afterworld. A cadre of hypnotized youth was thus created. When unleashed, they went around

---

1 There are three generally accepted books of the prophet's sayings-Bokhari, Muslim and Tirmizi-named after the respective compilers.

2 The four main schools of Sunni thought named after the jurists are Hanafi- followed by about eighty percent of Sunnis-Shafai, Malaki and Hanbali. Shias, who constitute approximately twenty percent of Muslims, follow Imam Jafar, a descendent of the prophet who was also Imam Abu Hanifa's mentor.

3 For a detailed analysis of the role of Britain, France, USSR and the US in promoting Islamic fundamentalism please refer to *Devil's Game* by Robert Dreyfuss.

targeting and attacking non-Muslims, and even Muslims who did not agree with their handlers.

In historical terms, recent setbacks like the establishment of Israel, the debacle of the 1967 Six Day War, the 1971 civil war in East Pakistan, the total reversal after early successes in the 1973 Yom Kippur War, the Afghan jihad and post Gulf War II demolition of Iraq, have driven Muslims further away from the path of development, sciences and enlightenment.

Students at the seminaries, many of whom were actually from Afghanistan, now popularly known as the Taliban, did not need much persuasion to cross over to the country to wage the jihad against the infidel. They got a new patron with messianic zeal, Osama bin Laden, who was worth $600 million. All sections and ethnicities of Afghans fought the war against the Soviets. The Taliban were the best organized, financed and led. The Soviet retreat left something of a vacuum in a part of the world of immense strategic interest to all the great powers. The Taliban eliminated other factions in short order and committed atrocities, especially on the minority Shias and women.[1] They closed girls' schools and sent all female workers, doctors, teachers, and office workers home. Incessant warfare over two decades had left innumerable widows and orphans with no means of support. No longer allowed to work, many resorted to begging and prostitution.

The Taliban imposed "religious" courts where destitute women and other disenfranchised populace were summarily tried without the benefit of defense, witnesses or even prosecuting attorneys. Fanatical clerics handed down judgments after a few minutes' deliberation. The punishment could be public beatings, amputation of a hand or foot or stoning to death. Thousands in Kabul's main sports stadium watched the spectacle. On the streets, religious police caned women who were found not covered from head to foot, or wearing high heels. Men were subject to measurement of beards, which had to be regulation length, and the more zealous security guards would check the pubic area to see if it was properly shaved. Men had to wear ankle-length pants to play soccer. Members of one Pakistani soccer team had their heads shaved because they wore shorts.

The virus spread to Pakistan where at the time a common slogan used to be, "Who will save Pakistan? Taliban, Taliban." Sectarian violence increased. Members of the "other" sect were murdered for the greater "glory of Islam." In Karachi alone, scores of young Shia physicians were killed in cold blood. Mosques were torched, clerics butchered, and kidnapped. Christians and Hindus were not spared either.

Things have actually been getting worse. The political wing of the extremist parties actually won elections in two provinces in Pakistan. Despite the inter-

---

1 The recent book *Kite Runner* by Afghan expatriate Khaled Hosseini, now made into a movie, describes it well.

vention of the US government after 9/11, the deadly virus of Taliban apparently would have engulfed Pakistan in an epidemic of extremism. It may still do so.

## PAKISTAN 1983–1991

### OBSERVATIONS ON HEALTH, EDUCATIONAL SYSTEMS AND SOCIETAL CORRUPTION

We left for Pakistan in November 1983. It had been 20° below freezing in Bath, New York. Karachi was 80° above. We went around in short-sleeve shirts and switched on ceiling fans. But the electric supply was capricious. Blackouts were frequent. Sarah would get very uncomfortable.[1] Phone service was poor. The country had not kept pace with the technological development of the rest of the world and whatever little gains it made, were overtaken by population explosion.[2]

The first priority, after we had more or less settled, was to find a school for our daughter Sarah, now three and a half. Public schools in Pakistan, like every other service, had declined in standard of education, social and cultural values and basic safety as well. Private schools varied enormously in standards; the best ones were academically better than the vaunted missionary schools. With the arrogance of a returning expatriate and that from US, we went to the premier Christian missionary institute of the town. The head mistress refused to be impressed. She was used to feudal families, the high and mighty of the land, and income tax officers.[3]

When leaving the headmistress's office, I felt heaviness in the chest, difficulty in breathing and profuse sweating. I asked my driver to take me to the nearby office of a close friend Dr. Aziz, who took me to the National Institute of Cardio-Vascular Diseases — the only heart hospital in a city of over ten million people and for that matter the only one in a country of a hundred million people.[4] The staff attended to me immediately and gave me an intravenous injection, which made me feel entirely better. I wanted to go home, but they wouldn't let me, as another doctor they had let go recently in similar circumstances had died on them. I was admitted under the care of Dr. Aslam, a British-trained cardiologist, kept in ICU for forty-eight hours and transferred to a private room on the third day. I was discharged home after a stay of five days. The hospital bills, including that for two days of intensive care, came out to be about $200.00. At the time

---

1 The infrastructure was antiquated and direct illicit connections with electric poles compromised the inadequate supply.

2 The country's population was 35 million in 1947. It had risen to 145 million. In 2007 it had risen to 165 million.

3 Income Tax inspectors can raise or reduce your bill and it is a hassle even the high and mighty to have it reduced.

4 Many more heart hospitals have been opened since, most in the private sector, and cater to the rich. Expatriate money has given them great boost.

in the US it would be a minimum of $10,000. Fortunately it turned out that my heart was fine.

After I got better our first quest was again to find a school for Sarah. A friend recommended a kindergarten pre-school run by a well-educated and well-turned out lady. In due course Sarah moved up through the grades, consistently making A grades, and it was time for to look for a high school. We chose Mama Parsi School,[1] but in the good old sub-continental fashion looked for connections to make sure that she will be accepted. We were elated when one of my friends told me that he knew the granddaughter of the founder who promised to put in a word for us.

Sarah took the admission test and we happily anticipated a letter of acceptance. The brief note that we got a few weeks later stating that the school would not be able to take her floored me. I called on the granddaughter. She called the school and was told that Sarah had done very poorly in the test. I decided to get to the bottom of the mystery. I discovered that schools did not do much by way of teaching but awarded A grades keep parents happy. We had to have intensive private coaching to get her up to par.

My second project after recovery from my heart trouble was getting the baggage out of the clutches of Customs and finding a piece of land to build a hospital on. Baggage clearance was assisted by an older brother of a friend who was a high customs official. I did end up paying a small fee, as doing otherwise would adversely affect the future business of my clearing agent.

## Hospital Project

The story of what I went through in the quest of building a hospital would merit a book in its own right.

A relative by marriage of one of my partners offered an apartment building he had built, but I soon discovered that all he wanted was dollars over which he would have full control. I got rid of the man with a great deal of difficulty. With that experience under my belt, I proceeded to contact real estate agents. I would tell the agents that I was interested in a commercial plot, not a house, which could be converted into a hospital or an amenity plot.[2] The agents from "reputable" firms continued to take me to homes and amenity plots which were going "cheap."

The wife of another partner introduced me to a fairly well-known architect. He offered to assist me in my search for land, if I would give him the architectural and construction work. I gave him the same instructions about a commercial

---

1 It is an old school founded by a Parsi-Zoarastrian- gentleman Mr. Mama

2 In order to facilitate construction of charity hospitals the government offered land at low cost to charitable trusts which, of course, were controlled by friends and relatives of civil servants. They sold the land by the easy expedient of transferring ownership to a new trust, which was under the control of the new owner.

plot. He turned out to be no better than the real estate agents. In fact he started escorting me to vacant plots. On enquiry, it turned out that many owners didn't want to sell; some had been out of the country for years.

I was at a dead end and ready to pack my bags. But the fates finally smiled on me. An acquaintance told me of a commercial plot in a posh area. A friend recommended a retired manager of a nationalized oil industry for the job of project manager. He negotiated with the owner and I finally bought the land.

The architect heard that I had acquired a piece of land and started pestering me to give him the construction contract. I allowed my partners to prevail upon me to engage the firm as he had made the lowest bid. The architect produced blueprints which were discussed (perfunctorily) by the partners and agreed to.

The partnership did not have sufficient funds to finish the whole project. I started looking for investors and found quite a few, but the most invaluable was Dr. Aslam, my cardiologist. He was a highly regarded heart doctor and counted the high and mighty among his patients. He took me straight to the chairman of the National Development Finance Corporation (NDFC), an agency charged with helping "nation building" projects. The dignitary promptly approved the loan subject to submission of a feasibility report. His assistants were put out as they had lost the bribe that was "due" to them on approval of the loan. They asked me for a lot of documents in addition to a feasibility report.

The architect offered help in obtaining a feasibility report as well and introduced me to an "expert." The expert promised a report within ten days, but gave it to me after several weeks, only after I had threatened to fire him.

A week after I had submitted the feasibility report, I got a call from an irate senior vice president (SVP) of NDFC[1]. Did I know what was in the feasibility report? I confessed ignorance. He demanded that I go to see him immediately. On arrival at his office he told me that the report I had submitted was a copy of the report for another hospital, and my expert had not even bothered to erase the NDFC note of approval from it. It was confidential government document. I told him that they should adopt better measures to keep such valuable papers safe and advised him to report the matter to the chairman. He subsided.

The loan was finalized, signed and sealed. It was to be released in installments at defined stages of construction. My architect advised me that I should pay three percent as kick back to the SVP in charge; otherwise I would have to face interminable delays. I angrily refused. I was to rue the refusal. Funds were not released in time to buy the air conditioning equipment then duty free for hospitals. By the time I got the check, the government had imposed 400% tariff. We were never able to buy the AC unit. My partners, wiser in the ways of their native land, did not thank me for my scruples.

---

1 The man had been a classmate of Benazir's husband Asif Zardari at prep school. When she became the Prime Minister in 1989, he promoted him to a high post in the ministry of finance and the man started ordering his previous boss around.

The stage was now set for construction. We needed all kinds of permits from the Karachi Development Authority (KDA) and other civic agencies and I did not have a clue as to how to go about it. The architect got KDA to approve plans, presented a contractor to me for formal approval and construction started. A rough and ready tin and mud hut built overnight served as our corporate HQ.

Much to my surprise, construction work proceeded at a fast pace for a few weeks. Then it came to a grinding halt. I asked the architect. He was initially evasive but after a lot of hemming and hedging he confessed that he had offered too low a rate, as he was scared that I would find another firm and requested revision of the contract. I was advised that acceding to his request would lead to ever escalating demands. Work stoppage was a regular subterfuge and pressure tactics to raise the rates. I threatened a lawsuit, but what worked was the intervention of a newly found friend who knew high ups in KDA and could make life difficult for any architect in town. Work resumed.

The project manager, sensing my inexperience, started acting up. I sought the advice of my uncle who had recently retired from the railways engineering department and was savvy in ways of the government and contractors. He brought along a retired construction engineer to assist us at a nominal consultation fee. Some months later the accountant, who was a distant family connection, also decided to grumble. I got a lucky break. I met an accountant in a wedding party, and asked him to visit me in the hospital the next day. He had low-level experience in the field but adequate for our work. I hired him, and fired the distant relative.

In 1986 I visited New York for a court appearance and took the opportunity to visit and talk to my US-based partners. We had made an informal agreement, that I would go to Pakistan first, and another partner would replace me after three years. No one was willing to return.[1] I told them that I would have to co-opt partners from Pakistan. They promptly agreed. On my return to Pakistan I started broaching the idea of partnership to doctors I had got to know and liked. In due course I was successful in bringing at least one doctor in every specialty on board. None of my local partners, except for anesthesiologist Akhtar Aziz and Syed Aslam, helped in any work.

It was a never-ending struggle, wheeling and dealing with various government agencies and private enterprises.

## PROFESSIONAL WORK AND LIFE IN PAKISTAN

With the influx of expatriate money from workers in Mid-East and Africa, demand for private health care had grown exponentially. Even before I had formally opened an office, I started getting calls to visit patients at home. The rich and the powerful deem it beneath their station in life to visit doctors' offices. In the kind of rigid class based society they lived in, even professors of medical

---

1 I learned later that a partner's wife prayed during the Hajj pilgrimage that she would not have to move to Pakistan. Allah granted her wish.

colleges had to visit patients at home or they stood to lose all their privileges. I, coming back from the US, did not feel I had to fawn on anyone.[1]

But I had reckoned without the tenacity of our upper class. A repatriate ear, nose and throat (ENT) surgeon whose acquaintance I had made in the US gave my name to one of his friends. This man's employer was the owner of a large tobacco firm, and had developed a backache. The employee called me with a request to see his boss at the latter's residence. I told him that I did not make house calls. He insisted. His chief was the owner of the biggest cigarette manufacturing company in the country. I told him that I had quit smoking. He finally asked me if I would agree to look at the x-rays of the great man. I invited him to join me at a restaurant the next evening.

The man turned up clutching a huge bunch of x-ray films. The restaurant manager offered me a spacious lounge. In the short time I took looking at x-ray films, I had gathered an audience from the patrons and employees of the business. Some even ventured to ask for my advice. The tobacco baron had consulted all the leading specialists of Karachi. He appeared to be suffering from a herniated disc.[2] I told the factotum that his boss was being treated correctly. That nonchalant remark, if anything, whetted the tobacco chief's desire even more to have me visit him at his home. He prevailed upon the ENT surgeon to call me. It could not do any harm, my friend told me. It could be a useful contact. I reluctantly agreed.

The man lived in a palatial house. But I also noticed a huge and rotting garbage dump right outside the gates. I was ushered into the presence of the luminary in his bedroom. About a score of solicitous well-wishers were sitting in a semi-circle around the bed. They all rose to greet me. The place looked more like an old time Durbar of a fair sized princely state than a sick room. I could visualize myself as a visiting plenipotentiary from another state rather than a doctor come to minister to a patient. I asked if I could examine him in private.[3] This turned out to be an unexpected and unusual request.

After I had examined the tobacco chief, I told him that he should be in a hospital. He said that he would really get more sick there. I had only to name it and he would get all that a hospital could provide. I gave his assistant a list of equipment we would need to convert his bedroom into a hospital room. With his resources, contacts and money, we had all the supplies, a hospital bed and a traction kit within forty-eight hours. The bed was available locally, but the kit had to be imported from Hong Kong.

---

1 At the time specialists used to be British trained, had little money and had to cater to the whims of the rich and powerful.

2 Discs are cushions between the vertebrae in the spine. If their cover bursts, usually due to injury, a highly irritant material comes out causing pain and spasm in the muscles of the back.

3 People in the East do not exhibit much reticence in matters medical, or any other.

I have been asked for advice in wedding receptions, at airport immigration desks, on trains and buses. The patient and his hangers-on would not mind a public examination.

A few years later I got another call from him. His wife had bad knees. His son came to fetch me. The huge garbage dump was still there right outside his home. I asked the son if it was the same garbage I had seen some years ago. He was a bit put out and said that I was making fun of him. I told him that his family had all the money in the world. Why did they not have the garbage cleared? His response was that it was the job of the Municipal Corporation. I felt like telling him that the corporation did not live there, but it would have been no use.

My biggest personal problem was that the traffic was chaotic. The only rule I could discern was that the bigger vehicle had the right of the way. Very rarely one would come across a person wearing a seat belt. Not many cars had them. We hired a full time driver. Labor was unbelievably cheap and unemployment high.[1] When I asked my driver to use the seat belt, he said that if he had an accident, by the time he could undo it, the other driver would have had time to punch him several times. Fist fights between drivers after an accident were routine. Road accidents were very common. If there were a grievous injury, the offending driver would speed away. If both drivers stopped, a street argument would inevitably ensue. An impromptu court comprising of the passersby will be held. Soon a small crowd would gather and serve as members of the jury. After half an hour of arguments going back and forth, one side would concede and pay for repairs and treatment on the spot. Nobody called the police.

My younger son Hasan was born in Karachi in a hospital owned and operated by a medical school classmate, Farzana Mahboob. She not only did not charge for surgery, but also made the anesthesiologist return the fee I had given her. The hospital stay was free too; she even sent food for my wife and all visitors. Hasan used to complain that I had not brought him over to be born in the US so he was ineligible to become the president. But he has not complained since George W. Bush assumed office.

Social life was going to wedding dinners and music parties. Dinners started and ended late. There were fairly frequent male-only drinking parties, though younger persons in affluent neighborhoods had mixed gatherings too. New Year and Christmas used to be festive occasions till fanatics took charge of public behavior and morals. Public parties were discontinued after obscurantist hooligans mobbed them. Restaurants, clubs and outdoor facilities in the Western mode, would actually close early on New Year's Eve lest the self-styled guardians of public morals demolish the place for the greater glory of Islam.

In the 1950s and 1960s Karachi used to be a city of coffee- and teahouses. Students, young teachers, poets, writers, aspiring politicians and intellectuals would sit there till midnight or after, then take a bus or walk home. It was perfectly safe.

---

1 During my visits to Pakistan I regularly came across university graduates who drove cabs, not to support themselves in higher studies but because they could not find an appropriate job. Once I asked one of them, "Why are you driving a taxi"? He smiled. "Would you rather I robbed a bank?"

One cup of coffee would last hours. They have all but disappeared because the city had grown so big and it has become difficult and unsafe to commute in the middle of the night. Mullahs had taken to stoning coffee houses as well.

## VISITS TO QUETTA

We took to driving to the town for two weeks during school vacations. Quetta boasts of some of the finest fresh fruits in the world. Besides apples, grapes and apricots, we have a local variety of melons called *sarda*, roughly translated "cold." I am sure nectar would not taste better. I have never enjoyed anything more than the plump, dark blue, almost black cherries of Quetta. At the risk of being accused of male chauvinism, I would compare them to the dusky beauties of South India. Natives made an especially delicious roast goat leg called *sajji*, and the chapli kebabs[1] were out of this world.

Afghan refugees had nearly overwhelmed the population. I have yet to see a more affluent group of shelter seekers.[2] They controlled nearly all transport business and had poached upon the profitable smuggled goods business, the lifeblood of local bourgeoisie. They sold American and Russian guns too. Vast tent markets had mushroomed in which you could buy blankets, army uniforms from many countries, electric appliances, generators, shoes, tinned food and drugs. They had opened many restaurants. The food was different and quite good.

Quetta also boasts of the second largest smugglers market in the country.[3] Before the advent of Kalashnikov assault rifle and the drug heroin, the economy of the area was based on goods smuggled across the border. When you left the town, Octroi and customs agents would try to extract bribes from you for carrying contraband. If you handed over the goods to agents you would get them hassle free in other towns, just as you bought them. The other distinguishing feature of the city is the huge cantonment adjacent to the town. It did support the city economy, but the people resented it as a tool of neocolonialism. But for their huge presence, and ease of deployment, Baluchistan would have been much more successful in its struggle against the government which they feel, was exploiting the natural resources of the province with little benefit to them.

After a few days in Quetta, we would drive to Ziarat, a hill station[4] eighty miles away. Ziarat owes its name to a fable. The word means pilgrimage. The story goes that the daughter of a king of Afghanistan fell in love with a saintly young man. The saint, as their type was wont to do in those long forgotten days,

---

1 Sajji is made out of goat carcass left out in the freezing cold through winter months. Chapli kebabs have special and secret spices.
2 I am not saying that all the refugees were rich, but a great many had brought a lot of funds and indulged in drug and arms trading and smuggling.
3 The biggest is in vicinity of the Khyber Pass, between north Pakistan and Afghanistan, now controlled by Taliban.
4 The British, like the Moghals before them, used to transfer the administration capital to the foothills of the mountains in the hot months.

shunned her advances. Incensed, she complained to her father that the man had made indecent suggestions to her. The king sent his soldiers to take him into custody. He took shelter in a forest. The trees closed their ranks around the pious youth. Soldiers tried to smoke him out by putting the trees to fire. The earth split and they were sent to well-deserved perdition. The trees with their precious refugee moved away. The saint chose the middle of a bleak and desolate region for his final destination. The fact that Ziarat is the only lush green area with hundreds of miles of parched desert around lends credence to the story.

I had first visited Ziarat in 1958. It was full of trees of all kinds. One was believed to be five thousand years old. The area shared the general population explosion. The inhabitants had to fell trees for fuel. Except for fruit orchards, the settlement was practically bare of trees.

We used to stay in the government rest house, courtesy of a friend who was the TV news chief in Quetta. One year, though, we found that our rooms had been occupied by army officers. We asked the district officer how could they take over the rooms booked for us. His laconic response was, "the same way they have taken over the rest of the country." It was Zia's period of martial law.

## Chapter 12. Hospital Management

Our hospital was built and finally went into operation on January 31, 1989. We had, by common consent, named it Hill Park General Hospital (HPGH). We chose a date for an "open house" and had a stream of visitors through a full day. Now I had the opportunity to impose my will and began starting Surgery at 7:30 a.m., as I was used to in the United States. In Pakistan that was an unearthly hour. It took six months to get the staff in line. Between clinical and administrative work, my personal schedule was very heavy. The staff took to calling on me for all kinds of problems. The only way I could get off time was to leave town.

We started looking for contracts from nationalized industries. I had treated many influential persons and they came in handy. Dr. Aslam was, as usual, an invaluable help. Other partners chipped in with links. The gynecologist Saeeda Rahman had close relations with Pakistan international Airlines. Akhtar Aziz exhibited rare facility in these negotiations. Overall, we were fairly successful.

A contractor approached Akhtar and offered to provide nursing, sanitary, janitorial, security and "lower" staff. Our DA&F[1] was enticed into making a deal with the street-smart crook. One morning I found the hospital abounding with men and women wielding all kinds of brooms and buckets. At the time only two patients constituted the entire inpatient census of the hospital. I told the contractor to leave four persons. A few months down the line, the man presented me with a bill for half a million. I was flabbergasted. I demanded proof of work done. He produced a document with a forged signature of the DA&F. I threw him out of my office.

---

1 We had a board of directors. I was the Chairman of the Board. Akhtar was Director Administration and Finance.

A few days later the manager of the night shift called me to say that the con-tractor and his strong-arm men were harassing the staff. It was late in the eve-ning. I went to the hospital and found a "law and order" situation. We tried call-ing the police. They were all busy as Benazir was addressing a public meeting. In desperation, I called a friend from NSF days who was now head of the national airline union. He brought about two dozen enforcers, beat up the contractor and his men, and threw out their office furniture.

A few days later the inspector in charge of the local police station asked us to visit him as he wanted to discuss the situation. A partner and I went to see the man. The police officer implied that very high police officers were friends with the contractor. If we knew what was good for us, we would pay up. We told him that we would get back to him. The inspector took to calling us every day. The police are nasty in Pakistan, much more than in the West, with little check on their behavior. I called a friend, Dr. Rizvi, in Lahore. His father had been a high police officer. He called back and asked me to go to police headquarters (HQ) the next day and see the deputy inspector general — an eminence indeed.

It was my first visit to the imposing colonial building. I duly presented myself at the man's office at the appointed time. As soon as he learned of my identity, the man's secretary greeted me effusively in Punjabi, "Sahib thwada intizar karde pai nain," (the big chief is waiting for you) and he escorted me to the inner sanctum with the remark, "Sir Ji Eai Dr. Rizvi de yaar nain." (Mr. Sir, this is the friend of Dr. Rizvi.) I was at a loss. If I spoke Urdu, the man might take it amiss. "Historic"[1] memory saved me. I talked to him in English.

The chief was equally ebullient. He greeted me with reassuring words. "Eai kera inspector ai je thwanu tang karda pya ai," (Who is this police inspector dar-ing to bother you?) I replied, "His name is so and so, in charge of the station in our area." My English, which had a hint of British and a lot of American accent, worked as magic. He said, "We can't have that," rang the bell, and asked his re-ceptionist to get the Superintendent (SP), so and so. The SP arrived in a minute and the DIG told him to take care of the inspector. He asked me to accompany him. In his office I found a collection of holy men in colorful drapery laden with beads of all kinds. I suppose the SP was cognizant of his intensive need of inter-cession with the Almighty. In any event the SP called the inspector and swore at him in three languages.

When I arrived back at the hospital, the Inspector was waiting for me. He lit-erally fell on my feet. I asked him to get off my shoes. He got up timidly, confessed that the contractor had gotten a different DIG (traffic) to get him to be rude to us. But I had gotten to a much more potent DIG, the one in charge of the headquar-

---

1 I once went to see a superintendent of customs who was a Gujarati-speaking person. He spoke
  to me in the language. I could understand a bit and instinctively decided to respond to him in
  English. The man forgave me all the dues and penalties.

ters. His fate was in my hands. The traffic DIG was, moreover, an Urdu speaker.[1] He could hurt only a traffic inspector but not those in charge of police stations. DIG (HQ) could transfer a station chief to a desk at the head office. It was getting to be like a scene from a B class Bollywood movie[2] and a few onlookers had gathered around us. Their senses were titillated by the spectacle of a police inspector bowing and scraping in front of an ordinary mortal.

The contractor saga does not end here. I got a visit from an MQM[3] don with a few gangsters in tow. His demeanor was deferential, but he insisted that I give the contractor half a million. A few days later, I got a very respectful letter from a member of the Sindh assembly requesting me to honor his office with a visit the next day. I took Akhtar with me. The assemblyman was holding court and pompously announced that the party stood for justice and fair play; the rich no longer had the right to exploit the poor in Karachi. We had to pay half a million, he told us. We left, promising to get back to him.

We started getting threatening calls at home. MQM were known to be tough customers. Rumors of their torture cells were rife. Some children had been abducted too. Our wives were very nervous. We were too. Fortunately for us, one of our partners had operated upon the wife of Azim Tariq, the number two in the MQM hierarchy. He called his patient. The effect was dramatic. The assemblyman called and apologized.

I must say the contractor was irrepressible. He filed a suit in a lower court. The judge was an ethnic Sindhi. One of my closest friends, eye doctor Dr. Saleh Memon, was a very influential Sindhi. I called him to find a contact. He sent word after a while that the High Court registrar, a very powerful personage indeed in the ranks of the judiciary, would visit me in the evening and discuss the problem. The man assured me that he would take care of it. The lower court judge called me the next day. It was the curtains for the contractor.

## HANDICAPPED CHILDREN, NUCLEAR DISARMAMENT: CONTRAST WITH CONDITIONS IN INDIA

While in Karachi, I co-founded the Pakistan chapter of International Physicians for Prevention of Nuclear War (PPPNW). I also served as Secretary General of Pakistan Orthopedic Association, wrote its byelaws (the original had been lost), and arranged regular monthly meetings and did volunteer work for a handicapped children's association called Al-Shifa.

Soon after arrival in Karachi, a friend told me about the charitable organization which looked after handicapped children. I called Al-Shifa. The President

---

1 Even when Urdu speakers got to high ranks, they did not enjoy as much authority as an equivalent of Punjabi origin.

2 The word Bollywood is a hybrid of Bombay the center of Indian film industry and Hollywood.

3 The man was in charge of the party in my area. Mentioned in the chapter on rise of Fundamentalism, MQM was the party of immigrants.

of the trust, on hearing that I had recently returned from the US, welcomed me with open arms. I started consultation clinics there. Within a few weeks I realized that the advice I gave for corrective surgery was not available to the patients. I proposed to the President that I would perform surgery pro bono if the trust picked up hospital charges. She pleaded lack of funds.

I would have under normal circumstances accepted the excuse, but this facility had air-conditioned and well-appointed offices, hosted lavish lunches and dinners and provided chauffeured transport for officers. I wrote to the wife of the chairman of the trust, a lady who had trained as a nurse. She also had the good sense to marry an army officer who had risen to the rank of a major general.[1] She asked me to come to the next trust meeting.

The president was rather taken aback to find me among those present and looked at me suspiciously. The general's wife quelled her with a glance, and a word that she had invited me to present my case. I laid it on. My host ordered the president to finance surgical procedures and requested me to try to persuade the hospital owners to give discounted rates. That did not make me very popular. But they dare not flout the wife of the chairman. Several hospital owners agreed to make nominal charges on the patients. After two years the general retired from his job. An Air Marshal replaced him. During his first visit he lauded my humanitarian work, but was not terribly interested in handicapped children His wife was led by the nose by the officers of the charity. The program was discontinued soon afterwards.

In 1986, Al-Shifa offered to send me and the senior physical therapist, Mrs. Pirzada,[2] to Bombay to observe the facilities for treatment of handicapped children there. We visited a federal government facility first. The director had a lavish office and entertained us royally but lost interest as soon we asked him to show us around. He called an underling, who took us on a perfunctory tour of the facility.

But the next day we visited a facility managed by a charitable organization supported only by public contributions. They ran a fifty-bed hospital performing, on the average, thirty surgical procedures a week. It supported a fully functioning and well-equipped physical therapy department manned by dedicated technicians. An orthopedic workshop with facilities for making all kinds of aids to locomotion from simple splints to artificial limbs was also located on the premises. The administrative office was unpretentious. The head of clinical service was a lady who had been the professor and head of the orthopedic department of a famous medical college. She was internationally known for her work on cerebral

---

1 The general was the chairman of the national airlines, which funded Al-Shifa. His wife functioned as the chairperson of Al-Shifa.
2 Mrs. Pirzada was one of the wives of the "eminent" attorney who advised all martial law administrators.

palsy.[1] During the visit a gentleman rode into the facility on a bicycle. I was taken aback when he turned out to be a fully trained orthopedic surgeon. I couldn't help contrasting what I saw there with conditions in Karachi. An orthopedic surgeon riding a bicycle to work would be laughed out of the town in Pakistan.

On the third day, we visited another non-government facility housed in a six-story building. Every floor had several cottage industries, printing, knitting, and carpentry, dress making, bookbinding, and electric equipment repair etc. You name it and it would be there. All workers were handicapped. One was even triplegic, that is paralyzed in three of the four limbs. The office in this facility was even more unassuming.

At the end of the visit I asked the charitable hospital management if they would be willing to train our physical therapists. They readily agreed, offered training at no charge and free lodging with cooking amenities as well. The federal minister of health in Pakistan at the time was a personal friend and an old NSF colleague.[2] He visited Al-Shifa soon afterwards. I told him of the offer. He was stunned. India was off bounds. Benazir would have a fit. Her detractors had already accused her of pro-India bias.[3]

One afternoon Mrs. Pirzada arranged a visit to a film shoot in which the delectable Rekha[4] was acting. She was more beautiful than she looked on the screen. She (my companion, not Rekha) took me shopping too. Fabric and handicrafts were much cheaper than they were in Karachi. Food was less expensive too, except in Chinese restaurants.

Another aspect of Bombay I was struck by was the traffic. People, pedestrian and in vehicles, followed the traffic rules. Even the buses stopped behind each other. One time about midnight, my taxi driver sped through a red light. I asked him if he was from Karachi. He grinned and said "Saab[5], I looked both ways."

In 1988, Al-Shifa sponsored a visit for me to an international conference on the management of handicapped children in Bangkok, Thailand. But we were taken to only to a few token lectures and workshops and spent most of our time in dinners, boat trips, and at tourist sites. We were also treated to a formal banquet and a stage show presided over by the younger daughter of the king, a girl in her early twenties. For two hours she sat haughtily, with not even the hint of

---

1 Cerebral palsy is caused by damage to the brain at birth due to a problem with supply of oxygen and often results in deformities, which require corrective surgery.
2 The minister, Amir Haider Kazmi and I among others, had spent time together as state guests during Ayub time.
3 Sikhs had organized an insurgency in India in Indra time. Zia had given them shelter and training facilities. Benazir Bhutto had closed the training camps and had given the list of the leaders to the then Indian Prime Minister, Rajev Gandhi.
4 Rekha is a marvelous and beautiful Indian film actress who played a memorable part of a courtesan of the declining years of Moghal rule in India in a movie "Umrao Jaan".
5 Bombay Wallahs abbreviate Sahib to Saab.

a smile on her face. All native persons presented to her, including the minister of health, would bow low to her and walk backwards.

We made a day trip to the famous Patayya beach and ate lot of shrimp and lobster and guzzled Singha beer. It was delicious. Prostitution male and female was overt. They knocked at hotel doors. We were wary. HIV was quite common there even then. Food and beer were incredibly cheap. A huge chicken rice dish was about $2.00. Shopping was oriental style. You haggled. One of my colleagues offered thirty *bhat* (local currency, then less in value than a Pakistani rupee) for a shirt marked two hundred. I was nervous. He and the shopkeeper both laughed good-naturedly, and a deal was finally made for forty *bhat*. Thai silk is famous; it was selling for two hundred *bhat* a yard in a swank shop. I bought identical material a few shops down the road in a less opulent house for eighty *bhat* a yard. Gold and silver plated cutlery and precious stones, rubies and emeralds were very cheap too. .

## Pakistan Orthopedic Association

The body was moribund. Except for an annual event which was spent in dinners and politicking, they hardly had any meetings. I re-instituted regular monthly meetings of the executive committee. I also managed to bring out a glossy, but well written Magazine. The entrenched interests in POA felt threatened by this burst of activity. They tried to sabotage the work. I ignored them. The professors, except for those in Karachi who were used to the belligerence of juniors, behaved like hegemons. They had inherited the supercilious manners of their British counterparts, without the saving grace of academic and professional excellence of the latter. They spent little time on teaching, less on patient care and negligible on research.

Confrontation was looming large. I had arranged to dismantle the opposition. They were saved by the bell. I left for the good old US to practice in Bath NY, a few days before the critical meeting I had arranged.

## International Physicians for Prevention of Nuclear War — The Delhi Conference

In 1987 a delegation of International Physicians for Prevention of Nuclear War (IPPNW), a Boston-based organization of which the Soviet Minister of Health and an American physician were co-presidents, visited Pakistan. The Pakistan Medical Association gave them a formal welcome. We decided to form a chapter of the organization in Pakistan. I was elected the General Secretary. We held regular chapter meetings. IPPNW used to hold international meetings in various world capitals. We sent delegations to Tokyo, Japan and Montreal, Canada meetings in successive years. I could not go to these conferences as I was very busy with hospital and private work.

I was, however, able to attend the regional meeting in Delhi. A young physician and his wife received us at the airport. The young man kept on praising Muslim food, culture, customs and language, etc. I thought he was doing it to please us. Eventually I told him that we were not that religious. With a twinkle in his eye, he said that he was a great admirer of Muslims. His wife blushed deeply. She was a Muslim.

The city was in the grip of upper–lower caste agitation instigated by right wing groups. The government under Prime Minister V.P. Singh had decided to implement the affirmative action provisions in favor of lower castes ordained by a government committee several years ago. The "untouchable" castes had remained wretched in spite of being called *Hari Jans* — progeny of the gods — by Gandhi Ji. The situation calmed down the next day, and we were able to visit the Red Fort and Chandni Chowk. People were very friendly. As soon as they learnt that we were from Pakistan, they welcomed us even more.

We had sessions and lunch in the parliament house. Just before the first formal session started, a man in his thirties with a cloth shopping bag in his hand walked in. I thought he must be a messenger. He proceeded to the dais, ascended the steps and approached the head table. To my utter surprise he was placed in the seat of honor. He turned out to be the Union Minister of Education. A government minister in Pakistan would not be seen dead in a ditch in that attire. V.P. Singh and Zail Singh, a former Sikh president of the country, addressed us. The latter, clad in a *shervani* and *chooridar* pajama,[1] spoke eloquently in Urdu of the purest diction I have heard, on the need for peace and lauded the prophet of Islam in glowing terms. If one closed one's eyes, one could easily have mistaken him for a Muslim scholar.

I took the opportunity of visiting a few surgical supply shops. You could buy first-rate "made in India" instruments, screws and plates to fix broken bones, artificial hips and knees and other equipment, at a fraction of the cost of what we had to pay in Pakistan. The government of Pakistan did not allow direct import from India. The very same equipment came to Pakistan via Dubai, and the intermediaries duly added their profit.

During a trip I started talking to a rickshaw driver. He turned out to be a Muslim. I asked him about the condition of his co-religionists in India. It was not so good, he replied, but this after a pause, certainly better than of the immigrants who lived in Karachi.

One of our delegates had a friend from childhood when both lived in Burma. This man was a member of an extremist anti-Muslim group. But friendship is only a little less potent than a love affair and certainly longer lasting in most cases. He took us to visit the hunger strike camp of his leader. The leader received us very

---

1 A long generally black coat and very narrow pleated trousers, it was the court dress during Moghal times.

graciously, even posed for photographs with us, but visibly shrank back when we told him that we were from Pakistan.

## Stockholm

In 1991, I went to Stockholm for an IPPNW annual meeting. Members of the host committee had very kindly arranged our stay in private houses. My hosts were a university professor of music and his physical therapist wife. Both spoke good English. The weather was gloomy, though. It was winter and quite cold. The sun rose, I think, at 11:00 a.m. and set at 1:30 p.m. People generally drank heavily. We were routinely offered hard liquor at lunchtime. On the final day we were treated to a cultural evening with songs, dances, skits and general revelry.

The conference was well organized and the attendance was impressive. General sessions were attended by several hundred delegates from practically all countries of the world and were treated to high oratory in different languages. I was designated chair of the Israeli–Palestinian session. The Israeli participants were all liberal left-leaning people openly sympathetic to the Palestinian cause. The Palestinians spoke of being "Red-Indianized." Smaller caucuses followed. The American co-chair met our delegation in an informal session. We told him that the problem of atomic weapons could not be taken or tackled in isolation. It was inextricably linked with colonialism and its new incarnation capital-imperialism. People in the West had to change their economic system before the governments would look after the general population.

From Stockholm I flew on to Philadelphia to visit my daughter Eram, who was a student at the University of Pennsylvania. At the Stockholm airport, though, a US security agent gave me a hard time. Why did I attend an anti-nuclear conference? I told him that it was none of his business. That annoyed him visibly. He asked me if I had packed my bags myself. I said I had forgotten to bring my valet along. He advised me that he would be flying with me on the same plane to the United States. I invited him to come along with me when I paid a call to my congressman and complained about his officious behavior. I did not come across the security man on the flight to Philadelphia. Mention of my congressman's name had put the fear of God in him.[1]

During the visit I availed of the opportunity to renew contacts with friends and acquaintances. I called my old hospital in Bath. The CEO was out of town but his secretary told me that my successor had left, and asked if would I like to come back. I did and flew to Bath the next day. The CEO offered the old practice back to me on enticing terms. I agreed to return.

Most of the time I had been frightened out of my wits in Pakistan. A few well-known doctors had been kidnapped for ransom, and worse, one had his child abducted. Before the trip I had discussed the situation with a partner who was

---

1 That was pre-9/11 time. If I did that now I would end up in Guantanomo Bay.

weighing anchor to go back to the United States. He told me that I was a prime target. They would look at the hospital and come to the very reasonable conclusion that I was loaded. It would be worse, as he knew that I did not have the wherewithal to meet their expectations. That convinced me, all right.

## Chapter 13. BB–NS Musical Chairs

### Musharraf and Altaf

I have used the term musical chairs advisedly. Though Benazir Bhutto (BB) and Nawaz Shareef (NS) took turns in occupying the Prime Minister's office for eleven years between Zia and Musharraf, except for the last two years when NS managed to sack a head of the navy and force the resignation of the army chief,[1] real power remained in the hands of the army. They controlled the band and made the politicians dance to their tune.

The Pakistani army allowed Ghulam Ishaq Khan (GIK), senate chairman under Zia, to take over the President's office. He inherited Zia's authority to nominate a person to the Prime Minister's office, and sack the parliament at will. The new president and both houses of the parliament got together, and amended the constitution to provide for party based elections. Elections were announced, prepared for and held at the end of 1988.

Pakistan People's Party (PPP) led by BB[2] won the largest number of seats. They were just shy of an overall majority. The party had done well in the Punjab

---

1 The naval chief was dismissed on corruption charges. The army chief had suggested that a Turkish style national Security Council comprising the President, Prime Minister, Joint chief and service chiefs, be constituted.

2 Benazir was and continues to be popularly called BB, an affectionate abbreviation of Benazir Bhutto. When out of TV lights and out of reach of radio recorders, she put down everyone in sight. The noted Pakistani columnist Ayaz Amir wrote in the Pakistan English Daily *Dawn* that PPP asked him to host a reception for BB to meet journalists. He wanted to invite a few friends from his village to show off, only to be curtly told that the party would provide him with a list of guests.
BB was very fond of ice cream. He ordered buckets of every kind he could find. BB had one teaspoon of ice cream. When seeing her off, he expressed gratification at the opportunity of helping her meet the newsmen. She retorted that it was his duty.

where the unnatural coalition of progressive elements and feudal lords cobbled by Zulfiqar Bhutto had got together again. Provincial elections followed a few days later. By making crass parochial appeals (a popular refrain was, "the Punjabis have been dishonored"), protégés of Zia led by NS won in the Punjab. Mohajir Qaumi Movement (MQM) swept the seats in urban Sindh.

MQM holds a special position in the musical chairs. At the time of independence in 1947, the Muslim minority provinces offered more than half of civil servants and an overwhelming number of businessmen, industrialists, bankers, and professionals and almost the entire leadership of the Muslim League that Pakistan inherited from the Raj. Muslims in the provinces, which came to constitute West Pakistan, could only offer army officers and soldiers, decrepit feudals lords, and their subservient peasants. The Eastern wing was no better off. It offered jute, which was processed in India, and one senior civil servant. Bitter turf wars broke out between the "sons of the soil" (SOS) — a term used for those born in the Punjab and non-sons of the soil — NSOS bureaucrats, born elsewhere. The SOS had the weaker hand. In 1951 practically all the heads of government departments were non-Punjabi immigrants. NSOS also had more representation in the officer corp. of the army, than their percentage in the population would justify.

This situation obtained till the advent of Ayub's takeover of the Government. Ayub broke the back of NSO bureaucracy by sacking all the immigrant senior officers, except for one who had married the only sister of three Punjabi senior civil servants. His successor Yahya did more of the same. Bhutto scraped the bottom of the barrel.

Bhutto had won more seats in the Punjab and diehard Sindhi nationalists openly derided him as a tool of Punjabis. All he could do was to deflect Sindhi unrest to the immigrants. He introduced a rural–urban quota system; Sindhis would be given preference to immigrants in all government jobs. He also nationalized large chunks of industry and business, further emasculating the immigrants. Worst affected were Sindhi-Immigrant relations. Immigrants controlled all the cities, cultural, social, educational, commercial, industrial, financial and administrative modes. Sindhis were relegated to the villages.

Zia had already effectively put an end to secular non-ethnic politics in Pakistan. Paying lip service to religion, he engineered dissension among all the groups, students included. Altaf Husain, the founder of MQM, had founded a Student Organization and had used the platform to unite the progeny of the immigrants. He had touched a sensitive nerve and had gathered considerable support. During his time at the university, Altaf distinguished himself by not attending classes, or taking tests. He managed to pass the pharmacy final examination, or more likely

---

A Pakistani-born Professor at Cornell University once invited her to give a talk at the campus. At the airport, she was all over his white assistant and ordered him to carry her bags to the car. The assistant hastened to pick up the bags. She tried to recover and asked him to become an adviser to her party.

was allowed to do so.[1] Soon after graduation, he left for the United States. To support himself he drove a cab in Chicago for a while. Not much is known about his whereabouts and activities in the next few years. During the mid eighties, he surfaced back in Pakistan, launched MQM and met with moderate success. But he had acquired a core of devout followers.

In 1984 a speeding bus had crushed a college girl named Bushra Zaidi. The victim was of immigrant origin; the driver and conductor of the bus were Pathans. Tension between bus drivers/conductors and the general public of Karachi was endemic. Like any large city, people of Karachi were also on an edge most of the time. Most of the buses were owned by Police officers. They rushed past other traffic, and were blatantly scornful of traffic rules. The Police looked the other way. Drivers worked long hours too. Accidents were consequently common. Drivers would seek shelter in the nearest police station.

But this was different. The victim was a young girl; she had died in the sight of hundreds of college students. The police had been complicit in keeping the culprits under wraps. Ethnic riots broke out in an area called Aurangi, a huge shantytown, which provided shelter to Pathan migrants from the North who lived in uneasy proximity with a large number of refugees from the erstwhile East Pakistan. Pakistan army had used the latter to fight the Bengali militia and had trained them in the use of small arms and in concocting Molotov cocktails.

In the first round Pathans were apparently taken by surprise. Scores were killed, and their huts put to torch. A few days later they retaliated. Hundreds lost their lives. Large swathes of the region were burnt down. Police were conspicuous in their absence. Veterans of the independence period riots claimed that Hindus/Muslims/Sikhs had not got at each other with such ferocity; as Pathans and Mohajirs did in Aurangi. Riots spread to other parts of the city. Large areas of town were put under curfew. Commercial, educational and all other activities came to a standstill. Rumors were rife and made life intolerable.

In mid 1985 the party announced that Altaf would address the public in Karachi. The day before the meeting I found the whole city was festooned with colorful MQM banners. I learnt later that a veritable swarm of well-led enthusiasts had worked in a very organized and disciplined manner, and had draped all exposed surfaces of the city with Altaf's proclamations. Many questions were raised on the source of MQM financing. Detractors openly expressed the idea that it was underwritten by the Inter services Intelligence (ISI) [2]A reported hun-

---

1 Academic institutions would do anything to get troublemakers out of their hair. At the time there was an acute shortage of pharmacists in the US. Altaf was obviously not able to pass the requisite licensing examinations.

2 The political guru of Altaf and I were together at a dinner. He told me that MQM been formed to (a) launch a middle class party, (b) displace the obscurantist Jamaat-e-Islami from Karachi, and (c) develop better relations with natives of Sindh. The first two objectives had been achieved. After a few abortive attempts at reaching an accommodation with Sindhis, Altaf had abruptly cut off all contacts.

dred thousand people attended it. It was actually a moderate number for Karachi, a city of many millions. But what was striking was the discipline of the crowd. It rained buckets during Altaf's speech. Not a person fled the downpour.

A few days later MQM announced a meeting in Hyderabad, a town about a hundred miles from Karachi. In an ostentatious display of solidarity, MQM decided to bus thousands of supporters to the town. The route of the buses passed through a Pathan drug mafia dominated area.[1] Gangster mobs attacked the tail end and stragglers. Several hundred were killed. The organized manner in which the dastardly deed was perpetrated led many to believe that it had been an officially abetted aggression. The Lt General Governor of the province was widely believed to have intimate connections with the underworld. The tragedy proved to be a tremendous boost to MQM fortunes.

Altaf soon grew bigger than life. MQM enjoyed massive support among Mohajirs and funds poured in. By the same token, the "sons of the soil" hated it. In the municipal elections held after Zia died in a plane crash, it swept the polls for the city council in Karachi. The city was transformed into one huge festive, ebullient and harmonious carnival. Total strangers, men and women, boys and girls greeted each other with the novel and secular avant-garde salutation "Long live Mohajir." MQM nominated Dr. Farooq Sattar, a recent medical graduate and member of the minority within the minority, the Gujerati business community, as its candidate for the Mayor's post. He lived in a two-bedroom town house in a modest settlement.

After the council elections I attended a private fundraiser for MQM addressed by Altaf. The host was a former member of the Brahmin class of Pakistan, the coveted Senior Civil Services.[2] Nearly all the hereditary and proletarian Mohajir leaders, the progeny of the founders of the country, were in attendance. Hoping to get nominations to the assemblies, they eulogized Altaf in extravagant terms. Raising his voice to a crescendo, he turned to the veteran power brokers and told them that they had chased power like dogs do a bone and done nothing for Mohajirs. They all clapped their hands rapturously. Even the prospect of power corrupts the soul.

MQM was organized on fascist lines. Altaf's cult of personality rivaled that of Hitler, with a dash of oriental superstition thrown in. His pictures were reported to have materialized in the tiles of the floors of Mosques and inside vegetables. He was frequently called Pir Sahib, a sort of live saint. Questions like where was the Quaid-e-Tahreek (Leader of the movement) born, or what was his mother's

---

1 Afghan refugee-drug dealers dominated the main exit from Karachi to interior Sindh and the rest of Pakistan. Zia had ushered in an era of drugs and arms in Pakistan. The technology of refining opium into Heroin was courtesy of the Soviet Union. Arms were the generosity of the US. The loot was so stupendous, a hereditary Nawab of the NWFP, offered to swap all his holdings and huge estates for the one-month take of the Lt General in charge of the province.

2 The man was dismissed by Zia as he had attended a meeting presided over by the dictator, somewhat the worse for drink.

name, etc. figured prominently in the formal doctrinal examinations held for the rank and file. Everyone who was anyone in Pakistani politics, BB and NS among them, visited Altaf in his tiny townhouse. BB gave him a copy of the Koran. He gave her a Dupatta.[1]

MQM had been given a few ministerial portfolios in Sindh, but were regarded as little more than a nuisance by the bureaucrats, fellow ministers and the governor of the province. They realized too late that PPP had given them oral assurances which they had no intention of honoring. The Mayor of Karachi was made impotent. Sindhi hatred of Mohajirs extended even to the sole Mohajir PPP minister Amir Haider Kazmi.[2]

BB appointed Naseerullah Babar as police minister. He had been indoctrinated in counter insurgency techniques by the best CIA could offer, and was the acknowledged godfather of the Taliban. He dispatched armed personnel to surround localities. A house-to-house search would follow. Young men and some young girls who took the fancy of the marauders would be picked up and taken away to police stations. The boys would be mercilessly beaten in full sight of parents, who would beg for a reprieve. If they could pay an adequate bribe, the victim would be released. Tens of hundreds of young men became victims of extra-judicial killing. Mohajir and Sindhi workers fought a gun battle in the steel mill. The army mediated the conflict. Police surrounded Purana Qila (old Fort), Hyderabad, which housed about half a million Mohajirs and severed the gas, water and electric connections to the area. The siege continued for several days till the COAS General Aslam Beg, a Mohajir himself, sent the army to break the siege.[3]

General Beg threw a party for his daughter's wedding, which in opulence would shame the ones thrown by Caliphs of Baghdad. BB, the President and all power brokers attended. After he retired, Aslam Beg told the Chief Justice (CJ) boldly, nay sneeringly, that yes he had collected and diverted a fabulous amount of money to prop up favorite groups in the elections. The CJ spluttered incoherently but subsided when Beg glared at him.

BB indulged in unprecedented jobbery. All government offices, nationalized industries, businesses and banks had to find a berth for people presenting themselves with a chit, a note from BB or one her senior minions. The person BB had chosen as her husband, Asif Zardari became known as Mr.10% percent,[4]

---

1 Presenting a headscarf to a girl is equivalent to the Hindu Rakhi ceremony of "adopting" a sister.

2 Accompanying BB to a function at a medical college, Sindhis would not let him share the stage with her.

3 The repression continued well into Nawaz Sharif's term.

4 She had been advised that her unmarried status would be a hindrance for her political career. She wanted to marry a Punjabi landowner, but the head of his clan vetoed the match. In a sly reference to the rumors that her father's parents had married only when he was eight or nine, the clan head cast doubts on BB's antecedents. She came across the stepmother of Asif in London who proposed the match and, desperate, she accepted.

after his reported facilitation fee. International press reported that he had commandeered a national airline plane to transport racehorses from Argentina. The couple bought a mansion in Surrey County in England. It boasted a helicopter-pad. He and BB were to be named in money laundering and other such cases in international court.

BB's government was never stable and barely tolerated by the army. A lieutenant general publicly snubbed her during a meeting presided over by her. The President was not a fan. He had nominated BB very reluctantly. NS, the chief minister of the Punjab, another spawn of Zia, was snapping at her heels. Altaf was disgruntled. Minority provinces were restive. MQM left the Government. Opposition parties got together to move a resolution of no confidence in the parliament against BB. She was able to fight it off by the good old method of bribing and purchasing votes. But the President dismissed her and the assembly soon afterwards and ordered new elections. She had served only twenty months of her five-year term.

NS's party won in the elections and he became the PM. MQM were again in the Government, this time with more clout. In the run up to the new elections, Altaf had demonstrated his complete control over the Mohajirs. Altaf had also accompanied the opposition leaders on a tour of Pakistan. He had mesmerized the crowds in the heartland of the Punjab. That gave him ideas. He could rule over the hearts and minds of not just the people of Karachi, but those of Punjabis as well. He changed the name of his party from Mohajir Qaumi movement to Muttahda Qaumi Movement (from the Immigrant National movement to the United National movement). That sealed his fate. The Army created a dissident wing in MQM and supplied them with arms.

This internecine tussle went on through the NS and the following BB tenure. Under BB, Naseerullah Babar sent in the army and tried to destroy the MQM infrastructure. Altaf was spirited out of the country. Armed forces unleashed a reign of terror with the same ferocity they had in East Pakistan. Sindhi–Mohajir riots restarted with a vengeance. There were armed skirmishes. Police looked on; they would not be much good anyway. The partisans were better equipped.

NS's father was a friend of the general who governed Punjab for Zia and had appointed him finance minister in the province. Opponents made fun of him in a fashion rather reminiscent of Khwaja Nazim of yesteryear, suggesting that he consumed a whole tray of yogurt in addition to kebabs, *parathas*, *pulao*, *chargha* and desserts at breakfast. His first tenure was marked by enhanced corruption, this time presided over by his younger brother Shahbaz. They bought four luxury apartments in the poshest of all London localities, Park Lane in the West End. Each apartment was, reportedly, worth £2.5 million (roughly $5 million) at the time.[1] In an effort to promote the family iron works concern, they tried to sabotage the works of the national steel mill.

The loss of precious and scarce foreign exchange was enormous. One of his more outlandish schemes was the duty-free government-financed import of taxis to develop new jobs. Banks were on the verge of bankruptcy. They had no hope of ever recovering all the bad loans. He had tried denationalization, probably in good faith, but the industries and businesses had taken so many loans, their staff had been so bloated and the balance sheets so much in the red, that there were no takers. Conversion of foreign currency deposits to local currency had made expatriate capital shy of the country.[2]

The only enterprises, which had mushroomed after denationalization were private schools and Hospitals. Zulfiqar Bhutto had undermined the state schools in Karachi by requiring them to teach Sindhi to Urdu speakers — without taking measures to provide teachers of the language. Parents took two jobs each and paid for tutoring at teachers' homes. People converted small houses into schools by the simple device of putting up a huge sign with an attractive title like "Advanced Cambridge Academy." Licenses for private schools were available from the education department for a modest bribe and a monthly retainer. The schools would be run by a nominal charitable trust.[3]

Hospitals also became a boom industry. Population had burgeoned. Government hospitals, which provided a very basic level of care, could not cope with the vastly increased numbers. People had gotten more health conscious too. An Inflow of expatriate money gave a tremendous boost to private health care as it did to private schools. As in the case of schools, small, medium and large houses in congested areas in already crowded neighborhood, were converted into hospitals. One such hospital, in a bunch of ramshackle buildings, evolved into a medical college and a while later into a medical university.[4] The owner is now Chancellor of the university. He did have the good grace to build a campus for basic sciences, but the bulk of clinical side is still housed in poorly planned residential homes.

Surprisingly enough, starting a hospital did not require any kind of license, registration or permission from any state agency. One had as great a liberty to allow performance of major surgery as one did to sell groceries. Hospitals sur-

---

1 Nawaz Sharif's brother Shahbaz was later "credited" with receiving a larger share and was dubbed Mr. 25%. Five million US dollars, at the exchange rate of the time, was an astronomical sum for Pakistan. He also indulged in financial shenanigans in the Persian Gulf states. The family developed a huge estate in the Punjab. It had a lake, parks and a full size zoo, with lions, cheetahs, and other exotic animals. They also built a large hospital for family and friends.

2 Post 1998 atomic explosion, Nawaz had converted $1.2 billion in deposits into rupees. It was believed that his cronies had transferred $50 to $100 million prior to the currency "nationalization" announcement.

3 One of my cousins inveigled me into becoming a trustee of the one he had started.

4 A well-known practitioner of oriental medicine, Hakim Said, originally from Delhi, became Sindh governor in Zia's time. He gave a university charter to many institutes including his own Hamdard University and to his friend Dr. Baqai's medical school.

vived on "panels".[1] Another glaring misuse of the system was that patients would wheedle, force or threaten — union officials would employ the latter method — doctors to write prescriptions for expensive medicines and exchange them for cosmetics at drug stores. Physicians and surgeons ran their offices from 5:00–6:00 p.m. to midnight and beyond, and would generally spend 4–5 minutes with each patient. The teaching staff employed by medical schools would spend an hour or two in the school and the attached hospitals. If you add non-existent quality control and no state regulation, there is no limit to avarice. The number of unnecessary surgical procedures was mind-boggling.

Higher education suffered the same fate as medical care did. At the time of independence there were only two medical colleges in West Pakistan, and one in the East wing. By the way of institutes of higher learning, all Pakistan could boast of was the Punjab University in Lahore and University of Karachi in the West and Dhaka University in the then East Pakistan. It had one each of engineering college, teachers training college, agricultural college and dental school on the West, none in the East. In 1962 there were six medical colleges in the West, three in the East and a corresponding number of other colleges/universities. For some curious reason, till the 1980s there was only one dental school in the Western wing. In 1991 there were half a dozen universities and innumerable "professional" colleges in Karachi alone.

The general spread of literacy increased the demand of these exalted houses of scholarship. All kinds of charlatans indulged in the game of opening institutes of "higher" learning. One day a doctor, who had been two years junior to me in the medical school called me and said that he wanted to open a medical college in his 400 square yard[2] hospital and wanted me to co-sign a letter asking for university approval.

Corruption rose to mind boggling heights. Examination halls were sold to entrepreneurs. They would provide answers to questions for a fee. The controller of examinations, in my presence, offered a leading Eye doctor of the town to get any position for his daughter in twelfth grade.

NS wanted to amend the constitution to take away the power of the President to dismiss the Prime Minister and the assembly. That required a two third support for the measure in the assembly. BB could provide that. She declined.[3] The President dismissed NS. NS challenged the dismissal. The Prime Minister and the President issued contradictory orders. The army chief of the staff, General Kakar intervened and forced both to resign and ordained an interim admin-

---

1 Hospitals approved for providing health care to employees of nationalized industries were put on the "panel".
2 It is less than a twelfth of an acre.
3 BB told a journalist that she had done so on Margaret Thatcher's advice that she should let the President and Prime Minister emasculate each other.

istration under an expatriate from the United States. Mid-term elections were arranged.

BB won the new elections and this time secured an overall majority. She had her erstwhile foreign minister Farooq Leghari elected as President. The man, another scion of a feudal family, had served as a junior minister under her father. She treated the man as a family retainer.[1] Jobbery and arbitrary governance reached ever-greater heights. The President warned her in a friendly fashion. She told him to mind his own business. The worm turned. The former retainer sacked her and ordered a new election. The voters were sick of frequent polls. NS could play the role of a victim very well. The public decided to give him a chance. In the ensuing elections in 1997 he won big. He and his minions went about crowing that they had an overwhelming mandate.

The CJ had the temerity to hear cases against the government. NS sent his family attorney to suborn a member of the Supreme Court bench to propose a vote of no confidence in the CJ. When that stratagem did not work, he sent gangsters to man handle the CJ while he was presiding over a trial. A minister in the Punjab provincial government, several members of the assembly and an adviser to the Prime minister, were actually caught on the camera leading the mob. The CJ was eventually hounded out of office. NS had a vote of no confidence passed against the President and filled the slot with the same attorney who had led the campaign for ouster of the CJ.. He had requisite number of votes in the houses of the assembly and was able to remove the offending clause from the constitution, which authorized the President to dismiss the Prime Minister and the assembly. He undeservedly and presumptuously took credit for the successful atomic bomb explosion in 1998.

He was riding high and overreached himself. He appointed Parvez Musharraf to succeed the sacked army chief in the office, under the mistaken belief that being a Mohajir he would not have roots in the army and would do his bidding without question. But the armed forces of Pakistan are a malevolent hydra-headed organism. You cut off one head; another grows in its place and is obeyed implicitly by senior officers. Without so much as by your leave to the Prime Minister, Musharraf attacked Indian positions in Kargil and manufactured a crisis. Standing on high ground, and taking the Indian troops by complete surprise, they were able to kill several hundreds of Indian forces and force them to retreat. NS foolishly chose to take credit for the misadventure.

When the Indian Prime Minister threatened an all out war, NS had to run, with tail between legs, to Washington and beg for US intervention. Clinton made him sit by while he placated Indian Prime Minister Bajpai on phone, and arranged a cease-fire. NS was made to give a pledge to keep his army on a tight

---

1 The hapless man told the press that once BB had asked him to leave his office, as she wanted a private word with her husband.

leash. As a consolation prize he was given a photo op at a family breakfast with the American President. As planned the army cried foul. What our Jawans had won with their blood and Shaheeds had given their life for, was lost by a pusillanimous Prime Minister. A concerted jingoist campaign was launched. But it did not catch the public imagination.

NS wanted to move quickly to replace Musharraf. Musharraf got wind of the impending axe. He consulted with his confidants, and confronted N S. N S is timid. He totally denied any scheme of replacing Musharraf. To placate him further, he gave the army chief additional charge of the head of joint chiefs of service committee.

Musharraf was scheduled to visit Sri Lanka on a good will mission. N S thought that would be a good time to replace him. He had found a general with impeccable antecedents. Like his own family, the man was of Kashmiri descent.[1] But Musharraf had taken precautionary measures. He had retired two Lieutenant Generals, and transferred another two suspected of being in league with the NS to impotent desk jobs. He had also moved loyal officers to key slots, one as deputy chief of army staff and three others as corps commanders of Karachi, Lahore and the capital area.

While Musharraf was on his way back, actually in the air en route to Karachi, NS announced his replacement by the new man on the radio and TV. The new man went to the GHQ to take over. The deputy chief apologized. Tradition dictated that charge be given by the old chief to the new one. In the meanwhile the deputy chief sent troops to surround the Prime Minister house and take over all the tactically important places. N S and the new chief were unceremoniously taken in custody and for good measure the latter was manhandled a bit too. TV and Radio stations were captured, and all programs suspended.

Now unfolds a scenario worthy of another Bollywood thriller. Musharraf's civilian plane was not allowed permission to land in Karachi. The plane was running low on fuel and was directed to an Indian airport not too far across the border. Musharraf said over his dead body. Government ordered the pilot to proceed to an airport further inland. Not enough fuel.

The local corps commander Lieutenant General Usmani was waiting at the Karachi airport to receive his boss. He saw the runway blocked by trucks and got worried. He somehow managed to get in touch with Musharraf's plane and ordered the pilot to keep on circling. In order to get the runway cleared and overpower the air traffic handlers, he needed his soldiers in a hurry. His cantonment was less than a mile away. He could not get hold of a phone, and had to drive to his base and bring his troops back with him. With the help of soldiers, he took over the Air Traffic Control office. His soldiers cleared the runway of the trucks. Musharraf landed with only minutes to spare.

---

1 This is an important consideration in the clan ridden Pakistani society.

This plot has more holes than the proverbial sieve. First, the Air Force has two large runways in Karachi. Both are capable of handling planes of all sizes. In fact, before the runway on the civilian airport was enlarged, big commercial airplanes had to use the facility at one of the bases. Musharraf was chairman of the joint chiefs of staff committee and could legally land his plane there. Second, no Pakistani in his right mind would deny a Lieutenant General the use of a phone. Usmani would inevitably be accompanied by an honor guard to receive the chief and could easily commandeer airport facilities without having to go to his base. Third, Usmani must have known of the appointment of a new chief. He was not a blithering idiot and must have come prepared. In any event, Musharraf landed safely and went into consultation with his fellow conspirators. A few hours later he made a formula speech on the TV and the radio that safety of the country was at stake. It was his duty as an officer and a patriot to protect the nation etc.

Musharraf's coup was in one way distinct from the previous usurpations of authority. Ayub took over when there was a real fear that the country might slide into anarchy. Ayub handed over the government to Yahya illegally and unconstitutionally but law and order situation was again fast deteriorating. Zia took over when the law and order had been subverted by the opposition and foreign agencies. It was left to Musharraf to invent a patently spurious excuse.

## MUSHARRAF OF PAKISTAN

Musharraf appeared to be what the country had been looking for a long time. Sophisticated, well spoken and urbane, he seemed to combine compassion with firmness. The enlightened progressive and educated element was happy that he was secular and invoked the name of Kamal Ata Turk, the founder of modern Turkey. He pledged to put the country on the road to modernization and industrial development. Cases of nepotism, corruption, bribery, fraud and loot of national assets were filed in courts in Pakistan and abroad against the deposed Prime Minister Nawaz Shareef and former Prime Minister Benazir. NS had been arrested at the time of the coup. BB was out of the country but her much more unpopular husband was duly locked up.

But what he faced was in many ways different from what Mustafa Kamal had to contend with in post World War I Turkey. Musharraf had inherited a people disillusioned and at odds with each other. They had seen a highly venal civilian rule in which heads of the government were beholden to the army. They had lived under military rulers who had widened the rich-poor divide (Ayub), lost half the country (Yahya) and Zia who had empowered clerics and promoted ethnic and sectarian conflicts and left a legacy of arms and drugs. They had been let down by that false Messiah Zulfiqar Bhutto, who had given a slogan of Islamic Socialism, but had only reinforced the rule of his feudal class.

Times had changed too. The public was no longer so frightened of the army. The judiciary put a time limit of three years for his rule. At the end of the period he would have to get public endorsement, if he wanted to continue in office and would have to shed his military uniform. Under international pressure he had to let go the Nawaz Shareef clan into a comfortable exile in Saudi Arabia. He easily managed an election. Erstwhile supporters of BB and Nawaz fell over each other to get in line for his favors. The Mohajir party (MQM) was his natural linguistic constituency. They joined hands with anti-BB elements, turncoats and the ever-ready feudals lords to form a government in Sindh. Fundamentalist parties were amenable to a deal that their members would vote for him to remain head of the state and keep his army rank as well.

Musharraf was an international pariah from the day he took over. His fortunes rose with 9/11. Now he could do no wrong. The US was pitted against the Taliban. They needed Musharraf to keep the Inter Services Intelligence of Pakistan (ISI), the creator of Taliban, on a tight leash. Musharraf, however, in a devilishly cunning manner, kept the Mullahs up his sleeve, to be taken out at proper times to reinforce the view that his mentors had no other choice.

Things went on pretty much on the pattern. Musharraf selectively favored certain sections of the power brokers and constantly made and remade alignments. He appointed a Baluch grandee as Prime Minister. The man, in a suitably colonial fashion, addressed him as Sahib. In an obvious attempt to placate the corporate interests, he ditched the Baluch Sirdar for a crony who was conveniently engaged in a mid level position in an American Bank. In order to take the wind out of the sails of the fanatics in the army and to please the overlords, he made peace overtures to India. The measure annoyed the Mullahs to no end, but made them realize that they had made a compact with a cleverer Satan.

Musharraf and his minions brandished the oxy-moronic slogan of enlightened moderation He was all for women's rights and even ordered the local security agencies to register a case against the perpetrators of Punchayat — local village government — ordained gang rape of the now celebrated Mukhtaran Mai. Mukhtaran was invited by a Human rights advocacy group in the US, Asian American Network Against Abuse (AANA) to visit the United States. Musharraf ended up trying to by prevent her from leaving.[1]

Musharraf continued to play a highly adroit balancing act. He kept Washington convinced that he was irreplaceable in the fight against terrorism. Political opponents kept themselves salivating for his favor. He even wrote (ghost written no doubt) — a book and the publisher cleverly arranged the release with an audience with Bush, pushing the ratings sky high. Detractors claimed that it was a move to launder his ill-gotten fortune.

He finally took a misstep, reportedly at the advice of the Prime Minister, and asked the Supreme Court Chief Justice (CJ) to resign. The CJ had blocked the

---

1 The excuse was that the dirty linen of Pakistan should not be washed in public. International opinion forced the government to let her go.

sale of the steel mill at fire sale price[1] and had asked that the "disappeared" be found and presented to the court. The man declined the suggestion. He had most likely sensed the regime's weakness or turned as the proverbial worm. The CJ was kept incommunicado for several hours, and finally sent home, allegedly manhandled in the process, to a virtual house arrest. Cases of his "corruption, nepotism and unfair use of prerogatives of office" were referred to the supreme judicial council[2] and he was "dysfunctionalized," whatever that meant. Uncharacteristically the attorneys went up in arms. The public and students disgusted and disillusioned as they were with the antics of power brokers, wished pox on all houses. Attorneys had however shown unusual staying power and continued to boycott court proceedings.

In the meanwhile some mullahs, in reenactment of the worst excesses of the Taliban regime in Afghanistan, "persuaded" a video shopkeeper to light a huge bonfire of his stock. The presiding mullah announced the formation of a Shariah court and threatened the very "Islamic" suicide bombings if the government dared to thwart his wishes. The prelude to all this resurgence was that women from a seminary in the capital city had "captured" a library, abducted the keeper of an alleged house of pleasure, overpowered and made hostage of the security agents sent to rescue the woman, all under Musharraf's enlightened nose in Islamabad.

After a lot of maneuvering and a vigorous public campaign the judicial council reinstated the CJ. A spate of anti-government decisions followed, including the release of several alleged terrorists. The brewing insurgency on the Pakistan-Afghan border tribal areas exploded. Musharraf had ordained that the outgoing assemblies would vote for presidential candidates for the next five years. Petitions were filed in the SC that outgoing assemblies not be allowed to elect the future President and that as the general held an office of profit, he be declared ineligible. The SC allowed the election to proceed, but in an extreme oxymoronic fashion ordered that the name of the successful candidate not be officially announced. Musharraf, of course, got all but two votes. The SC continued to delay a decision on his status.

The government had in the meanwhile allowed BB[3] to return and had issued an ordinance under which after all cases of corruption registered before Mush-

---

1 The Prime Minister, previously an employee of CitiGroup, was most likely a global capital implant and would not take blockage of the sale lightly.

2 The CJ was suspended on March 9, 2007 and the case referred to the supreme judicial council, a constitution ordained body, which at the referral of the head of the state, sits in judgment on senior judiciary. The man next in line Bhagwan Das a Hindu by faith was out of the country. The third man in line was hastily flown in from Karachi and sworn in as acting CJ.

3 Musharraf had been grievously weakened by the intemperate actions against the CJ and imposition of emergency rule on November 3, 2007, when he dismissed 63 members of the senior Judiciary. The United States, for their own strategic reasons, dispatched BB to prop him up, ostensibly on the rather shaky grounds that Musharraf was the best person to deal with "terrorists".

arraf had taken over in 1999 would be withdrawn. A huge crowd and a suicide bomber greeted BB.[1]

Rumors were rife that the SC was about to hand down a decision against Musharraf. SC judges pompously declared that they would no longer allow themselves to be coerced by the government. The CJ was reported to have told a friend that seven judges would decide against the general and three for him.[2] Musharraf apparently unable to bear the suspense declared a state of emergency, placed the dissenting SC judges under house arrest, suspended the constitution,[3] issued a provisional constitutional order and reconstituted the SC with persons of his choice.

An avalanche of protests by lawyers and political workers and an international uproar followed. The government put hundreds in jail. BB hastened back from Dubai[4] and made an abortive attempt to hold a protest meeting. The general climbed down a bit and once again made a pledge to hold elections and doff his uniform if the SC allowed his election to stand.[5]

---

1 The government claimed that a few of the released persons had been responsible for suicide bomb-ings on military personnel in which scores of lives were lost.

2 His phone was tapped.

3 The Pakistan constitution must hold a record for the number of times it has been suspended.

4 Nawaz had made an attempt to return earlier but was unceremoniously sent back to Saudi Arabia. Musharraf allowed him back at the intervention of the Saudi king, or more likely as a counter-poise to BB.

5 BB was assassinated by a suicide bomber. Scotland Yard detectives, asked to give an independent report, agreed with government security agencies that she died due to head injury as a result of aftershock of a bomb blast. Her husband Zardari inherited the mantle per her will. Such is the hold of the feudal system on the country that political parties become part of inheritance. Elections postponed from January 08, 2008 to February 18, 08 due to the assassination, produced a divided house. Zardari and Nawaz could not agree on restoration of the judiciary, the core of the platform they had contested the elections on, giving Musharraf another lease of life. They eventually agreed to impeach Musharraf.

---

## Chapter 14. America the Beautiful

When I arrived in the country in 1974, the United States of America was friendlier to immigrants and diverse ethnicities than any other country I have lived and worked in. I had also discussed the working conditions with friends in countries as diverse as Saudi Arabia, Iran, Nigeria, France, Holland and Germany. They all discriminated to various degrees against foreigners, minorities and new immigrants.

The US was entirely different. I was offered a senior position in a good hospital on the basis of my British qualification. I was made to feel at home in Brooklyn, was invited to homes of my co-workers, encouraged to develop a private practice and assisted in many other ways. I also came across several physicians of sub-continental origin in positions of authority in my hospital and other hospitals in the area. Immigrants from the subcontinent counted business tycoons, corporate heads, banking chiefs, partners in investment firms, members of think tanks and elected officials among their ranks.

By the waning years of the twentieth century, Muslims had made great political headway in the United States. Expatriates and local followers of the faith had united on a broad based platform and played a great part in raising public consciousness about the faith. Interfaith dialogue had become fashionable. They generously contributed to electoral campaigns. Organizations like the Council on American Islamic Relations and American Muslim Alliance earned public recognition and the former had access to the White House. Muslim haters like former congressman Suarez and a senator from South Dakota, lost re-election races largely due the work of Muslim activists, not the least among them the cabbies in New York City, who transported voters to election booths to vote against Suarez. A US senate candidate refused to accept a platform presented to him in New Jersey. A corps of volunteers manned the phones for seventy-two hours non-stop. The man lost.

US society is rather insular, though post 9/11 their perception of the outside world has undergone a change. Pre 9/11, an average person had little knowledge of anything outside his/her own region. New York City was as foreign to someone from the Midwest as to a person from Nagpur, India. The reasons for that lie outside the scope of this book.

The US has been ascendant since World War I and may only now be beginning to grow out of its resplendent (and reckless) imperial youth. It has gone to war in the Middle East twice in less than two decades. It has failed to realize that social and political awakening follow acts of both group and state terrorism.[1]

The illusions of invulnerability and invincibility, and for many, trust in their government, were shattered by 9/11. Rumors abounded about who did it, who knew, and who should have done what to prevent it.

After the disbelief, terror and numbness had worn off, unprecedented outrage took over in the United States. Every foreign-looking person was a suspect. The general line given was that this crime had been committed by a band of men under the leadership of a Saudi Osama bin Laden.

Muslim women with the traditional *hijab*[2] were harassed. Government agencies put out incomplete and misleading information that did nothing to underscore the fact that all Arabs/Muslims/brown people were not the same. George W Bush made an irresponsible remark about a "crusade"[3] against terror. A Sikh was killed because he had a long beard and a turban — like Osama bin Laden's. People of all shades of complexion between white and black were targeted.

Facts that were glossed over include the point that those named as the hijackers had been beneficiaries of the Saudis, who not too long ago were funding 22,000 religious seminaries in Pakistan, and the Saudi ruling family was as close to the American establishment as could be and acted as their surrogates in the region. There were links with US security agencies that had been trained fighters to oppose the Russian occupation of Afghanistan. Also ignored was the fact that the US government was supporting Israel in perpetrating a reign of terror on the Palestinians. Gross injustice breeds terrorism.

The US fanned the panic by cracking down on everyone: friends, foes, and its own citizens. All air space and harbors were closed.[4] The whole Western world was shocked. Someone had hit the two main citadels of US hegemony — the World Trade Center and the Pentagon. The US gathered a huge harvest of sym-

---

1 Terrorism is the war of the poor; war is the terrorism of the rich — Peter Ustinov.

2 Hijab, the head covering, was originally ordained for wives of the prophet so that other men would not pester them.

3 The word, referring to the massacre of Muslims in Jerusalem in one of the crusades, has historic anti-Muslim connotations.

4 But members of the Bin Laden clan, business partners and benefactors of the Bush family, were whisked out on secret flights.

pathy and the voters were happy thenceforth to approve any curb on their liberties in the name of fending off another such disaster. Bush gave an ultimatum to Afghanistan to hand over Osama Bin Laden and sent a belligerent notice to Musharraf: "You are with us or against us" (never mind that his first responsibility was the integrity of the Pakistani nation).

The Taliban rebuffed the ultimatum. Osama's forces were strong and he was an icon. Americans went into Afghanistan with great hubris and in the first round made short work of any organized resistance. But they did not get Osama.

It would all have been well, if the US had left it well enough alone. But apparently this was just one move in what was intended as a larger campaign. The Bush league now set out to pulverize what they painted as Islamo-fascists everywhere. It is curious that they chose to begin in the officially secular state of Iraq. Lies that Iraq had WMDs were invented, convincing the public that there were grounds for an attack. The Democratic Party, perhaps scared of being accused lack of patriotic fervor, fell in line. The US defense budget at $451 billion already exceeded the combined defense spending of the rest of the world.[1] More funds were allocated.

It was taken as a given that Iraqis would turn to America as a savior, and out of gratitude hand over the oil wells to US-dominated multi-national corporations (MNCs), elect a "democratic" government with a prime minister in the image of Tony Blair, and all would be well. Spinmeisters even staged the ecstatic scenes of Saddam's statue being toppled. There was apparently not much discussion of an exit strategy; perhaps there was no intention of exiting at all. Within the United States, all kinds of illegal and unconstitutional acts have been perpetrated under the blanket cover of national security.

The congress passed the draconian USA Patriot Act, which gave law enforcement agencies great leeway.[2] Legal Muslim charitable organizations sent money to the destitute in Middle East and South Asia, as Oxfam and others did to South America; but now the former were targeted, harassed and intimidated. Their leaders were often arrested and held without bail. People became shy to contribute to humane causes lest their motives be misconstrued.

Bush captured the White House for a second term. Iraq continued to spiral out of control. The US applied techniques perfected in Central and North America. They are funding, training and supplying arms to Iraqi equivalents of the Contra in Nicaragua with similar results — mass murders, kidnappings, torture, rape and mass displacement of population internally and out of the country, but on a far larger scale. About a million Iraqis had been killed by the end of 2007. Over three million in external and two million in internal exile had been rendered homeless. Altogether about a quarter of the country's population was affected. In

---

1 The nearest rivals are Russia at $65 billion and China $56 billion a year.
2 A mini 9/11, the event of 7/7 in the UK, gave an excuse to the neo-con government of Tony Blair to persuade British parliament to pass draconian anti-immigrant laws.

order to distract attention from the gaps between rhetoric and reality in Iraq, and the failure to achieve the apparent goals, debates were raised over the "need" to attack Iran on the totally spurious grounds that the country is developing atomic weapons — this in spite of repeated declarations of International Atomic Energy Agency that they had been unable to find any evidence to the effect.[1]

Successive US governments had used Al-Qaida, Taliban, and Saddam Hussein as surrogates to secure US interests. It made pragmatic sense, we were told. But no one likes being ditched after having been used. Thugs require aftercare. US government agencies failed to provide that.

The late aftermath of 9/11 was even worse for non-white foreigners. Smarting from their monumental failure, the security agencies went after the most vulnerable among the foreigners, hundreds of thousands of people who had overstayed their visas, etc., and were running grocery stores, cabs, restaurants, and doing other odd jobs. They were rounded up wholesale and held incommunicado. Families in many cases had no knowledge of the whereabouts of loved ones for weeks, even months. One of my friends, Sibghat U. Kadri, a barrister on the Queen's Counsel[2] no less, was interrogated on arrival at Chicago's O'Hare Airport and quizzed on an anti-Musharraf speech he had given. Criticizing satraps was also terrorism!

The quality of life of all South Asians and others has been badly affected. The image of the United States has been tarnished and it is highly debatable if security has been enhanced. Now some second-generation South Asian students in the US contemplate a future career in Canada, Europe or South Asia. And whereas very few first-generation immigrants used to plan to return to their native land, now most of them are giving serious thought to the matter. We might have to face the prospect of a reverse brain drain. The trend is conspicuous among doctors from Pakistan. After passing the requisite tests to qualify for a training program in this country, fully one third are denied visas. The usual excuse is that the Homeland Security Department has denied clearance.

Physicians working in the US on different kinds of visas accept appointment in remote, poor and under-served areas under an assurance that their status will be adjusted. They have been ordered to report to INS offices all over the country for "validation of visa," then were interrogated and harassed. They have been interviewed in a room next door to a hall with a prominent sign, "detention cell." A physician driving back to New York City from Florida stopped at a restaurant on the way. The waitress was not happy with the tip. She called the FBI and said that he looked like a terrorist. The man was picked up and held without the benefit of legal counsel for two weeks. His wife happened to know an attorney

---

1 Alan Greenspan, long serving Chairman of the Federal Reserve Bank, wrote in his post retirement autobiography that oil was the reason all along.
2 Highly regarded barristers are appointed to the rank. Only they are allowed to appear before the judiciary committee of the House of Lords, the British equivalent of the US Supreme Court.

who had been a public prosecutor. He pulled strings and got the doctor out of jail. Meanwhile one of the doctor's patients, who had been admitted in a hospital, sued him for abandonment.

An Oxford University student (of Indian origin) and his English girlfriend boarded a plane in London to attend a music festival in New York. The check-in clerk told her supervisor that the man looked like a terrorist. The Canadian and US governments were immediately warned. It was panic. Canadian air force planes escorted the flight to the US border where US F16 fighters took over and accompanied the airliner to JFK. Both passengers were arrested and kept in jail for three days.

Crossing the border from Canada used to be a breeze. Now visitors are stopped at random. My van was once checked for radiation and we were made to wait for a long time. Driving back on my next visit, I told the immigration agent that I had bought a bottle of whisky. He waved me on without a question. Alcohol had conferred good citizen status on me!

People who bore grudges reported on neighbors they did not like. One house in Pittsburgh was raided because a neighbor has seen the woman of the house putting something suspicious in the garbage can. They had exchanged harsh words a few months ago. The suspicious material turned out to be spoiled beef curry.

The Economy suffered. Whole neighborhoods were rendered desolate. To cite one example out of score of hundreds, numerous shops were shuttered and whole blocks of apartment buildings abandoned in Coney Island Avenue, Brooklyn, New York. None of these people supported terrorism. Airlines are going bankrupt, as people are scared of visiting the US. I know of several businessmen who were grilled because they had offices in South Asia and had to, of necessity, transfer funds overseas for employees' salaries and other expenses. Their clients panicked and the businesses failed, adding to unemployment.

Though the initial panic has subsided, conditions remain uncertain. Random harassment continues. The ill-considered and imprudent military adventure in Iraq has enhanced the sense of insecurity. Saddam was a brutal, fiendish and unregenerate tyrant. His removal was an undoubted act of humanity. But perpetuation of occupation is an unmitigated disaster. Measures to reduce US troop casualties inevitably lead to increased Iraqi civilian deaths and injuries. Private security forces have run amuck. They and fundamentalist cohorts react in kind. . Afghanistan is an exact parallel. Afghans are veterans of innumerable resistance movements. They humiliated Russians at the height of their power and the British when the sun never set over the Empire.

Immigrants always carry a baggage of norms, mores, traditions and customs from the old country. I have used the term "baggage" advisedly, and not in any derisory sense. It is a heavy load that they carry and it keeps them from moving ahead. The burden of racial, linguistic and religious differences can be even heavier. They might be vegetarians, *halal* meat eaters or observe other food restrictions. By and large they were comparatively sexually conservative. Their culture and religion may discriminate against women.[1]

For many, their home environment was post-colonial, feudal or tribal. They were caste- and sect-ridden. Only India had representative government, which was substantially marred by covert and lately overt mistreatment of Muslims and untouchables. Because of the baggage the first generation of all immigrants tend to ghettoize. That alienates them further from the locals. The second generation rebels against tradition and tries to assimilate. They are often thwarted in their longings. Insecurity breeds intolerance and fundamentalism widens the divide more.

Muslims specially do not assimilate easily. They do not drink and are not very tolerant of others faiths. They insist that women wear *hijab*, so hoodlums have no problem identifying them. This is reminiscent of Nazi fascists who forced Jews to wear the Star of David.[2] Charging or paying financial interest is proscribed in their dogma. They are forced to rationalize in order to get by in the Western world: mortgages involve interest so they stoop to such subterfuges as getting a loan which included a "mark up" calculated on what would been interest plus loan. Others keep the money under the mattress and get into trouble when they offer thousands of dollars in cash when buying a car. Saudis invest in interest-bearing accounts in the United States. Their women wear dresses from the most expensive boutiques under the traditional dress and take off the outer covering as soon they land at a Western airport. Saudi princes import liquor in boxes declared as furniture.[3]

South Asian immigrants were, by and large, educated and brought much needed skills in medicine, engineering and trade. They were welcomed and made much of in early years. They worked hard and distinguished themselves in the medical, financial and commercial fields. In the beginning they were far too few in numbers to congregate in ghettoes which were to mushroom in New York, New Jersey, Pennsylvania, Illinois and many other states. But with success came

---

1 Even in the comparatively enlightened versions of the Islamic faith, women have half a vote as witness in a court of law, half as much inheritance as male siblings and if a person has only female children the share that would have gone to a male child goes to a male cousin. A woman may be divorced by a simple device of the husband saying so three times.

2 A stark example of conditioning is that some European Jews took to exhibiting the sign of David with ostentation and as a right rather than as a symbol of victimization.

3 A newspaper reported that a prince arrived from Europe and declared that the wooden crates he had brought contained furniture. One crate crashed. Whisky started pouring out. The customs man called the palace to report, "Your Highness, your furniture is leaking." Amy Chua, a professor at Yale Law School in her book *World on Fire* contends that if "democracy" were to be introduced in the Mid East, fundamentalists and others who fail to admire the US, globalization and free markets, would easily defeat Hosni Mubarak and other rulers in the region.

jealousy on the part of the natives. Some South Asian students in university campuses are routinely called new colonizers by black youth.

South Asians can help avoid some of the misunderstandings by being circumspect — but honest — in discussions. To the extent they may have a different perspective on events, they can try to base such discussions on rational information instead of what may be termed instinct and conviction, that is, "gut" reactions and emotion. They can bring some knowledge of history and geography to the discussion while impressing upon all that they are as loyal to the country as the progeny of those who migrated a few generations before them. They should participate in civic affairs, shun and deplore extremist views vehemently, and counsel people with nefarious views to either shape up or ship out. There is little merit in ostentatious exhibition of such social customs as the *hijab*. They should also try to grow out of deliberate ghettoization of their communities. They must above all learn to separate religion from politics.

Muslims should also keep in mind that the US is still a more open and tolerant society than many in South Asia or Middle East, Europe and other continents. Incidents much less earth shattering than 9/11 have led to the annihilation of suspect communities — in Iran in 1953, Indonesia in 1965, the then East Pakistan in 1971, Karachi and Jordan in the 1980s, the Syrian town Hammas in 1986, Bosnia in the early 1990s, Gujarat in India in 2001. The list is endless. Ethnic cleansing is endemic in Israel, India, Pakistan, several African countries and sporadically elsewhere. And history suggests that events that set off such reaction sometimes turn out to be complicated affairs, involving provocateurs and false-flag operations intended to enflame a relatively stable situation.

CHAPTER 15. UK 2001–2002

HEALTH CARE AND SOCIAL CONDITIONS COMPARED WITH 1965–1972

I decided to explore the possibility of doing temporary work in the UK. I contacted several employment agencies and was soon inundated with offers. I eventually accepted a Locum Consultant position in a town called South Shields near Newcastle in the north of England. There was actually not much work[1] to do. Except for the department head who was from an African country, the other four consultants were from India. It was a drab town with derelict housing, high crime and drug addiction rates and rampant alcoholism. After several weeks I decided to take a break and returned to Bath, New York.

My next locum was in Glasgow in Scotland. I had to work in two hospitals about twenty miles from each other and conduct clinics in villages around, one in a sea resort seventy miles away. The roads went through valleys and hills. It was very picturesque in the summer and dismally bleak in the winter. For the amount of work I did the pay was good.[2] Scottish people are very friendly. I did have a problem understanding their accent. They do drink a lot in the country. Once during a clinical conference I made a remark on the signs of advanced loss of calcium on an x-ray of a relatively young patient. One of my colleagues said it was alcoholic osteoporosis.

I had come across an advertisement in the British Medical Journal that examiners for disability determination were urgently needed. This was right up

---

1 Doctors in the UK work on the average 25 to 30 hours a week. In the US they put in more than twice as many hours.

2 I was paid the equivalent of about $ 19,500 per month in the US. I had no office, insurance or malpractice expenses.

my alley, or so I thought at the time. I made an appointment with the director of the service. She was very impressed by the fact that I had performed IMEs[1] in the United States. The business of disability examinations had been outsourced to an American firm. She apologized that I would have to undergo didactic and on-hands training and gave me dates for the next course of lectures.

My fellow trainees in the course belonged to the fields of family practice, psychiatry and rehabilitation medicine. I was the lone orthopedic surgeon. During the lectures I was to discover that I would be expected not only to assess the claimant for physical deficits, but also examine all other body systems. I told the instructors that I had had no exposure to internal medicine or psychiatry at all. They told me not to worry. I would only have to report my findings according to a book of guidelines. A lay adjustor who had no clinical background, training or knowledge would determine the level of disability.[2]

Disability determination work exposed me to deterioration of social services and decline of living standards in the country much more than hospital work had done. The contrast to the conditions in the 1960s could not be greater. Gone were the social support systems which helped the unemployed and the sick live in a fair degree of comfort. They offered an incentive to work hard at rehabilitation. Now people lived in squalor and had lost self-respect.

In 2001, I was to discover many radical changes in the health service. In my training days the consultant (service chief in American parlance) had his own unit — hospital beds, nursing and trainee staff, and compliant operating room staff. No one dared admit a patient on his ward without his specific say so. No one dared protest that the surgical list had exceeded the allotted time. Now administrators could cancel a surgeon's operating list or admit a patient in his ward without his permission. Routine surgery stopped at 4:30 p.m. As the cut-off time approached, nurses would openly ask that cases be postponed to the next list.

The whole ambience has changed. The trust between patients and doctors, which both used to take pride in, was a thing of the past. Patients would often make a complaint to their member of the Parliament against their doctor or the hospital. Malpractice suits, nearly unheard of during my earlier service in the country, had become fairly common, though still far behind the rate in the US.

Waiting lists were horrendously long.[3] The waiting period used to be longer before the Parliament mandated a few years before 2001 that it had to be kept less than twelve months. They did not work the hours my consultants used to. General practitioners used to take their own emergency calls in rotation with their partners. Not now, come 6:00 p.m. calls were transferred to an emergency

---

1 Independent medical examination referred to in the chapter on Health Services in North America.

2 Hiring specialists in every field would have cost a lot more. They had to do it the US. In the less litigious UK society they could get away with it, so they did.

3 If a patient required a joint replacement, surgeons would literally wash the joint of debris and inject cortisone. This was unheard of in the US.

service, as would all the calls from 6:00 p.m. Friday to 8:00 a.m. on Monday. New regulation did provide welcome relief to junior staff who had their hours of work fixed to forty four hours a week, so that they would get one and a half day off every week, an unheard of luxury in my training days.

The deterioration was the direct result of the cost cutting, euphemistically called re-structuring, initiated by Margaret Thatcher as a part of her campaign to whittle away at social services.[1] The health service was starved of funds, partitioned into regions, and the heads of the regions were penalized if they could not scale their budgets down. The pattern was much like that of HMOs in the United States. Family practitioners in the UK could haggle with hospitals on the cost of hospitalization. Many in metropolitan areas resorted to such outlandish schemes as busing their patients to distant hospitals. Drugs were no longer free. American-style health insurance and private clinical care, virtually unknown outside of London where it was based essentially on rich Arabs, became a favored choice for those who could afford it. Doctors left the country in droves. The service had to pay more to temporary employees than they did to regular employees. Employment agencies took a hefty cut. Health care cost actually went up.

Social-economic conditions in the UK were very different in the 1960s and 1970s from what I found in 2001-2002. The Labor party had inducted a welfare state in post World War II years. Conservatives had ruled from 1951 to 1964 and had tried to dismantle the system but had only been able to nibble at the edges. Free market absolutism was only a gleam in the eyes of Margaret Thatcher.[2]

In 1965 health care was the best in the world and free. Medications were free too, till 1969 when a small charge was levied. The service included home visits by nurses for the chronically sick, post-operative cases and new babies. Physical therapists would call on patients for supervised exercises at their homes. Access to family physicians was easy. They took care of all routine problems and performed uncomplicated deliveries at home as well. Appointments with hospital-based specialists did not take too long either. The service attracted a lot of foreign doctors who formed the backbone of National Health. Most of them returned home after higher training. New ones replaced them.

In the field of orthopedic surgery in which I had direct experience, the UK was far ahead of the United States. Total joint replacements had been developed in Britain in the late fifties. The procedure was not to be commonly practiced in the larger centers in the US till late seventies. When I moved to Bath in 1980, I was the first to perform the procedures in the area. British surgeons took much less time to perform surgery than their counterparts in the US did. Anesthesia and turnover time between one surgery and the one following was also much

---

1 Margaret Thatcher went at the welfare state with hammer and tongs as it were, and badgered trade unions to submission.
2 She had, as the minister of education under Prime Minister Edward Heath, tried to withdraw state supply of milk in schools and was derided as Margaret Thatcher the "Milk Snatcher."

less. Unlike the US, there was not much to choose between a surgeon in a large metropolitan area and the one in a remote region.[1] My colleagues who moved to the US after working in the UK told me of experiences in their fields. They agreed with me that their specialty too was more advanced in the UK.

Percentage of jobless people, except in mining areas in Wales, Scotland and North Country was not higher than that in countries in comparable stage of development. Unemployment and disability benefits were quite adequate. Recipients of state aid were interviewed in privacy and social service workers visited homes of the sick. The Government provided incentives for vocational training and loans to start small businesses. Low cost housing was provided as a matter of right and not as charity. Old people's homes were managed by the state. There was surprisingly little abuse of the system.[2]

Salaries were low, but the cost of living was low too. Fish and chips were just over two shillings.[3] An average worker could have three meals a day, visit the pub on the weekends, buy a small house and afford a small car. In 1961 one of my friends bought a three-storey house in Balham in London for three thousand pounds. Now it would cost half a million. I worked as a GP in a working class neighborhood in London and made house calls. Homes were generally neat. They, however, did not have central heating or running hot water. Toilets were outside the living area, hence the term out-house

Race relations were generally amicable except in working class neighborhoods. The immigrants had come with a view to save as much as possible. They earned a bad name for slum living.[4] But the most important reason for bitter hatred that the working class bore to people of color was that the latter took the jobs away, worked all kinds of hours at low wages and obeyed orders unquestioningly.

Due to the early preponderance of Pakistanis among the immigrant workers all brown people came to be called Paki, and the act of harassing them was designated Paki bashing. The hoodlums who beat them up shaved their heads and were called skinheads. The predators concentrated on poorer neighborhoods in London, Birmingham and Bradford. Racial prejudice at a more subtle level was more in the nature of patronization. One fellow physician told me that he would not mind his sister marrying me, but would strongly object to her hitching up with an average Pakistani. I told him that I would not wish to put my children at a disadvantage.

Four years into Blair's time things had changed. Education to all levels had been free. Admission to famed institutions like Oxford and Cambridge was merit

---

1 Level of skills and expertise of physicians varies enormously between villages and cities in the US

2 Productivity depends a great deal on the care given to employees. Japanese run industries have much higher efficiency levels than the firms managed by white Americans.

3 Prices have sky rocketed. My friend took me out for lunch. The bill was over sixty pounds ($120). We had not consumed caviar and Champagne.

4 To save money to send home they would live twelve in a room, four at a time for eight-hour shifts.

based. Scholarships and grants from local, county and government agencies were plentiful. Books were of course free. Now College and University students paid two thousand pounds a year in England and Wales. Scotland had not started charging a fee. Books had to be purchased. Grants for living expenses were a remote memory.

The cost of living had gone sky high. Food was so expensive that a person on an average salary was hard put to feed a wife and two children. One job was difficult enough to get so they could not hope to find another. Even small houses in lowbrow areas were beyond the reach of the average person. Petrol was equivalent of $5.00 a gallon when it was under $1.00 in the United States. Eating out was a luxury beyond all but the very well heeled.

I had been used to walking around in London up to all hours of night in all kinds of areas. Soon after arrival my friends warned me that it was not the England of old days. Gangs, opportunistic marauders, drug dealers, racists and all kinds of unsocial elements were rampant. Police used to carry only a short stick. Now, in their armor, they would be the envy of a Chicago cop.

Race relations, directly related as they are to economic circumstances, were much worse. Some of the worst riots in the country happened in 2001. Bradford and other areas in the north were the worst hit. Among the expatriate population, Muslims were the worst affected by the neo-liberal foreign policy. Blair's wholehearted support for Bush in his Iraq misadventure, in spite of the overwhelming opposition of British voters, had spawned extremist groups. On a trip from Karachi to London I met a group of frustrated young college students. There was little prospect of a job after college. Change in the government meant little. The Conservative Party would follow the same policy. Most young people did not believe in terrorism but they felt that the July 7 train bombers were driven to it. No one gives up life voluntarily and happily.

Color prejudice had crept into health service too. I prescribed an injection for a South Asian patient. The pharmacist said that it was very expensive and not available. The next day I wrote a prescription for the same injection for a white person. She came back with it. I called the pharmacist; he denied that he had told me that the drug was unavailable. It must have been an assistant.

Poor had become poorer. Indian curry had overtaken all British dishes in popularity, but not because the natives have suddenly taken to spicy food. It was cheaper. I visited slums in the outskirts of many big cities. I could compare them favorably, in piles of garbage and stench, with the poorer sections of Karachi. The working class was fast regressing to a nineteenth-century level of wretchedness. They felt hopeless. Even card-carrying communists were not sanguine. Conditions would have to get much worse before the proletariat regained militancy.

The rich had become richer. You could not get a reservation in even a moderately fashionable restaurant or in the theatre for weeks. London was awash with Rolls Royces, Bentleys, Aston Martins, Jaguars, BMWs and Mercedes. Real estate in moderately good areas had gone beyond the reach of all but the very affluent. Business was booming. So were mental illness and the charm of messianic teaching.

# Chapter 16. Colonization to Globalization

## A Review of Metamorphosis

When I returned to upstate New York in 1991, I was struck by the change eight years had wrought on the economy of the region. Never very affluent, conditions could now be compared to those of post World War II England. Among the major employers, the Singer factory and Westinghouse had closed down. Taylor Wine, bought by Coca Cola, had moved away and Corning Inc. (formerly Corning Glassworks) had outsourced most of its work.[1] Agriculture, never very profitable, provided bare sustenance to farmers.

Unemployment was at an all time high. Too many homes were being foreclosed and more were on sale. People could not afford medicine. Blissfully unaware that 46 million Americans did not have health insurance and twice that number had inadequate coverage (leading to bankruptcies[2] in the event of prolonged illness), most people believed that they had the best health service in the world. Inexpensive education meant little to them as few wanted to go to college. The nearly unanimous opinion was that higher taxes were bad and people on welfare and the unemployed were wicked. They voted for the lesser Bush[3] in 2004 again because emotional issues like abortion were brought in to distract from er-

---

1 On the average two million jobs have been lost every year to outsourcing since early 1990s.
Five global corporations own ninety percent of "main stream" media. If a journalist, however prominent, dares to publish "deviant" views he/she is instantly fired.
2 Outstanding medical bills are the leading cause of personal bankruptcy in the US. The sub-prime mortgage crisis in late 2007 and 2008 has sent the number of foreclosures to an unacceptable high. This is a reflection of the way corporations exploit ordinary citizens. President George W. Bush blamed people for buying homes they could not afford.
3 I owe this term to Arundhata Roy. Please refer to her book, *An Ordinary Person's Guide to Empire.*

rors in economic and international policy. They would not accept that economic globalization was the main reason for their parlous state.

Globalization is a continuation of capitalist development. Capitalism is 400 years old and uneven development is inherent in it. Capitalism created uneven spaces within neo-colonies, so that the latter would serve as a market for its products. Using the religion of consumerism, capitalism also divides the minds of the people. Control over media helps it achieve global cultural uniformity.

Between 1757 and 1822, 5–6% of GDP of India was siphoned off.[1] Previously an exporter, India became an importer of British cotton as the British destroyed the indigenous industries of India by controlling production of raw material. Land revenue patterns along with de-industrialization created a semi-feudal society.

From the mid-nineteenth century the colonists started building railways, irrigation works and ports and developed mines, tea plantations and the jute industry. Between 1850s and 1918 India had a deficit with Britain and a surplus in trade with the rest of the world, which the latter used to balance their deficit with US and Europe.[2]

The term globalization encompasses trans-nationalization of information, culture, language, immigrants, feminist and Human Rights movements as well as exploitation of the working class, but when used without further qualifications it is meant to indicate the economic aspect of the integration of human society. It means that global corporations are no longer bound by territory under the respective government's nominal control.

The nineteenth century saw the rise of nationalism. People looked up to leaders of their own race in the fond hope that the latter would treat them fairly. Foreign rulers were branded as usurpers who exploited their natural resources for the benefit of their own people back home. The perception was true; the middle class in the UK lived better than the rich in India. Falling on their knees at the sight of an Indian Raja was fate. To bow to an Englishman was not.

With the demise of Soviet Union the floodgates of neo-colonialism were opened. The Indian governments, irrespective of the party in power, sold out forests, crops, patents, and water and built dams. At one point Indians could not grow ginger and turmeric or use their extract as medicine without paying royalty to patent holder, which, of course was a global corporation. Small farmers were forced out of their hearth and home. Quoting Jag Mohan, Union Minister in India 2006, India has the largest number of poor, illiterate and the undernourished in the world. Over 250 million of its people go to bed hungry. Out of 150 million children in the world who do not go to school, 130 are Indian. 640 million do not have access to sanitation, 170 million to safe water and 293 million to health services. From 1998 to 2003 one hundred thousand farmers committed suicide.

---

1 Bagchi, 1982.
2 Ibid.

Compared to China, India has 300 million under the poverty line to China's 30 million.

Capitalism has changed its essential character. National capitalists used to install manufactories and industrial plants in their own countries, loot the raw material from actual or virtual colonies and push the end product into captive markets. Industry and commerce in the West, US included, developed on this basis. Skilled and unskilled workers in the home country had to be employed and paid minimum wages. With empowerment of the workers, especially with the advent of communist rule in Russia, unionization of labor took rapid strides. Workers demanded and got living wages.

Then capitalists hit the jackpot. Jobs could be outsourced. Their virtual slaves in the legislatures, committed to serving their interests, reduced tariffs on imports.

Global corporations have industrial plants everywhere — in South Korea, India, Far Eastern countries, Latin America and China. Training local labor, logistics of the operation, and sending out operatives from mainland US (who may be obliged to travel abroad frequently or join unemployment lines) was cheaper than paying decent wage to workers at home.

But the most effective ploy has been purchase of the news media. All the mainstream TV channels, radio channels, newspapers are owned by global corporations and publish and broadcast news according to a well-defined program. They color events and slant the report in such a way that black seems white and white black. This is euphemistically called manufacturing consent. People believe whatever is repeated again and again. True, there is an independent media. But an average American has only heard vaguely of Free speech or Link TV or Pacifica Radio. Sometimes demonstrations are organized against world trade conferences. But the coverage they get is scant and industry leaders have taken to choosing obscure cities to meet in.

They have had remarkable success. A majority of people still believes that Saddam had weapons of mass destruction, that he played a leading role in 9/11 or that he had close links with Al-Qaida. They have never been told that he had been a key ally of the West for a long time or that US ambassador April Glaspie gave him a go ahead to invade Kuwait. They have not been told that Osama bin Laden was a full partner of the US government in the fight against the USSR's occupation of Afghanistan. That the US government agents trained and provided arms to the Taliban is not common knowledge. They are not made aware of the fact that Musharraf and Karzai, the US satraps, have negotiated with the Taliban and Al-Qaida to serve as a bulwark against the Shia in Iraq and Iran.

Insurgencies in Iraq and Afghanistan, demonstrations against globalizations all over the world, the resurgence of radical forces in South America and the Caribbean, have slowed the pace of globalization. But critical mass will develop only when workers in the developed countries, especially the United States, wake up. They will gradually feel the pinch. Jobs are going away to cheap labor countries.

One hopes that when they have remained unemployed for long enough, they will forget the animosity they bear for workers in less developed countries and will make common cause with the wretched in the Third World. Being situated in core countries, they will have less difficulty in overthrowing the system.

# Bibliography

Ahmad, Syed Akbar. 1997. *Jinnah, Pakistan and Islamic Identity: The Search for Saladin*. London: Routledge.

Ahmad, Iqbal. 2001. *Terrorism: Theirs and Ours*. New York: Seven Stories Press.

Akbar, M.J. *The Shade of Swords: Jihad and the Conflict between Islam and Christianity*. London: Routledge.

Ali, Ameer. 1984. *The Spirit of Islam: A History of the Evolution and Ideals of Islam*. Karachi: Allied Book Company.

Ali, Tariq.1983. *Can Pakistan survive? The Death of a State*. London: Verso.

Ali, Tariq. 2002. *Street Fighting Years: An Autobiography of the Sixties*. London: Verso.

Ali, Tariq. 2002. *The Clash of Fundamentalisms*. London: Verso.

Ayar, Mani Shankar. 2006. *Confessions of a Secular Fundamentalist*. Penguin Global.

Azad, Maulana Abul Kalam. 1960. *India Wins Freedom*. New York: Longmans, Green and Co.

Batalia, Urvashi. 2000. *The Other Side of Silence*. Durham: Duke University Press.

Bhutto, Zulfikar Ali. 1979. *If I Am Assassinated*. New Delhi: Vikas Publishing House Pvt. Ltd.

Bose, Mihir.1984. *The Agha Khans*. Kingswood: World's Work.

Chomsky, Noam. 2000. *Rogue States: The Rule of Force in World Affairs*. New Delhi: India Research Press.

Chomsky, Noam. 2002. *Understanding Power: The Indispensable Chomsky*. New Press. NY

Choudhury, G.W.1974. *The Last Days of United Pakistan*. London: C. Hurst & Co.

Chua, Amy. 2004. *World On fire*. New York: Anchor Books.

Collins, Larry and Dominique Lapierre.1975. *Freedom at Midnight*. New York: Simon and Schuster

Dreyfuss, Robert. *Devil's Game*. Metropolitan Books Henry Holt and Company NY

Dalrymple, William. 2002. *The White Moghals*. New York: Penguin Books.

Duncan, Emma. 1989. *Breaking the Curfew*. London: Arrow Books.

Edwardes, Michael.1967. *Raj*. London: Pan Books.

Frawley, David. 1995. *Arise Arjuna: Hinduism and the Modern World*. New Delhi: Voice of India.

Gandhi, Mohandas Karamchand.1927 *An Autobiography: The Story of my Experiments with Truth*. Ahmedabad: Navajivan Publishing House.

Gardezi, Hasan and Rashid Jamil. 1983. *Pakistan: The Roots of Dictatorship: The Political Economy of A Praetorian State*. Zed Press, 57 Caledonian Road, London N I 9DN

Gopal, Ram. 1976. *Indian Muslims: A Political History*. Lahore: Book Traders.

Grandin, Greg. 2006. *Empire's Workshop: Latin America, The United States, and the Rise of the New Imperialism*. New York: Henry Holt and Company.

Hodson, H.V. 1969. *The Great Divide, Britain-India-Pakistan*: Karachi: Oxford University Press.

Hosseini, Khaled. 2003 *The Kite Runner*: The Berkeley Publishing Group.

Jalal, Ayesha. 1994. *The sole Spokesman: Jinnah, the Muslim League and the Demand for Pakistan*. Cambridge: Cambridge University Press.

Johnson, Alan Campbell. 1985. *Mission with Mountbatten*. Macmillan Publishing Co.

Keay, John. 2000. *India: A History*. London: Harper Collins.

Khan, Abdul Jamil. 2006. *An Artificial Divide*. New York: Algora Publishing

Khan, Muhammad Ayub. 1997. *Friends not Masters: A Political Autobiography*. Oxford University Press.

Korejo, M.S. *Soldiers of Misfortune*. Karachi: Feroz Sons Pvt. Ltd.

Lenin, Vladimir. 1996. *Imperialism: The Highest Stage of Capitalism*. London: Pluto Press

Luce, Edward. 2007. *In Spite Of Gods: The Strange Rise of Modern India*. Maine: Abacus

Mascarenhas, Anthony. 1986. *Bangladesh: A Legacy of Blood*. London: Hodder and Stoughton

Mishra, Pankaj. 2007. *Temptations of the West: How to Be Modern in India, Pakistan, Tibet, and Beyond*. New York: Picador

Nehru, Jawaharlal.1959. *The Discovery of India*. New York: Anchor Books.

Nehru, Jawaharlal. 1963. *Autobiography*. Boston: Beacon Press.

Perkins, John.2004. *Confessions of an Economic Hit Man*. San Fransisco: Berrett-Koehler Publishers, Inc.

Qureshi, Ishtiaq Hussain. *The Muslim Community of the Indo-Pakistan Subcontinent*. Karachi: Bureau of Compilation and Translation University of Karachi. Pakistan

Roy, Arundhati. 2004. *An Ordinary Person's Guide to Empire*. Cambridge: South End Press

Seervai, Hormashi Maneckji. 1989. *Partition of India Legend and Reality*. Bombay: Emmenem Publications.

Sebastian, Thomas. 2007. *Globalization and Uneven Development*. New Delhi: Rawat Publications.

Shahab, Qudratullah. 1999.*Shahabnama*. Lahore: Sang-e-Meel Publications.

Shiva, Vandana. 2005. *Earth Democracy: Justice, Sustainability, and Peace*. Massachusetts: South End Press.

Siddiqa, Ayesha. 2007. *Military Inc.: Inside Pakistan's Military Economy*. New York: Pluto Press.

Sen, Surendra Nath, 1957. *Eighteen Fifty-Seven*. Calcutta: Government of India Press.

Wolpert, Stanley. *Jinnah of Pakistan*. Karachi: Oxford University Press.

Zakaria, Fareed. 2003. *The Future of Freedom: Illiberal Democracy at Home and Abroad*. New York: W.W. Norton.

# GLOSSARY

In India in the olden days one did not address one's mother and father with Amman (Mom) or Abba (Dad), as it was supposed to be embarrassing. I called my mother Bajya (elder sister) and father Bhayya (elder brother).

Wives did not address their husbands by their names, nor did the latter call the former by name. Each addressed the other as "Woh, Yeh," rather difficult to translate but roughly "that one", "this one." Among the less literate classes they would be addressed as father or mother of a child, for example if the child's name is Kallan, the husband will call his wife "Kallan ki Amman" (Kallan's mother). By the same token, she would call him "Kallan ke Abba" (Kallan's father).

The following pertains to Hindustani culture which was a synthesis of Urdu-Hindi secular heritage and was prevalent among educated adherents of both Hindu and Muslim creeds in North India-UP, Delhi and Bihar and Hyderabad in the South. It survives among the immigrants in Pakistan and has made inroads among indigenous Sindhis and North Pakistani residents of Sindh. In India fanatics successfully branded it Muslim and only vestigial pockets exist in such cities as Lucknow, Delhi and Hyderabad.

- Aap — to address elders.
- Abba, Abbu, Abba Jan, Abbu Jan for father. In a few families father is called Baba. In others Baba is reserved for father's elder brother.
- Amman, Ammi, Ammi Jan — mother.
- Bahu — daughter-in-law.
- Begum, Bibi — wife, Begum Sahiba used as a title for wives of the elite
- Beta — son — also used to call younger men by elders
- Beti — daughter — also used to call younger women by elders

- Baji, Bajya, Aapa — older sister, also generic for an older woman, respectful address for one in higher station of life.
- Bhai — brother. Bhai Jan, Bhai Sahib, Bhayya for an older brother, cousin, acquaintance and address of respect for one of a higher station in life.
- Bhabi, Bhabi Jan, Bhabi Sahib — older brother's wife. Also used for wives of friends, acquaintances and employers.
- Chacha, Chacha Jan, Ammo Jan, Ammo Sahib — uncle father's brother, cousin, friend. Also used for an elder family connections. Adding Sahib indicates that the person is older than one's father. Taya is also older than father.
- Chachi, chachi Jan — father's brother's wife. Also used for wives of father's cousins and friends. Tai for Taya's wife.
- Doolha — groom; Doolha Bhai — elder sister's husband.
- Dulhan — bride. In the past a mother-in-law and her family and friends would continue to call her Dulhan even when her own children were grown up.
- Dada — Father's father; his cousin's father is addressed in the same way. Par Dada — Grandfather's father. "Par" means wing, implying that the person is about to fly/pass on.
- Dadi — father's mother. Father's cousins' mothers are addressed in the same way. Par Dadi for grandfather's mother.
- Khala (Mousi, Bua in Hindi), Khala Jan, Khala Ammi — mother's sister and cousins and friends. Adding Ammi indicates that the person is older than one's own mother.
- Khaloo, Khaloo Jan — Khala's husband.
- Nana — mother's and her cousins' father. "Par" is added on for the next generation.
- Nani — Mother's and her cousin's mother. Add Par as above.
- Phuphi, Phuphi Jan, Phuphi Ammi — father's sister and cousins.
- Phupha, Phupha Jan — Phuphi and her cousin's husband.
- Saas — mother-in-law and her cousins. Bahus address them as Ammi or continue to call them as they did before marriage, if a relationship predated the wedding (as it did in most cases among Muslims in the subcontinent). Expatriates call them auntie.
- Tum — you, for equals or juniors
- Sasur — father-in-law and his brothers and cousins. As with mother-in-law, the past mode of address was retained. Expatriates call them uncle.

## ACKNOWLEDGMENTS

I am indebted to many friends in the US, Pakistan, the UK and India for advice and criticism. Some of my benefactors are outstanding scholars in their own right; others are fellow travelers and political activists.

My daughter Sarah took time out of her own busy academic life to transcribe my long hand notes. My son Umar and daughter-in-law Zarina have been of invaluable technical help. My youngest, Hasan, devoted many hours of his vacation time to go over the text, checking spellings and diction. My eldest, Eram, and her husband Adnan and Laila-Sana went over the draft and encouraged me. Rashid Memon gave me invaluable technical help. My wife Paro (Rafat), expecting to spend more time together after I retired, nevertheless put up with my preoccupation with her usual cheerful demeanor.

I would also like to offer my thanks to Andrea Secara of Algora Publishing for all her encouragement, advice and guidance.